The Seattle Classic Cookbook

The Seattle Classic Cookbook

The Junior League of Seattle

PHOTOGRAPHS BY JOSEF SCAYLEA

MADRONA PUBLISHERS
THE JUNIOR LEAGUE OF SEATTLE
Seattle · 1983

FIRST EDITION
10 9 8 7 6 5 4 3 2 1

Published by Madrona Publishers, Inc.
113 Madrona Place East
Seattle, Washington 98112
and the Junior League of Seattle, Inc.
1803 42nd Avenue East
Seattle, Washington 98112

Library of Congress Cataloging in Publication Data
Main entry under title:
The Seattle classic cookbook.
Includes index.
1. Cookery, American—Washington (State)
2. Seattle (Wash.)—Social life and customs. I. Junior
League of Seattle.
TX715.S4447   1983   641.5   83-9433
ISBN 0-914842-00-5

Composition: The Franklin Press, Seattle
Printing and binding: North Central Publishing Co., St. Paul

Acknowledgments

THE Manuscript Committee wishes to extend its gratitude to the many members and friends of the Junior League of Seattle who submitted and tested thousands of recipes, over 500 of which ultimately resulted in *The Seattle Classic Cookbook*. In addition, we would like to express thanks to our patient families, who encouraged and supported us throughout the four years of writing and publishing this book.

The purpose of the Junior League is educational and charitable: to promote volunteerism, to develop members' potential for voluntary participation in community affairs, and to demonstrate the effectiveness of trained volunteers.

Proceeds from sales of *The Seattle Classic Cookbook* will be returned to the community through projects of the Junior League of Seattle, Inc. It is to our community that we proudly dedicate *The Seattle Classic Cookbook*.

MANUSCRIPT COMMITTEE

Steering committee

Carol Willers White, chairman
Laurie Weaver Austin, design and editorial consultant
Pam Best Chicoine and Jane Polwarth Ekberg, coordinators of book chapters
Marilyn Dillard Coons, assistant to the chairman
Carlyn Koch Steiner, contract negotiator
Peggy Moore Steward, publishing consultant
Jill Belknap Armstrong, manuscript committee secretary
Katherine Jones Raff, editorial consultant

Chairmen of book chapters

Usha Nayudu Burns
Ginny Souza Clarke
Sally Peters Davidson
Dianne Michaelson Dilling
Linda Johnson Greer
Jane Cooper Hardin
Sue Hutton Hellar
Gail Westover Helms
Pam Rauscher Krug

Faye Bush McCollum
Deborah Evans Nelson
Gail Mortensen Richards
Barbi Monroe Robinson
Julie Cartano Rourke
Jo-Anne David Shanahan
Carlye Hawkins Teel
Myrna Montgomery Torrie

Committee members

Charlotte Eliason
Cori Allmano Hawes
Sonya Hanson McLaughlin
Cinda Steenhof Morrison
Charlee Hutchinson Reed

Ellen Beacot Myers Richardson
Francesca Louis Schultz
Grace Gulliver Thompson
Robin Adair Warjone

Marketing coordinators

Marsha Stroum Sloan and Karen Warren Wickstrand

Preface

><:=><:=><:=><:=><:=><:=><:=><:=><:=><:=><:=><:=><:=><:=><:=><:=><:=><:=><:=><:=><:=>

ON A November day in 1851—the year the *New York Times* appeared on the newsstands and *Rigoletto* was first performed, the year of Queen Victoria's Great Exhibition and the publication of *Moby Dick*—a small group of weary people stepped ashore at Alki Point, on the south end of what is now Elliott Bay in Puget Sound. They built a fire in the rain (as difficult to do then as now) and ate a meal of clams and salmon. Their landing marked the founding of Seattle, Puget Sound's major city. A hundred and thirty years later, people who make their homes around Puget Sound still pull their boats ashore on rainy days, build fires, and cook clams and salmon on the beach.

The history of Seattle and Puget Sound in the intervening years has been closely tied to agriculture, fishing, and ranching. At the same time, in the space of only a few generations, our region has achieved world leadership in the aerospace, lumber, and high-technology industries. Yet our history is so short that there are people here who remember the great gold rush and the Alaska–Yukon–Pacific Exposition that followed it.

Within a few years of the Alki landing, waves of new immigrants began arriving. Along with their desires for new lives, they brought with them the dairy herds, seeds, trees, and vines that have earned Washington a preeminent place in North America's food production. Over the years, immigration to the Puget Sound region became not slower but broader, each group bringing its foods and recipes and dining customs. These have been modified and modernized as cultures have met and mingled and as new residents have begun to use native ingredients. The ethnic traditions of the various groups are vigorous. In Seattle one often hears the languages and dialects of Scandinavia, Italy, Greece, China, and Japan. More recently, we have begun hearing those of Laos, Cambodia, and Vietnam.

Washington's abundance astounds the casual reader of statistics: We are the nation's first in production of apples, hops, spearmint, and summer potatoes; second in production of green peas, Bartlett pears, and apricots; third in production of winter wheat, asparagus, prunes, winter pears, strawberries, sweet cherries, and alfalfa seed; fourth in production of cranberries, grapes, and barley. Together, Washington and Oregon produce 95 percent of the raspberry crop in the United States, and Washington milk production exceeds that of any other state.

Seattle-area cooks rarely need to use imported ingredients for even the most complex recipes. Fresh strawberries, blueberries, mushrooms, apples, pears, peaches, cherries, raspberries, honey, and mint—luxuries so dearly bought elsewhere—are obtained with ease and economy from our gardens, forests, farms, and markets.

This richness has led to anything but complacency. One of Seattle's great civic battles concerned the preservation of the Pike Place Market, a public market stocked generously with the products of local farms. In the 1960s, attempts to raze the market for urban renewal aroused the citizenry, who realized that the Market symbolized the heart and spirit of Puget Sound and Seattle. Now, hard work and dedication have resulted in a thriving, renovated marketplace, a jewel in the city's crown, luring the visitor with the almost-forgotten pleasures of colorful, flavorful, unpackaged fruits and vegetables; just-caught fish; still-hot breads and pastries; assortments of sausages and hams; thick, raw cream—products once available all over America and now largely a memory. But at the Pike Place Market, the freshest and best local foods in season are still alternatives to the plastic-packaged fast foods prescribed for our future by those to whom shelf life is more important than taste.

The self-sufficiency of Puget Sound grows yearly as new food industries make our area their home. Washington's maturing wine industry is fed by ever-expanding vineyards and increasingly sophisticated vintners. Encouraged by our desire to explore different tastes, cheese merchants regularly stock their tables with new varieties. Fish heretofore left for Japanese and Soviet trawlers are now welcomed by newly adventurous buyers. And the demand for the freshest and the best has generated prepared goods of unexcelled quality—authentic pâtés and quiches, fresh pastas, croissants, pastries, and ice creams are made locally. Game farms supply restaurants and food shops with hare, duck, goose, and pheasant, while coffee, tea, and spice shops, ethnic groceries, pastry bars, and bistros widen our culinary experience.

For *The Seattle Classic Cookbook,* we have selected recipes that represent our varied and seasonal lifestyles. During the winter we sail, ski, and fish, making the most of the rainy but temperate climate. That is the season for hot soup, oyster stew, and homemade bread after a day's outing. When winter-blooming camellias and rhododendron give way to the cherry blossoms and hyacinth of early spring, we begin preparing our gardens. Often we discover the first asparagus shoots as early as February, and our menus turn to pasta primavera and green salads. Late spring (known elsewhere as summer) brings wonderfully long days and the beginning of a harvest that doesn't taper off until November. As the days shorten and the rain increases, forests abound with mushrooms and mushroom-hunters. Seafood is at its best; half a dozen varieties of salmon, as well as crab, mussels, and oysters, appear in the Market in the fall.

Cooks have responded with the style that characterizes life in the Puget Sound region. We often entertain on or near the water (per capita, more people own boats in this area than anywhere else in the U.S.) and our thriving boating traditions urge us to entertain under sail or at yacht club outstations across the Sound. Opening day of the boating season in May calls for parties on anything from skiffs to seagoing yachts. In December, the annual parade of lavishly decorated Christmas ships around Lake Washington means bonfires and hot toddies.

The possibility that their seafood, fruits, mushrooms and fast-growing vegetables would form the basis for what we now call our Northwest cuisine might not have occurred to the pioneers for whom these foods simply meant survival. We do know, however, that they were grateful for the abundance of natural, readily obtainable foods in the Puget Sound area, and in that respect we and they are very much the same.

Contents

INGREDIENTS

During the testing of the recipes in this book, the freshest ingredients available were used, assuring the highest possible quality in the final results. Unless otherwise stated, the ingredients are:

Butter: used throughout, rather than margarine, for flavor. Margarine may be substituted, but the quality of the flavor will change.

Citrus juices: freshly squeezed.

Eggs: large, grade AA. Eggs should be at room temperature before use.

Fish and shellfish: fresh.

Flour: white, all-purpose.

Fruits and vegetables: fresh.

Herbs: dried. If fresh herbs are available, use triple the amount specified in the recipe.

Parsley: fresh. Leaves only.

Zest of citrus fruit: the outer, colored peel, with none of the bitter inner white part, which should be avoided. To remove the zest, we recommend using a zester, available in most hardware stores, rather than a grater.

Opening day of the yachting season. With the Cascade Mountains in the background, boats return to Portage Bay from Lake Washington after the opening day parade and regatta.

Classic Menus
for Seattle Living

━━

AN invitation to share Seattle's classics should begin long before the table is set, with a proper introduction of the city. The best first impression is from the air—not only because it is the most appropriate way to greet an aerospace city, but because to look north or south or east or west from any point over Seattle is to catch one's breath at the beauty of the setting. From this distance, the overwhelming impression is of a cluster of buildings surrounded by immense mountains and limitless water.

The Cascade Mountains, to the east, are part of a geologically youthful range that includes Mount St. Helens. But it is the compelling, magnificent Mount Rainier, rising 14,000 feet from sea level, that rules the city. The quality of a day is often described in terms relating to the mountain, whether obscured by overcast skies, partially visible through low clouds, or, on a brilliant day, unexpectedly bigger than life.

Directly west, the rugged and heavily forested Olympic Mountains jut sharply along the Pacific Coast, protecting Seattle and Puget Sound from cold Pacific blasts and absorbing much of the rainfall off the ocean. Lying beyond the shadow of the mountains, Seattle receives 34 inches of rain a year, compared with the Olympic Rain Forest's annual 140.

Elliott Bay, on which Seattle's deep-water port was built, is an arm of Puget Sound, which was shaped and protected by the massive Olympic Peninsula. The Sound is dotted with boats: ocean-going cargo and passenger vessels, fishing boats, tugs, sailboats, and the ubiquitous green-and-white ferries that faithfully cross and double back day and night. Waterways and bridges seem to appear everywhere. Lake Washington, the largest of many glacier-carved lakes, lies to the east of Seattle, extending the full length of the city and surrounding the residential community of Mercer Island, which is connected to Seattle by a floating bridge. To the north, another floating bridge connects Seattle with the city of Bellevue. Nearer the heart of the city are Lake Union, a commercial center, and Green Lake, a recreational center. There is a man-made ship canal where salt water meets fresh water at the Hiram Chittenden Locks; there is the Duwamish River, headquarters for the heavy shipping industry; and the waterfront itself, its piers pointing northwest toward the Strait of Juan de Fuca and the Pacific Ocean. The Port of Seattle is one of the busiest international ports on the Pacific Rim.

Although Seattle was built on seven hills, only five can be counted, the two nearest the business district having been sluiced into the bay early in this century by the children of pioneers whose vision of Seattle's future called for moving mountains. Each remaining hill has a distinct character and is a landmark unto itself; each has at least one park or boulevard or tower that is a perfect spot for viewing distant splendors.

The mountains, the Sound, the lakes, and the hills give up only enough space for a city that is long and narrow, compressed in the middle where buildings are most dense and commerce most active. Here Seattle becomes a walkers' city, and that is an appropriate place to put aside first impressions and begin what we hope will be a lasting friendship.

WHEN GOOD FRIENDS GET TOGETHER

Menus that say the most about Seattle cuisine and lifestyle include easy-to-get local ingredients, and provide pleasure in marketing as well as in preparation. An essential for good meals is good company, and the three menus that follow are for those occasions when friends get together for the simple pleasure of seeing one another.

Waterfront Luncheon

BLOOMER DROPPERS

CHICKEN AND SPINACH CRÊPES
TOMATO ROSE GARNISH
RASPBERRY MANDARIN MOLD
NUT MUFFINS
Wine: White Beaujolais or *Chenin Blanc*

CHOCOLATE TRUFFLE CAKE
Wine: Champagne

To be enjoyed in the spring sunshine within view of one of Seattle's lakes, this menu is appropriate for the last gathering before summer or for greeting a newcomer to the neighborhood. The Bloomer Droppers will be the icebreaker.

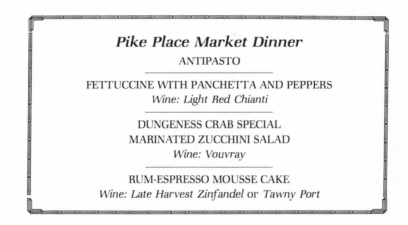

Pike Place Market Dinner

ANTIPASTO

FETTUCCINE WITH PANCHETTA AND PEPPERS
Wine: Light Red Chianti

DUNGENESS CRAB SPECIAL
MARINATED ZUCCHINI SALAD
Wine: Vouvray

RUM-ESPRESSO MOUSSE CAKE
Wine: Late Harvest Zinfandel or *Tawny Port*

For this, dinner preparation begins during lunch hour with a walk through the Pike Place Market to choose the freshest produce and seafood. The menu has to be flexible enough to allow for substitutions in case one of the merchants has special recommendations.

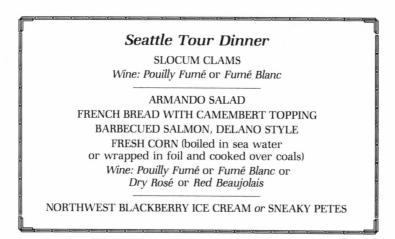

Seattle Tour Dinner

SLOCUM CLAMS
Wine: Pouilly Fumé or Fumé Blanc

ARMANDO SALAD
FRENCH BREAD WITH CAMEMBERT TOPPING
BARBECUED SALMON, DELANO STYLE
FRESH CORN (boiled in sea water
or wrapped in foil and cooked over coals)
*Wine: Pouilly Fumé or Fumé Blanc or
Dry Rosé or Red Beaujolais*

NORTHWEST BLACKBERRY ICE CREAM *or* SNEAKY PETES

The Seattle Classic's all-Northwest dinner for out-of-town visitors brings to a climax a day that could include a tour of the Boeing plant, a walk around the University of Washington campus, or an all-day trek to Mount Rainier. Such a day might also feature a visit to the Space Needle, the Pacific Science Center, or a streetcar ride along the downtown waterfront.

GETTING AWAY

One of the nice things about living in a city is the occasional pleasure of getting away. Frequently, for those who live in Seattle, it's to a mountain cabin with wood-burning stove or one of Puget Sound's lovely small-town or country inns. For many of us, such a day or weekend has the psychological effect of a three-week vacation. Wherever one goes, the occasion is right for sharing an unhurried meal.

Bounty of the Beach

BARBECUED OYSTERS

SEATTLE'S CAESAR SALAD
CIOPPINO
CHEDDAR CROWN LOAF
*Wine: Dry Gewurztraminer or Red Chianti or Barbaresco or
Sauvignon Blanc*

LEMON FLUFF PIE

A traditional cioppino offers a fine sampling of a variety of the Northwest's abundant seafoods. Puget Sound is one of the few places in the world where one can rise before the sun to dig clams at low tide and later gather mussels and pull crabs from crab pots for the evening meal.

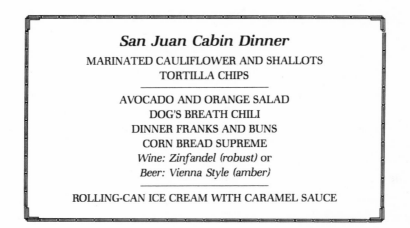

San Juan Cabin Dinner

MARINATED CAULIFLOWER AND SHALLOTS
TORTILLA CHIPS

AVOCADO AND ORANGE SALAD
DOG'S BREATH CHILI
DINNER FRANKS AND BUNS
CORN BREAD SUPREME
Wine: Zinfandel (robust) or
Beer: Vienna Style (amber)

ROLLING-CAN ICE CREAM WITH CARAMEL SAUCE

Numerous small islands in Puget Sound and the Strait of Juan de Fuca, some of them accessible only by private boat or seaplane, lend themselves to weekend retreats and summers of leisure. Protected by the Olympic Mountains and heated by the Japanese Current, the islands are sunny and warm most of the year.

Apple Harvest Picnic

Box Lunches
SAUSAGE EN CROUTE
KENT VALLEY APPLE SLAW
MARINATED TOMATOES
Wine: Northwest Chardonnay or *Tavel Rosé*
or *Anjou Rosé* or *Red Beaujolais*

Apple Tasting

Apples	*Cheeses*
RED DELICIOUS	BRIE
JONATHAN	BLUE CASTELLO
GRAVENSTEIN	GJETOST
CRITERION	COUGAR GOLD CHEDDAR

Descriptions of Washington's apples always contain such words as *crisp, shiny, healthful,* and *abundant.* Celebrate the fall harvest with this apple-tasting party in an orchard, back yard, or gazebo. After the box lunch and apple tasting, let guests take turns at the cider press.

Winery Picnic
SAUSAGE-FILLED ITALIAN BREAD
PICKLED MUSHROOMS
CARROT-CUCUMBER RELISH
Wine: Red or *White Chianti* or *Red Nebbiolo*

FRESH FRUIT
DUWAMISH MUD BARS
Wine: Champagne or *Late Harvest Riesling,* or
Late Harvest Chardonnay

Grapes for Washington State's burgeoning wine industry thrive in a long growing season of warm days and cool nights. Washington produces such varieties as Cabernet Sauvignon, Pinot Noir, Zinfandel, Pinot Chardonnay, and Sauvignon Blanc, all of which compare favorably with their European and California counterparts. Some unusual sophisticated fruit wines have also met with success. After a tour of one of Seattle's nearby wineries, enjoy this colorful outdoor feast.

THE SPORTING LIFE

Physical activity always provides a good excuse for bringing people together, whether to challenge each other or the elements. Often one of the biggest challenges is how to feed the crowd. To solve that dilemma we offer menus that lend themselves to days when the cook is bicycling, skiing, sailing, or arm wrestling—but not in the kitchen.

Snoqualmie Summit Fireside Supper
BEEF VINAIGRETTE
FRENCH FONDUE SEATTLE STYLE
CRUSTY FRENCH BREAD
Wine: White Burgundy or *Red Beaujolais*

FRESH FRUIT
DIRTY MOTHERS

With winter sports in the Cascade Mountains as near as an hour's drive away, Seattleites can spend the day downhill or cross-country skiing, snowshoeing, or tobogganing, and then return to a winter cabin or a home in the city for this warm, intimate dinner.

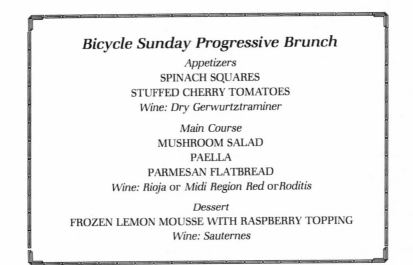

Bicycle Sunday Progressive Brunch

Appetizers
SPINACH SQUARES
STUFFED CHERRY TOMATOES
Wine: Dry Gerwurtztraminer

Main Course
MUSHROOM SALAD
PAELLA
PARMESAN FLATBREAD
Wine: Rioja or Midi Region Red or Roditis

Dessert
FROZEN LEMON MOUSSE WITH RASPBERRY TOPPING
Wine: Sauternes

Whether biking a trail such as the Burke-Gilman, which follows an old railroad line along the shores of Lake Union, Portage Bay, and Union Bay, or joining friends on a Bicycle Sunday, when major roadways are temporarily restricted to bikes only, try a meal that can be enjoyed in stages at stops along the way.

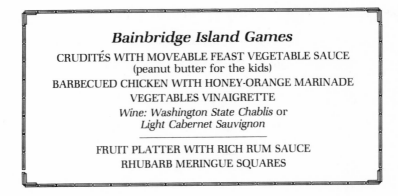

Bainbridge Island Games

CRUDITÉS WITH MOVEABLE FEAST VEGETABLE SAUCE
(peanut butter for the kids)
BARBECUED CHICKEN WITH HONEY-ORANGE MARINADE
VEGETABLES VINAIGRETTE
Wine: Washington State Chablis or
Light Cabernet Sauvignon

FRUIT PLATTER WITH RICH RUM SAUCE
RHUBARB MERINGUE SQUARES

The distance between Seattle and Bainbridge Island is measured not in miles but in the thirty minutes it takes a ferry to cross Elliott Bay. This serene suburb is our setting for a Fourth of July family celebration featuring such old standbys as croquet, badminton, and three-legged races.

ARTFUL GATHERINGS

Seattle is a mecca for artists who are drawn to at least a dozen theaters, to orchestra, opera, and dance companies, and to an immense variety of visual arts and craft studios as well as the highly respected Seattle Art Museum. PONCHO (Patrons of Northwest Civic, Cultural, and Charitable Organizations) sponsors an internationally known annual fund-raising auction, while other arts organizations sponsor imaginative parties throughout the year. With such entertaining in mind, we offer three contrasting buffet menus.

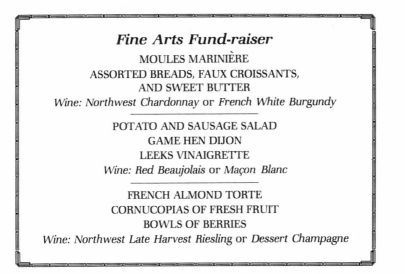

Fine Arts Fund-raiser
MOULES MARINIÈRE
ASSORTED BREADS, FAUX CROISSANTS,
AND SWEET BUTTER
Wine: Northwest Chardonnay or French White Burgundy

POTATO AND SAUSAGE SALAD
GAME HEN DIJON
LEEKS VINAIGRETTE
Wine: Red Beaujolais or Mâçon Blanc

FRENCH ALMOND TORTE
CORNUCOPIAS OF FRESH FRUIT
BOWLS OF BERRIES
Wine: Northwest Late Harvest Riesling or Dessert Champagne

A rhododendron-filled garden on a late spring afternoon would be an ideal setting for this buffet. Invite a string quartet or guitarist to provide music and a celebrity artist to mingle with the guests.

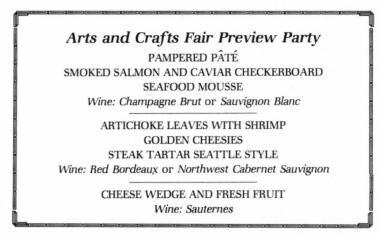

Arts and Crafts Fair Preview Party

PAMPERED PÂTÉ
SMOKED SALMON AND CAVIAR CHECKERBOARD
SEAFOOD MOUSSE
Wine: Champagne Brut or *Sauvignon Blanc*

ARTICHOKE LEAVES WITH SHRIMP
GOLDEN CHEESIES
STEAK TARTAR SEATTLE STYLE
Wine: Red Bordeaux or *Northwest Cabernet Sauvignon*

CHEESE WEDGE AND FRESH FRUIT
Wine: Sauternes

The Pacific Northwest Arts and Crafts Fair draws visitors to Bellevue each July to view the work of visual and performing artists, both professional and nonprofessional. Juried shows, demonstrations, performances, and the stir and commotion of countless visitors give the fair an atmosphere of excitement and festivity.

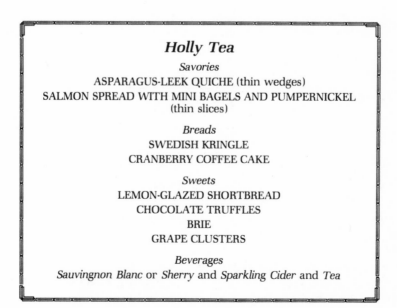

Holly Tea

Savories
ASPARAGUS-LEEK QUICHE (thin wedges)
SALMON SPREAD WITH MINI BAGELS AND PUMPERNICKEL
(thin slices)

Breads
SWEDISH KRINGLE
CRANBERRY COFFEE CAKE

Sweets
LEMON-GLAZED SHORTBREAD
CHOCOLATE TRUFFLES
BRIE
GRAPE CLUSTERS

Beverages
Sauvingnon Blanc or *Sherry* and *Sparkling Cider* and *Tea*

Many of Seattle's performing arts groups maintain holiday-season traditions with productions such as the Pacific Northwest Ballet's *Nutcracker; A Christmas Carol,* performed by A Contemporary Theatre; Intiman Theatre's *Christmas Sampler;* and Seattle Opera's *Amahl and the Night Visitors.* In anticipation of one of these performances, gather parents and children in their holiday finery for a traditional tea.

SPECTACULARLY SEATTLE

Meals planned around special events are often easiest to arrange; for the guests, the meal becomes part of the event itself. These menus for brunch, lunch, dinner, and dessert highlight events that are characteristically Seattle and generate parties having universal appeal.

Opening Day Lunch Afloat
HALIBUT PATE WITH RAW VEGETABLES AND CRACKERS
CHEESE TWISTS
Wine: Sauvignon Blanc or *White Graves*

PARMESAN CHICKEN
CONFETTI OVERNIGHT SALAD
WHOLE WHEAT REFRIGERATOR ROLLS
Wine: Dry White Riesling or *Pinot Noir*

DISAPPEARING MARSHMALLOW BROWNIES
FRESH FRUIT

With boat owners comprising a large percentage of Seattle's population, the annual opening day of the yachting season in early May is one of the city's most festive occasions. Whether joining the parade of decorated boats or setting anchor to watch, run up a wind sock and enjoy this lunch with friends. No on-board preparation is required.

Husky Fever Brunch

HAM AND CHEESE SANDWICH PUFF
PENNSYLVANIA-DUTCH TOMATOES
RASPBERRY STRUDEL
Wine: Sparkling Wine (with a dash of bitters)
or Sparkling Wine and Orange Juice

Autumn brings a season-long celebration for University of Washington football fans, and the cheering begins at a pregame brunch. Home games are played at the university's Husky Stadium, adjacent to the campus on the shore of Lake Washington and accessible by both boat and car.

Fat Tuesday Dessert Buffet

CHOCOLATE MOUSSE PIE
SWEDISH RASPBERRY CREAM
MOUNT ST. HELENS SPECTACULAR
ORANGE-CRANBERRY CAKE
CHEDDAR CHEESE CHEESECAKE
CHOCOLATE-CARAMEL COOKIES
ASSORTED CHEESE AND FRESH FRUIT
Wine: Champagne or Asti Spumante or
Late Harvest Gewurztraminer

The former heart of the city and the site of the original Skid Road (down which logs were skidded into Elliott Bay), Pioneer Square suffered a major fire and, eventually, virtual abandonment before renovation began in the early 1970s. Now its cobblestone streets and parks are the scene of a yearly public carnival on Fat Tuesday, the day before Lent begins.

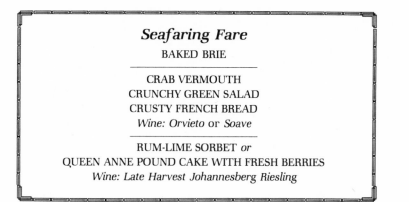

Seafaring Fare
BAKED BRIE

CRAB VERMOUTH
CRUNCHY GREEN SALAD
CRUSTY FRENCH BREAD
Wine: Orvieto or *Soave*

RUM-LIME SORBET *or*
QUEEN ANNE POUND CAKE WITH FRESH BERRIES
Wine: Late Harvest Johannesberg Riesling

Seafair is Seattle's spectacular, week-long summer festival, featuring parades and ethnic neighborhood activities and climaxed by hydroplane races. After watching the races, share this casual meal with good friends on a patio as the sun sets over the Olympic Mountains.

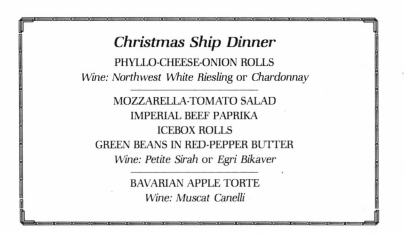

Christmas Ship Dinner
PHYLLO-CHEESE-ONION ROLLS
Wine: Northwest White Riesling or *Chardonnay*

MOZZARELLA-TOMATO SALAD
IMPERIAL BEEF PAPRIKA
ICEBOX ROLLS
GREEN BEANS IN RED-PEPPER BUTTER
Wine: Petite Sirah or *Egri Bikaver*

BAVARIAN APPLE TORTE
Wine: Muscat Canelli

As Christmas draws near, Seattleites decorate their boats with evergreen boughs and colored lights. The annual Parade of Ships can be seen from Lake Union, Lake Washington, and Elliott Bay, from bridges, parks, houseboats, and hillside homes. Friends gather to watch the boats and share an informal meal followed by caroling.

Piles of oyster shells cover the beach in Washington's oyster country near Westport, at the coastal town of Ocosta.

Appetizers, First Courses, & Beverages

>=-=<

Baked Brie

small wheel (about 1½ pounds)
    herbed Brie cheese, rind intact
8 sheets phyllo

1 cup butter, melted
8 blanched almonds

Preheat oven to 375 degrees.

Brush each phyllo sheet with butter, fold in half, and brush top. Wrap the entire wheel of cheese in a folded sheet and seal. Turn the wrapped cheese over and continue until all phyllo sheets are used. Arrange almonds on top and brush with remaining butter. Bake for 20 minutes and let stand for 15 minutes so cheese will not run.

SERVES 12

Note: Use only a whole, uncut wheel.

Fried Brie

7 to 8 ounces firm Brie cheese, rind
    intact
3 tablespoons butter
⅓ cup fine bread crumbs

½ teaspoon thyme
1 egg
chopped green onions for garnish
French bread

Allow Brie to stand at room temperature for 15 minutes. In a small skillet, melt butter over medium heat. Mix bread crumbs and thyme. Beat egg and coat cheese first with beaten egg, then with bread crumbs. Sauté coated cheese in melted butter, 1 or 2 minutes on each side. Let stand 5 to 10 minutes (so cheese will not run), garnish with green onions and serve with sliced French bread.

SERVES 4

Cheese-Filled Won Tons

Cheese Filling
½ pound ricotta cheese
½ pound feta cheese, crumbled
½ pound Romano cheese, grated
½ teaspoon white pepper
1 tablespoon Worcestershire sauce
¼ cup finely chopped parsley

Won Tons
1 16-ounce package won ton skins
1 egg, beaten
1 to 1½ cups vegetable oil

To prepare filling: Mix all ingredients together to make filling. Place a heaping teaspoon of this mixture in the center of each won ton skin. Brush two edges of skin with beaten egg and fold won ton over to form a triangle, tightly sealing the two edges together. Place won tons on a tray.

When ready to cook, heat vegetable oil in a deep frying pan or wok. Fry won tons for 1 to 2 minutes, until golden brown on both sides. Drain on paper towels, and keep warm in 200-degree oven.

YIELD: ABOUT 50 WON TONS

Cheese Thins

16 slices white bread
2 cups mayonnaise
1 medium Walla Walla sweet or white

onion, grated
1 cup grated Parmesan cheese
paprika

Preheat broiler.

Cut 3 to 4 circles out of each slice of bread with a small glass. In oven, toast bread on one side. Grate onion and mix with mayonnaise; spread on untoasted side of bread rounds. Sprinkle cheese and paprika on top, and broil until bubbling.

SERVES 6 TO 8

Golden Cheesies

2½ cups flour	seasoned salt and pepper to taste
1 cup margarine (butter would burn)	3 cups grated sharp Cheddar cheese
1 cup sour cream	paprika

Preheat oven to 350 degrees.

Thoroughly mix flour, margarine, and sour cream. Divide into 4 portions, wrap in waxed paper, and chill. When dough is firm, roll it out, a portion at a time, on well-floured board. Roll each portion into a 6-x-12-inch rectangle, then sprinkle lightly with seasoned salt and pepper and with ¾ cup cheese. Roll up lengthwise, jelly roll fashion. Seal edges and place seam side down on ungreased cookie sheet. Score each roll slightly, making 14 marks on each. Sprinkle with paprika, bake for 30 to 35 minutes, and slice through to serve.

YIELD: 56 PIECES

Note: Rolls may be frozen before baking. If they are frozen, do not thaw, but bake for 45 minutes at 350 degrees.

Phyllo-Cheese-Onion Rolls

½ cup butter	2 cups shredded Swiss cheese
3 large white onions, sliced thin	¾ teaspoon caraway seed (optional)
6 ounces cream cheese at room temperature	12 sheets (½ pound) phyllo

Melt 3 tablespoons butter in a wide frying pan. Add onions and cook over moderate heat, stirring frequently, until onions are limp and pale gold, about 20 minutes. Remove from heat and let stand until luke warm. Then mix onions thoroughly with cream cheese, Swiss cheese, and caraway seed. Melt remaining butter.

To make a cheese roll, stack 4 sheets of phyllo, brushing very lightly between layers with melted butter (streaking the phyllo, not coating the entire layer). Along the widest edge of the phyllo, spoon in a third of the cheese-onion mixture in an even band and roll to enclose. Cut roll in half and place halves seam side down, a few inches apart, on a buttered baking sheet. Brush entire surface of roll well with butter to prevent drying. Repeat to make 2 more large rolls that will then be halved. Cover with foil and chill a few hours or overnight.

Preheat oven to 400 degrees.

Cut rolls on pan into 1-inch pieces, leaving in place. Bake for 12 minutes or, if still chilled, for 17 minutes. Let cool slightly before serving.

YIELD: 5 DOZEN

Note: May be frozen before baking. Unwrap before thawing.

Cheese Twists or Palmiers

This recipe comes from Gretchen Mathers, noted Seattle restaurateur, caterer, and cuisine artist.

½ cup grated Cheddar or Parmesan
   cheese
1 tablespoon paprika
1 teaspoon cayenne
1 teaspoon salt

1 egg
1 tablespoon water
1 17½-ounce package frozen puff
   pastry, or your own recipe

Preheat oven to 400 degrees.

Combine cheese, paprika, cayenne, and salt. In a small bowl beat egg with water until blended. Roll out chilled puff pastry dough very thin, using some of the cheese mixture to flour the board. Brush with egg wash. Sprinkle evenly with half of the cheese mixture, pressing lightly so that cheese adheres. Turn dough over and repeat on other side.

To make twists: Cut coated dough in 3-x-6-inch strips. Twist each strip corkscrew fashion and then roll tightly, with hands, on board. Bake on ungreased baking sheets for 10 minutes or wrap and freeze until needed. If these have been frozen, they can be unwrapped, placed directly in oven, and baked for 20 minutes.

To make palmiers: Roll 1 side of the dough lengthwise (jelly roll fashion) to the center of the rolled-out dough; roll other side to the center in the same way. Refrigerate until firm, or wrap and freeze until needed. To bake, cut into ¼-inch slices, place on ungreased baking sheet, and bake for 5 to 7 minutes (or 10 to 12 minutes if frozen).

SERVES 6 TO 8

Seafood Mousse

1 tablespoon unflavored gelatin
3 tablespoons cold water
1 can condensed cream of mushroom
    soup or 1 cup White Sauce
    (following recipe)
6 ounces cream cheese
½ cup mayonnaise
½ cup sour cream
½ cup chopped parsley

½ cup chopped celery
¼ cup sliced green onion
2 tablespoons lemon juice
¼ to ½ teaspoon Tabasco sauce
1 teaspoon dill
7 ounces crabmeat, fresh or canned
¾ cup fresh shrimp
parsley for garnish

Oil a 1½-quart fish-shaped mold. Soften gelatin in water for 5 minutes. Meanwhile, heat soup or White Sauce in saucepan. Add gelatin and stir until dissolved, then add cream cheese, stir until melted, and allow to cool. Stir in remaining ingredients, pour into prepared mold, and chill for 4 hours. Garnish with parsley and serve with crisp crackers.

SERVES 12 TO 15

White Sauce

2 tablespoons butter
2 tablespoons flour

1 cup milk
salt and freshly ground pepper to taste

In a saucepan, melt butter and add flour. With a wire whisk, stir over low heat for 2 to 3 minutes. Slowly pour milk into mixture, whisking constantly. Continue to whisk over low heat until mixture bubbles and thickens. Remove from heat.

YIELD: ABOUT 1 CUP

Bacon-Wrapped Scallops

1 pound medium-sized bay scallops or
    halved sea scallops

1 cup teriyaki sauce
½ pound bacon

Poach scallops for 2 minutes, drain, and marinate in teriyaki sauce for 2 hours.

Preheat broiler.

Cut each bacon slice into 3 pieces, wrap bacon around scallops, and secure with toothpicks. Broil wrapped scallops until bacon is crisp.

SERVES 6 TO 8

Northwest Favorite

Arrange a fillet of smoked salmon on a platter surrounded by thin-sliced Walla Walla onions, lemon wedges, and sprigs of watercress. Sprinkle capers over the salmon and serve with thin slices of pumpernickel bread. Allow ¼ pound salmon for 3 to 4 people.

Salmon Spread

7 ounces cooked salmon
8 ounces cream cheese
1 tablespoon lemon juice
1 tablespoon grated onion
1 teaspoon horseradish

¼ teaspoon liquid smoke
½ cup chopped walnuts
3 tablespoons chopped parsley
1 dozen bagels

Combine salmon, cream cheese, lemon juice, onion, horseradish, and liquid smoke in food processor or blender. Process until smooth. Stir in chopped nuts and parsley and transfer to a crock. Refrigerate until ready to serve. Serve with bagels sliced into bite-size wedges.

YIELD: 2 CUPS

Hot Seafood Melt

8 ounces cream cheese
⅓ pound fresh tiny shrimp
⅓ pound fresh crabmeat
2 cloves garlic, minced
½ cup mayonnaise

2 teaspoons dry mustard
2 teaspoons powdered sugar
½ medium onion, minced
¼ cup dry vermouth
2 English muffins

Soften cream cheese in top of double boiler. Add all remaining ingredients except vermouth and stir gently until blended and heated. Add wine and transfer to chafing dish. Toast muffins, cut them into bite-ize wedges, and use them to scoop seafood melt from the chafing dish.

Serves 6 to 8 as an hors d'oeuvre or 2 when served on toasted muffin halves for lunch.

Deviled Crabmeat

1¼ cups dry bread crumbs	¼ teaspoon dry mustard
½ cup milk	6 drops Tabasco sauce
1 cup sour cream	¼ cup olive oil
1 tablespoon Worcestershire sauce	¼ pound fresh mushrooms, sliced
1 tablespoon minced onion	2 cups crabmeat
½ teaspoon salt	2 teaspoons butter

Butter 6 seafood shells. Soak 1 cup of the crumbs in milk for 10 minutes. Add sour cream, Worcestershire sauce, onion, salt, mustard, Tabasco sauce, olive oil, and mushrooms. Mix well. Gently fold in the crab. Divide the mixture into prepared seafood shells or ramekins. Refrigerate, covered, overnight.

Preheat oven to 400 degrees.

Sprinkle crab mixture with remaining crumbs and dot with butter. Bake 15 minutes; serve immediately.

SERVES 6

Clams Oreganato

1 tablespoon minced onion	1 teaspoon oregano
2 cloves garlic, minced	½ cup dry bread crumbs
1 cup chopped mushrooms	2 8-ounce cans minced clams and juice
2 tablespoons vegetable oil	salt and pepper to taste
2 tablespoons chopped parsley	¼ cup freshly grated Parmesan cheese

Preheat oven to 375 degrees.

Sauté the onion, garlic, and mushrooms in vegetable oil. Add parsley, oregano, and half of the bread crumbs. Sauté a few minutes to blend the flavors. Add the clams, including the juice. Taste for seasoning and continue to cook until most of the liquid has been absorbed, leaving the mixture moist. Spoon into clam or seafood shells and sprinkle with remaining bread crumbs and cheese. Bake 25 to 30 minutes for large shells, or 15 to 20 minutes for smaller shells.

Served in clam shells or cocktail-size patty shells, this is an hors d'oeuvre; in seafood shells or ramekins it becomes a first course.

SERVES 4 AS A FIRST COURSE

Slocum Clams

Clams and Nectar

5 pounds clams in shells
⅓ cup finely chopped onions
⅓ cup finely chopped celery
½ cup chopped parsley
¼ cup butter
¼ cup dry white wine
freshly ground pepper to taste

Dipping Sauce

¼ cup melted butter
¼ cup chili sauce
1 tablespoon Dijon-style mustard
¼ teaspoon thyme
¼ teaspoon basil
¼ teaspoon marjoram
¼ teaspoon onion salt
1 small clove garlic, minced
1 teaspoon lemon juice
½ cup clam nectar

To prepare clams and nectar: Wash clams. Place remaining ingredients in bottom of steamer or large kettle, and put clams on top. (There *is* sufficient liquid, and the clams will soon add more.) Cover and steam over high heat for 20 minutes or until clams are fully opened.

Serve in bowls with Dipping Sauce or melted butter on the side. Serve clam nectar separately in cups.

SERVES 6

To prepare dipping sauce: Combine ingredients in a small saucepan and stir until blended and warm. Serve immediately.

YIELD: ABOUT 1¾ CUPS

Geoduck Fritters

This is a specialty of Francois and Julia Kissel's Maximilien-in-the-Market, a restaurant located in the Pike Place Market, and commanding a spectacular view of Elliott Bay.

Batter

1 cup flour
2 tablespoons peanut oil
1 egg
¾ cup beer
½ teaspoon salt
½ teaspoon sugar

Geoduck mixture

1 tablespoon chopped onion
2 tablespoons butter
½ teaspoon curry powder
1 cup chopped geoduck
½ cup peeled and grated sweet potato
¼ cup peeled and grated carrot

To prepare batter: Combine all batter ingredients and mix well. Batter should be made 5 hours in advance and kept at room temperature.

To prepare geoduck mixture: Sauté onion in butter until brown, then stir in curry and geoduck. Add sweet potato and carrot, stir 1 minute, and chill immediately to keep crisp. Blend geoduck mixture into batter at the last minute and drop the combination in little balls into hot peanut oil for deep-frying. Serve with Ginger Mayonnaise (following recipe).

Serves 8 as an hors d'oeuvre or first course, or 4 as a main course.

Note: The geoduck, a specialty of the Northwest, is a clam whose shell can measure up to 8 inches, with a neck equally long. If geoduck is unavailable, substitute minced clams.

Halibut Pâté

¾ pound halibut
2 lemon slices
2 onions, sliced
1 bay leaf
8 ounces cream cheese, softened
2 tablespoons lemon juice
2 teaspoons grated onion

1 teaspoon Worcestershire sauce
dash of Tabasco sauce
¼ teaspoon garlic salt
½ teaspoon salt
¼ teaspoon dill
parsley for garnish

Place halibut in boiling salted water to cover and add lemon slices, onions, and bay leaf. Cover and simmer for 5 to 10 minutes. When fish flakes if pressed with a fork, drain. Remove skin and bones. Flake fish and combine with the remaining ingredients, except parsley, in food processor or blender and process until smooth. Pour into 4-cup mold lined with buttered waxed paper and allow to set for several hours or overnight.

Unmold onto serving plate, garnish with parsley, and serve with crisp crackers.

SERVES 8

Ginger Mayonnaise

Also created at Maximilien-in-the-Market, this is a delicious accompaniment for fritters, croquettes, fried fish, or cracked crab.

1 tablespoon grated fresh ginger   ¾ cup mayonnaise
3 tablespoons soy sauce

Combine ingredients and mix thoroughly.

YIELD: 1 CUP

Cold Barbecued Loin of Pork

5 to 6 pounds pork loin, boned and
    tied
1 tablespoon dry mustard
1 tablespoon thyme
toasted sesame seeds

Marinade Sauce
½ cup sherry
½ cup soy sauce
3 cloves garlic, minced
2 tablespoons grated fresh ginger

Sherry Sauce
1 8-ounce jar currant jelly
1 tablespoon soy sauce
2 tablespoons sherry

Snappy Apple Sauce
2 cups applesauce
¼ cup horseradish

Hot Mustard Sauce
2 tablespoons dry mustard
2 tablespoons boiling water
¼ teaspoon vegetable oil
pinch of salt

To prepare sauces: Combine ingredients for each and blend until smooth.

Rub roast with mixture of mustard and thyme. Marinate in Marinade Sauce for 2 hours, turning occasionally.

Preheat oven to 325 degrees.

Roast for 25 minutes per pound, basting with marinade during cooking. Remove from oven, cover with Sherry Sauce and allow to cool for several hours before slicing very thin. Serve with Snappy Apple Sauce or Hot Mustard Sauce, with toasted sesame seeds for sprinkling on top.

SERVES 25 to 30

Sweet and Sour Meatballs

Meatballs

1 pound ground turkey
1 pound pork sausage
3 tablespoons cornstarch
4 green onions, chopped
2 teaspoons sherry
1 egg
3 tablespoons soy sauce

Sweet and Sour Plum Sauce

2 tablespoons cornstarch
¾ cup sugar
⅓ cup vinegar
⅓ cup water
2 tablespoons soy sauce
1 teaspoon sherry
1 tablespoon oriental plum sauce

To prepare meatballs: Combine all ingredients, mixing well. Spoon mixture, a heaping teaspoonful at a time, onto shallow pan and bake for 15 minutes. Remove from tray, drain, and cool.

To prepare sauce: Combine cornstarch and sugar. Add vinegar, water, soy sauce, and sherry. Heat in heavy pan, stirring until thickened. Stir in the plum sauce.

Add meatballs to sauce and serve in chafing dish. The meatballs can also be served with Ginger Mayonnaise (page 27) instead of the Sweet and Sour Plum Sauce.

YIELD: ABOUT 32 MEATBALLS

Fried Ginger Chicken

1 2½-to-3-pound fryer or 3 whole
   chicken breasts
2 tablespoons soy sauce
1 teaspoon salt
dash of pepper
1 tablespoon gin or brandy

1 egg
2 tablespoons minced green onions
1 tablespoon grated fresh ginger
¼ cup flour
2 tablespoons cornstarch
4 cups vegetable oil

Cut up the fryer or, if chicken breasts are to be used, bone the breasts and cut into 1-x-2-inch pieces. Mix together all remaining ingredients except oil and marinate chicken in this mixture for 15 minutes. Heat oil in frying pan and fry chicken until golden brown.

SERVES 8

Pot Stickers

CHINESE FRIED AND STEAMED DUMPLINGS

Dumplings
4 leaves Nappa cabbage, or ¼ small
    cabbage
1 teaspoon salt
½ medium onion, chopped fine
2 green onions, chopped fine
1 teaspoon grated fresh ginger
1 tablespoon soy sauce
1 tablespoon sake or cooking sherry
¼ cup chopped chives (optional)

½ pound ground pork
1 package oriental dumpling skins
    or won ton skins
2 tablespoons vegetable oil
½ cup water

Gyoza Sauce
½ cup rice vinegar
1 teaspoon dry mustard
½ cup soy sauce

To prepare dumplings: Mince cabbage and add salt. Rub vigorously in hands to squeeze out moisture. Place in bowl and add onions, ginger, soy sauce, sake, chives, and pork and mix well.

Place 1 heaping tablespoon of the pork mixture in center of each dumpling skin and fold in half, shaping so that top is rounded and bottom is flat. Wet edges with water and seal. Heat oil in frying pan or electric skillet set at 350 degrees. Boil water. Place pot stickers in frying pan so that they are in rows, side by side and touching. Fry until golden brown, and pour in the water. Immediately place lid on pan and steam until water is gone.

To prepare Gyoza Sauce: Combine vinegar, hot mustard, and soy sauce until blended.

Serve pot stickers warm with Gyoza Sauce and Sweet and Sour Plum Sauce (top of facing page).

SERVES 10 to 12

Steak Tartar Seattle Style

Patty
⅓ pound fresh very lean ground beef
1 egg
salt and freshly ground pepper to taste
6 dashes Tabasco sauce
8 dashes Worcestershire sauce
lemon juice to taste
¼ cup mayonnaise

Garnishes
2 tomatoes, chopped
1 green bell pepper, coarsely chopped
1 white or Walla Walla sweet onion,
    chopped
¾ cup chopped black olives
2 lemons cut in wedges
red-leaf lettuce leaves

To prepare patty: Mix all ingredients except mayonnaise and mold into patty. Place patty on a bed of red-leaf lettuce and cover patty with mayonnaise. Circle with a ring of chopped tomatoes, then a ring of green pepper, a ring of white onion, and finally a ring of black olives. Serve with lemon wedges and Melba toast rounds.

SERVES 2 to 4

Note: To serve a crowd, increase ingredients proportionately and mold into a single large patty. It's the mayonnaise that makes this Seattle style.

Sausage en Croute

Pastry
8 ounces cream cheese
1 cup butter
2¼ cups flour
1 teaspoon salt

Filling
1 onion, chopped
1 cup chopped celery

½ cup butter
2 cups cooked, crumbled pork sausage
1 cup minced parsley
salt and pepper to taste
2 eggs, beaten
egg white for sealing edges
1 egg, beaten, for brushing top before baking

To prepare pastry: Beat cream cheese and butter until smooth and creamy. Add flour and salt; knead dough until it clings together. Wrap and refrigerate 2 to 3 hours or overnight. When ready to assemble, remove dough from refrigerator and let stand at room temperature 30 minutes.

To prepare filling: Brown onion and celery in butter. Add the cooked sausage, parsley, and salt and pepper. Sauté lightly, drain, and add 2 beaten eggs. Cool before putting into pastry.

Roll out a quarter of the dough at a time on a lightly floured cloth. Roll each quarter into a rectangle measuring approximately 20 x 4 inches and about ⅛ inch thick. Put 1 cup of the filling along the center. Fold dough in half, using egg white to moisten and seal the edges. Place on cookie sheet seam side down; chill 1 hour.

Preheat oven to 325 degrees.

Slice roll into 1-inch pieces, leaving in place on cookie sheet. Brush slices with beaten egg. Bake 25 to 30 minutes until lightly browned.

YIELD: 4 ROLLS, EACH SERVING 4 TO 6

Note: To freeze, place long roll on foil, cut in 1-inch slic[...] tightly, and freeze. Do not thaw before baking, but increase bak[...] time 5 minutes.

Pampered Pâté

1½ tablespoons butter
¼ pound salt pork, diced
1 medium onion, minced
1 pound chicken livers
1 teaspoon lemon juice
3 whole cloves
1 bay leaf

¼ teaspoon nutmeg
salt and freshly ground pepper to taste
3 tablespoons dry sherry
2 tablespoons heavy cream
cornichons for garnish
toast squares or a baguette of French
    bread sliced thin

Melt butter in skillet over medium heat; sauté salt pork with onion, chicken livers, lemon juice, cloves, bay leaf, nutmeg, salt, and pepper until liver is cooked but still slightly pink inside. Remove from heat, stir in sherry, and, when cool, add cream and mix in a food processor or blender until smooth. Serve in a small crock or tureen, garnished with cornichons. Spread on toast squares or thin slices of French bread.

YIELD: ABOUT 2 CUPS

Hot Artichoke Dip

1 cup mayonnaise
1 cup freshly grated Parmesan cheese

1 8½-ounce can artichoke hearts, not
    marinated, coarsely chopped
1 7-ounce can chopped green chilis

Preheat oven to 375 degrees.

Combine all ingredients and pour mixture into a shallow baking dish. Bake 10 to 15 minutes or until bubbly and heated through. Serve with tortilla chips.

YIELD: ABOUT 2 CUPS

Artichoke Leaves with Shrimp

2 fresh artichokes
6 ounces cream cheese
4 cloves garlic, minced

2 tablespoons lemon juice
dash of Tabasco sauce
½ pound fresh tiny shrimp

Steam artichokes until tender—about 45 minutes. Drain and chill. Blend together cream cheese, garlic, lemon juice, and Tabasco until smooth. Remove artichoke leaves, dip each one in cream cheese mixture, arrange on a platter, topping each leaf with baby shrimp.

SERVES 6 TO 8

Artichoke-Vegetable Melange

Serve this as a first course, a luncheon entrée, or an appetizer.

Dressing
¾ cup mayonnaise
½ cup unflavored yogurt
1 small clove garlic, minced
1 tablespoon minced parsley
1 teaspoon onion powder
½ teaspoon salt
pinch of thyme

Vegetables
4 large artichokes

¼ cup oil
¼ cup chopped onion
¾ cup cocktail onions
1 small clove garlic
¾ cup zucchini, quartered and sliced
    diagonally
½ cup diced green bell pepper
1 cup sliced carrots, blanched
¼ teaspoon salt
dash of pepper
¾ cup diced tomatoes

To prepare dressing: Combine dressing ingredients in a blender and mix until smooth. Cover and chill for several hours.

To prepare vegetables: Steam artichokes over boiling water seasoned with garlic until tender—about 45 minutes. Drain and chill. Heat oil in large skillet; add onions and garlic and sauté approximately 2 minutes, stirring constantly. Remove garlic. Add zucchini, green pepper, carrots, salt, and pepper, and sauté until vegetables are just tender, approximately 2 more minutes. Remove from heat and stir in tomatoes. Transfer to a bowl, cover, and chill. (May be prepared ahead to this point.)

Remove the center and choke of each artichoke by careflly spreading the leaves. Cut stem so that each artichoke sits upright. Spoon some of the vegetable mixture into center of, and some around, each artichoke. Stir dressing and spoon over artichokes. Serve remaining dressing separately.

SERVES 4

Crisp Artichoke Hearts

¾ cup buttermilk
3 tablespoons flour
½ teaspoon Beau Monde seasoning
1 8½-ounce can artichoke hearts
  (not marinated)

½ cup seasoned bread crumbs
½ cup grated Parmesan or Romano
  cheese
oil for deep-frying

Combine buttermilk, flour, and Beau Monde. Mix thoroughly to make a batter. Quarter artichoke hearts, dip into batter, coating well, and roll in bread crumbs.

Heat oil in deep skillet to 350 degrees. Deep-fry artichokes until golden. Remove from oil, drain on paper towels, and sprinkle with cheese. Serve warm with Garlic Hollandaise Sauce (following recipe) as a dip.

SERVES 8

Garlic Hollandaise Sauce

¾ cup butter
3 egg yolks
2 tablespoons lemon juice
1 tablespoon cold butter

1 tablespoon heavy cream
salt, white pepper, and minced garlic
  to taste

Melt 2 tablespoons butter in a small pan. Set aside and keep warm. In a 2-quart saucepan, beat egg yolks with a wire whisk. Beat in lemon juice. Place pan over very low heat and stir in 1 tablespoon cold butter. Using wire whisk and stirring constantly, add remaining butter a tablespoon at a time until butter melts and mixture is thick and coats whisk lightly. Remove pan from heat and *slowly* add cream, beating constantly. Season with salt, pepper, and garlic.

YIELD: 2 CUPS

Antipasto

Marinade
6 tablespoons tarragon vinegar
¼ cup olive oil
½ cup vegetable oil
2 tablespoons lemon juice
1 teaspoon sugar
1 tablespoon salt
freshly ground pepper to taste
2 teaspoons oregano
2 cloves garlic, minced

Vegetables
1 cucumber
3 carrots

½ head cauliflower, blanched
½ pound mushrooms, sliced
½ pound string beans, blanched
4 green onions
1 red bell pepper
1 green bell pepper

Accompaniments
Italian dry salami
Italian dry olives
pimiento peppers
pepperoncini
capers
red-leaf lettuce

To prepare marinade: Combine ingredients and mix well.

To prepare vegetables: Cut vegetables into serving-size pieces. Place in a shallow dish and cover with marinade. Refrigerate and marinate at least 3 to 4 hours, stirring occasionally. Drain vegetables and arrange on red-leaf lettuce leaves with choice of accompaniments.

SERVES 8 TO 10

Stuffed Cherry Tomatoes

2 cups marinated artichoke hearts,
    drained and chopped fine
½ cup chopped celery
½ cup chopped green onion
1 cup mayonnaise

salt and pepper to taste
2 cups cherry tomatoes
12 slices bacon, cooked and crumbled
2 bunches parsley for garnish

Chop artichokes; mix with chopped celery, green onion, mayonnaise, salt, and pepper.

Cut each tomato in half, remove seeds, and drain upside down on paper towels. Stuff each tomato half with artichoke mixture and sprinkle with crumbled bacon. Refrigerate. Serve on a bed of parsley to keep tomatoes from rolling.

SERVES 10 TO 12

Spinach Squares

2 10-ounce packages frozen chopped
   spinach
3 tablespoons butter
1 small onion, chopped
¼ pound mushrooms, sliced
4 eggs
¼ cup bread crumbs

1 cup White Sauce (page 22) or 1 can
   condensed mushroom soup
¼ cup freshly grated Parmesan cheese
⅛ teaspoon pepper
¼ teaspoon oregano
¼ teaspoon basil

Preheat oven to 325 degrees. Butter a 9-x-13-inch pan.

Cook spinach and squeeze out moisture. Set aside. Melt butter over medium heat; add onion and mushrooms and sauté until limp.

In a bowl, beat eggs with fork. Stir in crumbs, White Sauce, 2 tablespoons cheese, pepper, oregano, basil, drained spinach, and onion-mushroom mixture. Turn into prepared pan and sprinkle with remaining cheese. Bake uncovered for 35 minutes. Cool before cutting. To serve warm, reheat 10 to 12 minutes.

YIELD: 48 PIECES

Sugared Nuts

2 teaspoons cinnamon
½ cup sugar

2 cups pecans or walnuts
2 unbeaten egg whites

Preheat oven to 350 degrees.

Mix cinnamon and sugar. Roll nuts in egg whites and then in sugar-cinnamon mixture. Bake for 5 to 10 minutes or until golden brown.

SERVES 4

Cocktail Pecans

2 tablespoons butter, melted
½ teaspoon seasoned salt
2 dashes Tabasco sauce

1 pound pecans
3 tablespoons Worcestershire sauce

Preheat oven to 300 degrees.

Combine butter, salt, and Tabasco and stir in pecans. Spread in a 9-x-13-inch pan. Bake for 20 minutes, stirring occasionally. Add Worcestershire, stir, and bake 15 minutes more.

SERVES 6 TO 10

Beer Nuts

¾ cup dry roasted peanuts
½ tablespoon butter

1½ tablespoons brown sugar
½ teaspoon curry powder

In a heavy frying pan, melt butter and mix in brown sugar and curry powder. Stir in peanuts and cook for 3 to 4 minutes over medium-low heat, stirring constantly. Cool on aluminum foil, separating the nuts. Store in a covered jar.

YIELD: ¾ CUP

Spinach Dip in Red Cabbage

1 red cabbage

Filling
1 10-ounce package frozen chopped
    spinach, thawed
½ cup minced parsley
½ cup chopped green onion
½ teaspoon dill
½ teaspoon Beau Monde seasoning
1 cup mayonnaise
1 cup sour cream
2 tablespoons lemon juice

Vegetables
carrot sticks
cauliflower flowerets
zucchini spears
broccoli flowerets
celery sticks
turnip slices
white radishes
red bell pepper slices

To prepare cabbage: Cut stem so cabbage sits level. Then cut a hole 3 inches in diameter in top of cabbage to provide a cavity for the filling.

To prepare filling: Squeeze spinach to remove moisture. Combine with remaining ingredients, mix well, and spoon into cabbage. Chill until ready to serve.

Place cabbage in center of a serving platter, surrounding with assorted vegetables to be dipped in the spinach filling.

Smoked Salmon and Caviar Checkerboard

1 loaf (about 10 slices) wheat bread,
    sliced thin
1 loaf (about 10 slices) home-style
    white bread, sliced thin

½ cup unsalted butter, softened
8 ounces cream cheese, softened
freshly ground pepper to taste

1 pound smoked salmon (Nova Scotia
lox or Scottish salmon), sliced thin
2 to 3 jars Beluga caviar

juice of 1 lemon
parsley or watercress for garnish

Trim crusts from bread, butter each slice, and cut into 1½-inch squares. This will yield about 40 squares per loaf. Cover with a damp tea towel to prevent drying.

Spread wheat squares with cream cheese. (Cream cheese must be spread on *after* bread is in squares; otherwise bread will tear when cut.) Sprinkle these squares lightly with pepper and top with sliced smoked salmon. Spread white squares with caviar and sprinkle with lemon juice. Arrange squares on trays, alternating wheat and white squares to form a checkerboard pattern. Garnish with parsley or watercress.

SERVES 20 TO 30

The Triangle

A refreshing afternoon cooler.

Equal parts of
grapefruit juice

orange juice
ginger ale

Mix and pour over ice cubes in tall glasses.

Sneaky Petes

1 6-ounce can frozen daiquiri
concentrate or 1 6-ounce can
frozen lime concentrate combined
with ¼ cup superfine sugar

6 ounces vodka (use empty
concentrate can to measure)
3 scoops vanilla ice cream
crushed ice

Blend daiquiri mix, vodka, and ice cream in a blender. Add ice and blend briefly. Serve in coupe glasses or champagne glasses.

SERVES 4

Orange Vermouth

1 bottle dry vermouth
1 6-ounce can frozen orange juice
   concentrate

1½ cups water
orange slices

Mix vermouth, orange juice concentrate, and water. Serve over ice cubes in tall glasses, with an orange slice floating on top of each drink.

SERVES 4

Lullaby

½ 6-ounce can of beer
1 6-ounce can frozen lemonade
   concentrate

3 ounces (2 jiggers) whiskey
crushed ice
soda water to taste

Mix first 4 ingredients in blender. Add soda water and stir. Serve in whiskey-sour glasses or old-fashioned glasses.

SERVES 4

Strawberry Margarita

1 6-ounce can frozen daiquiri
   concentrate
1 10-ounce package frozen
   strawberries

4 ounces tequila
2 ounces Triple Sec
crushed ice
sugar

Mix first 4 ingredients in a blender, and add ice while blender is on. Serve in stemmed glasses whose rims have been moistened and dipped in sugar.

SERVES 4

Dirty Mother

An after-dinner drink.

2 ounces Kahlua
¾ ounce tequila

milk
crushed ice

Pour Kahlua and tequila into a double old-fashioned glass. Add crushed ice and fill the glass with milk.

SERVES 1

Margarita Wine Punch

A summer cooler for a crowd.

1 12-ounce can frozen lemonade
    concentrate
1 6-ounce can frozen limeade
    concentrate

2 quarts dry white wine
ice cubes
½ lemon
¼ cup salt

In a punch bowl, stir together the concentrate and wine and add ice cubes. Serve in punch glasses whose rims have been rubbed with lemon and dipped in salt.

Coffee Nudge

To be served after dinner instead of dessert.

1 ounce brandy
1 ounce creme de cacao
1 ounce Kahlua

coffee
heavy cream, whipped

Mix liqueurs in warm cup and fill with coffee. Top with whipped cream.

SERVES 1

Bloomer Droppers

1 6-ounce can frozen lemonade
    concentrate
6 ounces vodka

6 ripe peaches, peeled and sliced
crushed ice

Mix ingredients in blender; pour into stemmed glasses.

SERVES 6

Winter snow blankets the village of Fir, with Mount Baker in the distance and the Fir Lutheran Church in the foreground.

Soups

━━━

Puget Crab Chowder

1 pound fresh crabmeat
3 tablespoons dry sherry
¼ cup butter
1 medium onion, chopped
½ green bell pepper, chopped (about
   3 tablespoons)

1 green onion, chopped
1½ teaspoons chili powder
2 tablespoons flour
2 cups light cream
fresh lemon juice to taste
salt to taste

Heat crabmeat and sherry in a double boiler. In a frying pan sauté onion and green bell pepper in butter until softened but not browned. Combine chili powder and flour and add to onion-pepper mixture. Cook over medium-low heat for 3 minutes, then slowly add cream, blending thoroughly. Pour over crabmeat and sherry in double boiler, stir gently, and add lemon juice and salt.

SERVES 4

San Juans Seafood Chowder

Chowder

1 yellow onion, chopped
1 cup chopped leeks (white part only)
½ cup chopped celery
¼ cup butter

2 cups clam nectar
2½ cups dry white wine
3 cloves garlic, minced
1 bay leaf
½ teaspoon thyme

¼ teaspoon freshly ground pepper
dash of Tabasco sauce
½ cup chopped parsley
1 pound scallops
10 fresh steamer clams
1 pound fillets of sole, cut into 1½-inch
    squares

1 pound medium shrimp, shelled and
    deveined
1 cup heavy cream, scalded
croutons and white pepper for garnish

Croutons
½ baguette of French bread
½ cup butter

To prepare chowder: Sauté onion, leeks, and celery in butter in a large heavy saucepan until tender. Add clam nectar, wine, garlic, bay leaf, thyme, pepper, Tabasco, and parsley. Bring to a boil, reduce heat, and simmer uncovered for 5 minutes. Add scallops and clams and cook over medium-low heat for 3 minutes. Add sole and shrimp and cook until shrimp just turn pink. Remove bay leaf and stir in cream until warm.

To prepare croutons: Slice bread into ¼-inch slices, sauté in butter over moderate heat until golden brown, and drain on paper towels.

Serve soup in wide bowls and garnish with croutons and pepper.

SERVES 4

Manhattan Seafood Stew

½ cup butter
2 medium onions, chopped
3 cloves garlic, minced
1 cup chopped parsley
1 28-ounce can tomatoes, chopped
3 cups chicken broth
1 bay leaf
1 tablespoon basil
½ teaspoon thyme
¾ teaspoon oregano

½ teaspoon salt
1¼ cups dry white wine

Three of the following:

1 cup fresh crabmeat
1½ pounds medium shrimp
1 pound sea scallops, halved
1½ pounds steamer clams or ½ pound
    chopped clams, drained
1 pound white fish fillets, cubed

In a medium-size heavy saucepan, melt butter and add onion, garlic, and parsley. Cook until onion is limp. Add tomatoes, broth, bay leaf, basil, thyme, oregano, and salt. Cover and simmer 1 hour.

Add wine and simmer stock another 20 minutes, uncovered. Add seafood and simmer, uncovered, about 20 minutes more or until shrimp are pink, scallops are opaque, clam shells are open, and fish flakes easily. Serve in large individual bowls.

SERVES 8

Oyster–Spinach Soup

7 tablespoons butter
¼ cup chopped onion
1 clove garlic, minced
1 pint oysters and liquid
¼ cup flour
3 cups light cream

1 cup chicken broth
¾ cup spinach purée
salt and pepper to taste
¼ teaspoon nutmeg
chopped parsley for garnish

In a medium saucepan, melt 4 tablespoons butter, add onion and garlic, and sauté. Add oysters and their liquid and cook until oysters curl. Set aside.

In a 4-quart pan melt remaining butter, stir in flour, and cook gently about 5 minutes, until foaming but not brown. Gradually add cream, stirring until mixture thickens. Stir in chicken broth, spinach purée, and oyster-onion mixture, and bring to a boil. Cool slightly.

Purée entire mixture in batches in food processor or blender, return to pan, reheat, and taste for seasoning. Stir in nutmeg and garnish with parsley.

SERVES 6

Note: This soup may be made ahead and frozen.

Seafood Chowder

3 cups water
2 cups chopped, peeled red or white
    potato
1 cup chopped celery
1½ teaspoons salt
¼ teaspoon pepper
¼ teaspoon allspice
¼ cup butter
¼ cup flour
2 cups milk
1 pound cod fillets, cut into ½-inch
    pieces

1 teaspoon dill
1 cup grated or chopped cucumber,
    peeled and seeded
½ teaspoon paprika
2 tablespoons lemon juice
1 hard-cooked egg, sliced

Optional garnishes
½ cup chopped parsley
½ cup white wine or clam juice
1 14-ounce can tomatoes, chopped

Bring water to a boil and add potato, celery, salt, pepper, and allspice and return to boiling. Reduce heat, cover, and simmer 10 to 12 minutes. Drain, reserving 2 cups of broth. Set vegetables aside.

Melt butter in a large kettle. Stir in flour and cook over low heat until bubbly. Remove from heat and stir in milk and reserved broth. Return to heat, boil, and add cod and dill. Reduce heat and simmer, uncovered, about 8 minutes or until fish is just opaque.

Stir in cucumber, paprika, lemon juice, and reserved vegetables, and heat thoroughly. If desired, add parsley, wine, clam juice, or tomatoes. Garnish with egg slices.

SERVES 6 TO 8

Black-Tie Tomato Soup

When something elegant should start the meal, this soup, with the pungent flavor of gin, is recommended.

1 tablespoon unflavored gelatin
¼ cup cold water
1¾ pounds tomatoes, peeled and
    seeded
1 teaspoon sugar
salt and freshly ground pepper to taste
2 large cloves garlic, minced
4 slices bacon
5 tablespoons butter at room
    temperature

⅛ teaspoon thyme
pinch of basil
¼ pound fresh mushrooms, sliced
¼ cup gin
½ cup heavy cream
minced parsley and sliced mushrooms
    for garnish
½ cup heavy cream, whipped, for
    garnish

In a small pan, put gelatin in water and let stand until softened. Place over low heat, stir 3 minutes, and set aside.

Purée tomatoes in blender or food processor until smooth. Add sugar, salt, pepper, and half of minced garlic. Blend in softened gelatin, mix well, and set aside. Sauté bacon until crisp, drain well, and crumble. In a small bowl whip butter; add bacon, remaining garlic, thyme, and basil, and blend thoroughly.

Place bacon mixture in large frying pan and melt over medium-high heat. Add mushrooms and sauté lightly. Warm gin in small pan, add to mushrooms, and ignite. Reduce heat and add tomato mixture, stirring until blended. Pour in cream; simmer gently 20 minutes.

Garnish with parsley, thin-sliced mushrooms, and a dollop of whipped cream.

SERVES 4

Light Mushroom Soup

2 tablespoons butter
3 medium onions, chopped
1 pound mushrooms, sliced
2 tablespoons chicken bouillon
    dissolved in 3 cups hot water
½ cup chopped parsley
2 tablespoons tomato paste
1 clove garlic, minced

¼ teaspoon freshly ground black
    pepper
½ cup dry white wine
1 cup cheese-garlic croutons for
    garnish
¼ cup freshly grated Parmesan cheese
    for garnish

In a heavy 3-quart saucepan, melt butter over medium heat; add onions and sauté until almost tender, and add mushrooms and sauté lightly. Stir in bouillon mixture, parsley, tomato paste, garlic, and pepper. After bringing soup to a boil, reduce heat and add wine. Cover and simmer 5 minutes.

Garnish with croutons and cheese and serve immediately.

SERVES 4 TO 6

Chinese Mushroom Soup

7 cups chicken stock
½ pound mushrooms, sliced
3 ounces spinach, chopped
2 slices fresh ginger (size of quarters),
    peeled and minced
2 cloves garlic, minced
2½ tablespoons soy sauce
½ teaspoon sugar
⅛ teaspoon freshly ground pepper
⅛ teaspoon crushed red pepper

¼ cup dry sherry
2 tablespoons cornstarch
2 ounces vermicelli, cooked and
    drained
1 egg, lightly beaten
½ tablespoon sesame oil
½ pound bean sprouts, slightly
    chopped
½ bunch green onion, chopped

Bring stock to a boil in a large pot, reduce heat, and add mushrooms, spinach, ginger, garlic, soy sauce, sugar, and both kinds of pepper. Simmer uncovered for 40 minutes.

Combine sherry and cornstarch to make thin paste and set aside. Before serving, bring soup to a boil. Stir cornstarch mixture again, removing any lumps, then slowly blend into soup, stirring constantly until soup is thickened and clear. Add vermicelli and remove from heat.

While stirring soup gently, pour in egg, blending until light strands appear. Stir in sesame oil. Divide bean sprouts and green onions evenly among individual bowls and fill with hot soup.

SERVES 8 TO 10

Cream of Mushroom Soup

½ cup butter
2 pounds mushrooms, sliced
½ cup flour
3¼ cups chicken stock
1 quart heavy cream
1 quart light cream
1 cup sherry

2 bunches green onions, chopped
   (about 2 cups)
2 teaspoons salt
2 teaspoons freshly ground pepper
1 tablespoon lemon juice
½ cup chopped parsley

In a heavy 4-quart saucepan, melt butter and sauté mushrooms about 3 minutes over medium-high heat. Stir in flour and mix well. Slowly add chicken stock, stirring constantly until thickened. Reduce heat, add remaining ingredients, and simmer 2 hours over very low heat, stirring occasionally.

SERVES 8 TO 10

Cream of Broccoli Soup

2 pounds broccoli
¼ cup butter
2 onions, chopped
1 cup chopped celery
1 clove garlic, minced
½ cup flour

4 cups milk
4 cups chicken broth
½ teaspoon thyme
½ teaspoon marjoram
salt and freshly ground pepper to taste
1 tomato, chopped, for garnish

Trim broccoli; peel and slice stems and break tops into flowerets. Steam until tender but still slightly crisp; then plunge into cold water to stop cooking.

In a 4-quart pot, melt butter and sauté onions, celery, and garlic. Stir in flour and cook gently about 5 minutes. Gradually add milk, broth, and herbs, stirring constantly over low heat until thickened and bubbly. Add cooked broccoli, salt, and pepper, and heat thoroughly but do not boil. Garnish with chopped tomato.

SERVES 8

Garden Tomato Soup

3 tablespoons butter
2 tablespoons olive oil
1 large onion, sliced thin
½ teaspoon dill
½ teaspoon thyme
8 medium tomatoes, peeled and
    quartered, or 1 28-ounce and
    1 15-ounce can Italian plum
    tomatoes, drained
3 tablespoons tomato paste

¼ cup flour
3½ cups chicken broth
2 tablespoons sugar
1½ teaspoons salt
¼ teaspoon freshly ground pepper
1 cup heavy cream
½ cup freshly grated Parmesan cheese
yogurt, fresh dill, or croutons for
    garnish

In a large kettle combine butter, oil, onion, and herbs; cook over medium heat until soft and golden. Add tomatoes and tomato paste and simmer uncovered for 10 minutes.

Blend flour and ½ cup chicken broth in small bowl. Add to tomato mixture with remaining broth. Increase heat to high and bring almost to a boil. Reduce heat and simmer uncovered for 30 minutes, stirring frequently.

Using a blender or food processor, purée soup in batches and add sugar, salt, and pepper. At this point, soup can be refrigerated for up to 3 days or frozen.

When ready to serve, whip cream until stiff and fold in the grated cheese. Ladle soup—hot or cold—into individual bowls and place a dollop of cream mixture on top of each. Broil 6 inches from heat for 45 seconds or less, until cream mixture is melted. Garnish with yogurt, dill, or croutons.

SERVES 6

Cream of Zucchini Soup

6 cups chicken stock
4 small zucchini, sliced
3 stalks celery, sliced
1 small onion, chopped
2 shallots, chopped
¼ cup butter
3 tablespoons uncooked Cream of
    Wheat

¼ teaspoon chervil
¼ teaspoon basil
¼ teaspoon rosemary
2 egg yolks, beaten
½ cup heavy cream
¼ teaspoon white pepper for garnish
3 sprigs parsley, chopped, for garnish

Heat stock in a large pot. Meanwhile, sauté zucchini, celery, onion, and shallots in butter until transparent. Sprinkle Cream of Wheat, chervil, basil, and rosemary over vegetables and cook another 2 minutes. Add vegetable mixture to stock, simmer 20 minutes, and purée in batches in food processor or blender.

Whip together egg yolks and cream with wire whisk. Spoon ¼ cup hot soup into cream and then gradually return cream mixture to hot soup. Garnish with white pepper and parsley and serve immediately.

SERVES 8

Autumn Cream Soup

1 cup heavy cream
1 cup sour cream
4 medium carrots, grated
2 onions, chopped
1 large apple, peeled, cored, and
    grated

½ cup butter
4 cups chicken broth
2 tablespoons sugar
¾ cup dry vermouth
¼ cup chopped parsley for garnish

Combine cream and sour cream and let stand for 4 hours.

Sauté carrots, onions, and apple in butter until soft. Combine this mixture with chicken broth, sugar, and vermouth, and purée in blender or food processor. Add cream mixture, reheat (do not boil), and serve immediately. Garnish with parsley.

SERVES 6 TO 8

Cream of Artichoke Soup

1 cup butter
1½ medium onions, finely chopped
3 celery ribs, coarsely chopped
1 leek, white and green parts, washed
    and chopped
½ cup flour
3 quarts chicken broth
8 large artichokes, bottoms and peeled

stems only (what remains after
    leaves and chokes have been
    removed), cut into small pieces
1 large red or white potato, peeled and
    halved
1 cup broccoli flowerets
1¼ cups heavy cream
salt and pepper to taste

In a large deep pan, melt butter. Add the onions and sauté until soft but not brown. Add celery and leek and simmer over medium heat for 10 minutes, stirring frequently, until the vegetables are soft but not brown.

Blend in flour, stirring with a wooden spoon, to make a smooth *roux*, and cook for 2 minutes. Gradually stir in broth, being careful not to let lumps form. Bring soup to a boil, stirring constantly. Add the artichoke bottoms and stems, potato, and broccoli flowerets. Lower heat and let soup simmer gently, uncovered, for 2 hours. The long simmering brings out the full artichoke flavor.

Force the soup through the fine disk of a food mill or through a coarse sieve—do *not* put the soup in a food processor or blender. Return soup to saucepan, reheat gently, and stir in the cream and salt and pepper.

SERVES 10 TO 12

Note: The leaves that have been removed from the artichokes can be steamed—don't dispose of them simply because they're no longer attached.

Black Bean Soup

Soup

2 cups dried black beans
2½ quarts water or broth
1½ tablespoons salt
3 tablespoons olive oil
1 large onion, chopped
5 cloves garlic, minced
2 tablespoons white vinegar
1½ teaspoons cumin
1½ teaspoons oregano

Garnishes

1 cup yogurt
8 ounces dry sherry
1 cup minced green bell pepper
1 cup minced red bell pepper
    (optional)
1 cup minced green onion
2 lemons, sliced thin
1 cup sour cream
1 cup chopped ham

In a 4-quart saucepan, soak beans in water or stock overnight. After they have soaked, add salt and bring to a boil over medium heat. Cover and simmer, stirring occasionally, until soft (about 2½ hours).

Heat oil in a medium skillet; add onion and garlic and sauté 2 minutes. Add to soup along with vinegar, cumin, and oregano. Cover and simmer 1½ hours, stirring occasionally.

Ladle soup into individual bowls and serve garnishes separately.

SERVES 8

Split Pea Soup

2 cups dried split green peas
3½ quarts water
1 ham hock
4 medium red or white potatoes,
    peeled and sliced
4 teaspoons salt
1 cup chopped leeks
2 cups chopped onion

1 celery root, peeled and chopped
½ cup chopped celery leaves
1 bay leaf
1 cup diced ham
1 smoked sausage ring, sliced
3 tablespoons chopped parsley for
    garnish

Place dried peas in a large heavy pan, add water, and soak at least 12 hours.

Add ham hock and bring to a boil; reduce heat and simmer, covered, for 1 hour, stirring occasionally. Add all remaining ingredients except sausage and parsley; return to a boil, then reduce heat and simmer, covered, for 2½ hours, stirring occasionally. Soup should be thick and smooth.

Remove bay leaf and ham hock. Stir in sausage and cook until sausage is heated through, about 5 to 10 minutes. Serve garnished with parsley.

SERVES 8

Greek Chicken–Lemon Soup

8 cups chicken broth
½ cup lemon juice
½ cup grated carrot
½ cup chopped celery
½ cup chopped onion
¼ cup chicken stock base (powdered
    seasoning for dissolving in water)
¼ cup butter, softened

¼ cup flour
7 egg yolks at room temperature
1½ cups cooked white rice
1 cup diced cooked chicken
white pepper to taste
1 lemon, sliced thin, for garnish
chopped parsley for garnish

In a large pot, combine the first 6 ingredients and bring to a boil. Reduce heat, partially cover, and simmer 30 minutes.

Mix butter and flour in a shallow bowl until smooth. Add to soup in small amounts, blending thoroughly after each addition. Simmer 15 minutes, stirring frequently.

With electric mixer on high speed, whip egg yolks until light and lemon-colored. At medium speed, add 2 cups hot soup very slowly, in a thin stream. Slowly return mixture to remaining soup and heat but do not boil. Add rice, chicken, and pepper. Ladle soup into individual bowls and garnish with lemon slices and parsley.

SERVES 8 TO 10

Mulligatawny

Stewing broth

6 cups water
1 teaspoon salt
1 teaspoon whole coriander seeds
1½ teaspoons poppy seeds
2 whole cloves
½ cup grated coconut
1 onion, coarsely chopped

Soup

1 whole chicken, about 3 pounds
    (giblets removed)
stewing broth

¼ cup butter
3 tablespoons turmeric
1 onion, finely chopped
3 cloves garlic, minced
3 tablespoons flour
1 16-ounce can garbanzo beans
salt to taste
cayenne to taste
3 to 4 cups cooked white rice
lemon wedges
lemon slices for garnish
1 cup yogurt for garnish

To prepare stewing broth: In a large pot, combine all ingredients and bring to a boil. Reduce heat and simmer 30 minutes, covered.

To prepare soup: Place chicken in stewing broth and simmer, covered, 45 minutes. Remove chicken and cool, reserving broth. When chicken is cool, remove bones and skin from meat, and shred meat coarsely, and chill. Place bones and skin in stewing broth and continue to simmer, covered, 1 hour. Strain broth and chill. When chilled, skim off fat.

In a large pot, melt butter over medium heat and add turmeric, onion, and garlic and sauté until onion is soft. Stir in flour, cook until bubbly, reduce heat, and gradually stir in strained broth. Cook, stirring constantly, until thickened. In a blender or food processor, purée garbanzo beans in their liquid and add to soup along with chicken meat, stirring frequently. Add salt and cayenne and heat thoroughly.

When ready to serve, place ¼ cup rice in each bowl and ladle soup over rice. Squeeze wedge of lemon over each bowl and garnish with lemon slice and dollop of yogurt. The lemon juice and lemon slices are important, so don't skimp.

SERVES 6 TO 8

Mexican Chicken Soup with Rice

Soup

5 large cloves garlic, minced
¼ teaspoon ground cloves
4 teaspoons oregano
11 cups water
1 3-pound frying chicken
1 tablespoon chicken stock base
   (powdered seasoning for dis-
   solving in water)
1 tablespoon salt
5 teaspoons cumin
1½ teaspoons freshly ground pepper
3 bay leaves
4 large fresh basil leaves or 1 teaspoon
   dried basil
2 cups sliced zucchini
1½ cups sliced carrots
1¼ cups diced green bell pepper
1 onion, sliced

Rice

1 cup uncooked rice
lemon juice to taste
2 tablespoons vegetable oil
1 medium tomato, chopped
1 medium green bell pepper, chopped
1 large clove garlic, minced
1 tablespoon chicken stock base
1¼ cups hot water
1½ teaspoons cumin
¼ teaspoon salt
⅛ teaspoon freshly ground pepper

Condiments

1 bunch green onions, chopped
¾ cup chopped parsley
1 fresh jalapeno chili pepper, chopped
2 firm tomatoes, chopped
1 cup sour cream
1 avocado, sliced
4 corn tortillas cut into ¼-inch strips
   and fried

To prepare soup: In a small bowl, preferably a mortar, crush or mash together garlic, cloves, and oregano until they form a paste. In a soup pot, bring water to a boil and add chicken base, salt, cumin, pepper, bay leaves, basil, and garlic paste. Return to boiling, reduce heat, and simmer until chicken is cooked, about 1 hour. Remove chicken to cool.

Put zucchini, carrots, green pepper, and onion in pot, bring to a boil, reduce heat, and simmer about 15 minutes, or until vegetables are tender but still crisp. Remove skin and bones from chicken and shred meat coarsely. Return meat to soup and heat thoroughly.

To prepare rice: Combine rice with enough hot water to cover. Squeeze a wedge of lemon over the water and let stand for 5 minutes. Drain.

In a large heavy skillet, heat oil over medium-high heat. Add rice and sauté until golden. Add tomato, green pepper, and garlic and sauté 7 minutes. Dissolve stock base in 1¼ cups hot water and add, along with remaining ingredients, to rice. Reduce heat, cover, and simmer 15 minutes.

To serve, put ¼ cup rice in bottom of each bowl. Ladle soup over rice and garnish with 1 or more condiments.

SERVES 12

Note: Soup may be partially prepared ahead of time. Cook chicken in seasoned broth until tender. Remove and cool chicken, refrigerate broth, and, when chicken can be handled, remove skin and bones and shred meat coarsely. Refrigerate until ready to reheat; then add vegetables.

Hearty Turkey Soup

8 to 9 cups turkey broth or, for less
    filling soup, 10 to 12 cups
½ cup long-grain rice
3 medium carrots, sliced
3 stalks celery, sliced
6 tablespoons butter
6 tablespoons flour
2 cups light cream

3½ cups cooked turkey, chopped
3 small zucchini, sliced
½ pound mushrooms, sliced
½ cup chopped green onion
salt and freshly ground pepper to taste
1 egg yolk
½ cup chopped parsley for garnish

In a large kettle, heat broth to boiling. Add rice, carrots, and celery; reduce heat and simmer for 20 minutes, covered, or until vegetables are tender.

Melt butter in a small saucepan; add flour and cook until bubbly. Pour in cream and about 1 cup soup broth. Heat and cook until thickened, stirring constantly. Add this mixture to soup broth.

Stir in turkey, zucchini, mushrooms, green onion, salt, and pepper. Heat thoroughly until zucchini is tender but still crisp. Place egg yolk in a small bowl and pour ½ cup soup in a very thin stream into egg yolk. Stir yolk mixture into soup. Garnish individual servings with parsley.

SERVES 6 TO 8

Ground Steak Soup

4 cups water
1 cup cubed carrots
1 cup sliced celery
1 cup chopped onion
1 cup cubed red or white potatoes
1 pound coarsely ground round steak

6 tablespoons butter
6 tablespoons flour
1 16-ounce can whole tomatoes, cut up
1 10-ounce package frozen mixed
    vegetables

1½ tablespoons beef stock base
    (powdered seasoning for dis-
    solving in water)
½ teaspoon oregano

¼ teaspoon coarsely ground pepper
¼ cup burgundy
salt to taste
¼ cup chopped parsley

In a Dutch oven, bring 1 cup water to a boil and add carrots, celery, onion, and potato. Reduce heat and simmer 20 minutes or until vegetables are tender but slightly crisp. Drain vegetables, reserving liquid. In a frying pan, cook beef until it loses its red color.

In a small saucepan, melt butter, add flour, and stir until smooth. Combine 1 cup water with butter mixture, then add reserved liquid, stirring until smooth. Pour into vegetables, mixing well. Add remaining 2 cups water to vegetables. Drain fat from beef and add beef to vegetables along with remaining ingredients. Bring to a boil, reduce heat, and simmer, stirring occasionally, for 30 to 45 minutes.

SERVES 6 TO 8

Savory Beef-Vegetable Soup

1 tablespoon vegetable oil
1½ to 2 pounds beef shanks
1 pound stew beef
10 cups water
2 16-ounce cans tomatoes and liquid
1 sliced onion
1 tablespoon salt
½ teaspoon freshly ground pepper
1¼ cups barley

2 tablespoons beef stock base
    (powdered seasoning for dis-
    solving in water)
3 stalks celery, sliced
3 small carrots, sliced
1 large zucchini, sliced
½ pound broccoli, stalks peeled and
    sliced, and tops broken into
    flowerets

In a large soup pot, heat oil and brown shanks and stew beef well on all sides. Remove fat and add water, tomatoes, onion, salt, and pepper. Bring to a boil over high heat; reduce heat; cover and simmer 1 hour, stirring occasionally.

Take out meat and cut into pieces, removing fat and bones. Skim fat from broth. Return meat to pot and stir in barley and stock base. Heat to boiling, reduce heat, cover, and simmer 40 minutes. Soup may be set aside or refrigerated at this point to await vegetables.

A half-hour before serving, add celery and carrots. Bring to a boil, then simmer for 15 minutes. Add zucchini and broccoli and cook another 10 to 15 minutes until vegetables are tender but slightly crisp, stirring occasionally.

SERVES 6 TO 8

Oxtail Soup

3 pounds oxtails
¼ cup flour
2 tablespoons cognac or brandy,
   warmed
6½ cups chicken broth
1 carrot, sliced
1 large white onion, sliced

1 stalk celery, sliced
1 teaspoon thyme
1 bay leaf
2 sprigs parsley
salt and pepper to taste
1½ cups white wine
chopped parsley for garnish

Preheat oven to 450 degrees.

Sprinkle oxtails with flour and roast in a shallow pan for 30 minutes, turning oxtails several times.

Pour cognac or brandy over oxtails, ignite, and remove to large pot. Reduce oven temperature to 350 degrees. Pour chicken broth into roasting pan, stir to deglaze, and pour stock over oxtails. Add remaining ingredients, cover, and bake for 3 hours. Reduce oven temperature to 325 degrees and bake for an additional 3 hours.

Cool, remove meat from bones, discarding any fat, and remove bay leaf and parsley sprigs. Refrigerate overnight. Skim off fat. Reheat soup slowly but do not boil. Transfer to soup tureen or large individual soup bowls and garnish with parsley.

SERVES 4 TO 6

Note: Prepare several days ahead for best blend of flavors. This soup freezes well.

Minestrone

1½ pounds mild Italian sausage, casing
   removed, sliced
2 cloves garlic, minced
2 large onions, chopped
2 16-ounce cans Italian stewed
   tomatoes
4 cups beef broth
1¼ cups water
1½ cups dry red wine

½ teaspoon basil
¼ cup chopped celery
1 green bell pepper, chopped
2 medium zucchini, sliced
1½ cups cooked small pasta shells
1 tablespoon tomato paste
¼ cup chopped parsley
¼ cup freshly grated Parmesan cheese
Pesto for garnish (page 253)

In a large kettle, sauté sausage until cooked. Pour off fat and add garlic, onions, and tomatoes. Mix thoroughly. Add beef broth, water, red wine, and basil and cook, covered, for 45 minutes.

Add remaining ingredients except Pesto and cook 15 minutes more. Garnish with small dollops of Pesto, if desired.

SERVES 6 TO 8

Spuds-and-Sausage Chowder

1 pound mild Italian sausage, casing removed	1 cup water
1 tablespoon butter	4 medium red or white potatoes, peeled and diced
½ cup chopped onion	1 cup milk
½ cup chopped celery	1 cup grated Cheddar cheese
3 cups chicken broth	salt and pepper to taste

In a large pot, brown sausage, breaking into small pieces. Drain off excess fat, remove sausage from pan, and set aside. Melt butter in same pan, add onion and celery, and sauté but do not brown.

Add chicken broth, water and potatoes. Bring to a boil, reduce heat, and simmer, covered, for about 40 minutes or until potatoes are tender and begin to break apart. Drain. Mash about a quarter of the potatoes in the pan, leaving remaining potatoes in chunks.

Add browned sausage to soup, stirring until sausage is heated thoroughly. Just before serving, add milk, stirring constantly. Add cheese and stir until melted and well blended. Season with salt and pepper.

SERVES 4 TO 6

Creamy Vichyssoise

A variation of a classic.

5 medium red or white potatoes, peeled, diced, and boiled	3½ cups milk
12 ounces cream cheese, softened	salt and pepper to taste
3 green onions, chopped	⅛ teaspoon dill
1¼ cups chicken broth	chopped chives for garnish

Place all ingredients except chives in blender and purée. In a 3-quart saucepan, cook puréed mixture over medium heat until heated through, stirring frequently. Do not boil.

Garnish with chives and serve hot or cold.

SERVES 6

Gazpacho Seattle Style

4 cloves garlic, peeled
½ cup parsley, stems removed
1 small onion, peeled and quartered
2 large tomatoes, peeled, seeded, and
　　quartered
1 small green bell pepper, peeled,
　　seeded, and quartered
1 46-ounce can tomato juice

2 teaspoons ground coriander
cayenne to taste
1 teaspoon Worcestershire sauce
salt and pepper to taste
green bell pepper, green onions,
　　cucumber, and chives, all
　　chopped, for garnish

In a food processor, with machine running, drop garlic, parsley, and onion, 1 at a time, through the feed tube. Add tomatoes, green pepper, ½ cup tomato juice, coriander, cayenne, and Worcestershire, and purée until smooth. Pour soup into pitcher or tureen and add remaining tomato juice and salt and pepper. Refrigerate several hours or overnight.

Serve ice-cold in chilled bowls, garnishing with any combination of the green pepper, green onions, cucumber, and chives.

SERVES 4 TO 6

Variation: Serve in tall glasses with a jigger of vodka and an asparagus spear or celery stick as a refreshing Bloody Mary.

Frosty Watercress Soup

1 bunch green onions, chopped
1 cup minced chives
3 tablespoons butter
4 cups peeled, seeded, and diced
　　cucumber
3 cups chicken broth
1 cup watercress leaves
1 medium red or white potato, peeled
　　and sliced

½ teaspoon salt
lemon juice to taste
white pepper to taste
1 cup plain yogurt
½ cup light cream (optional)
watercress leaves, thin slices of
　　cucumber, or snipped chives, for
　　garnish

In a large saucepan, sauté green onions and chives in butter until soft. Add cucumber, chicken broth, watercress, potato, salt, lemon juice, and white pepper. Simmer 25 minutes or until potato is tender.

Cool 10 minutes, then purée in blender in batches. Transfer to a large bowl to cool. Add yogurt, mix thoroughly, and, if desired, thin with light cream. Chill at least 4 hours. Garnish with watercress, cucumber, or chives.

SERVES 8

Landlord Soup

1 28-ounce can tomatoes, chopped, and liquid
1 12-ounce can frozen orange juice concentrate

minced chives or watercress leaves for garnish
slice of orange for garnish

Thoroughly combine tomatoes and juice and refrigerate for at least 24 hours. Serve chilled with garnish.

SERVES 4

Chilled Plum Soup

1 20-ounce can purple plums and liquid
1 cup water
⅔ cup sugar
1 cinnamon stick
pinch of salt
¼ teaspoon white pepper
½ cup heavy cream

½ cup dry red wine
1 tablespoon cornstarch
2 tablespoons lemon juice
1 teaspoon grated zest of lemon
1 cup sour cream
3 tablespoons brandy
sour cream and ground cinnamon for garnish

Reserving liquid, drain, pit, and chop plums. In a large saucepan, combine plums with reserved liquid, water, sugar, cinnamon stick, salt, and pepper. Bring to a boil over moderately high heat. Reduce heat to medium and simmer, stirring occasionally, for 5 minutes.

In a medium-sized bowl, slowly mix ½ cup of soup into cream, stirring constantly. Return this mixture to saucepan. Combine red wine with cornstarch and pour into soup, stirring until soup is thickened. Stir in lemon juice and zest and remove from heat.

In a small bowl whisk sour cream into ½ cup of soup, add brandy, mix well, and stir into soup. Chill soup at least 4 hours. Serve with dollops of sour cream sprinkled with cinnamon.

SERVES 6, OR IF SERVINGS ARE SMALL, 8

Note: This soup can be served either as an appetizer or dessert.

Cheese Chowder

2 small zucchini, in ¼-inch slices	1 teaspoon basil
2 yellow onions, chopped	1 bay leaf
1 16-ounce can tomatoes, chopped,	1½ cups grated Cheddar cheese
and liquid	⅓ cup grated Romano cheese
¼ cup butter	1 cup heavy cream at room
1¼ cups dry white wine	temperature
2 teaspoons salt	1 pound asparagus (optional)
¼ teaspoon freshly ground pepper	8 ounces fresh crab (optional)
1 clove garlic, minced	

Preheat oven to 400 degrees.

Combine zucchini, onions, tomatoes, butter, wine, salt, pepper, garlic, basil, and bay leaf in a 3-quart baking dish. Cover and bake for 1 hour, stirring occasionally. Add cheeses, cream, and, if desired, asparagus and crab. Bake until asparagus is almost tender—about 12 minutes. Serve immediately.

SERVES 6

Hinterberger's Hot Peanuts Envy

This very tasty soup was created by popular Seattle Times *columnist John Hinterberger.*

½ cup diced or slivered pork	5 teaspoons miso paste, preferably red
2 tablespoons oil	(available at Asian specialty shops)
1 tablespoon soy sauce	½ cup dry-roasted peanuts
1 tablespoon cornstarch	dash cayenne
3 tablespoons chopped onion	⅓ cup peeled, seeded, and diced
6 mushrooms, sliced	cucumber
4½ cups water	2 green onions, chopped
½ large dried ancho pepper, seeded	1 cup vegetables (diced green beans,
and deveined	yellow squash, zucchini) in any
1 large clove garlic, minced	combination
1½ cups chicken broth	1 egg, beaten
1 tablespoon rice vinegar	2 ounces brandy

In a 3-quart saucepan, fry pork in oil over medium-high heat. Remove with slotted spoon. Dredge in soy sauce, then in cornstarch, and set aside. Using the same saucepan, sauté onion over low heat for 15 minutes. Add mushrooms and sauté 5 minutes more.

In a separate saucepan, bring 1 cup of water to a boil and add ancho pepper; simmer 15 minutes and set aside. Stir pork and garlic into onion-mushroom mixture, then add chicken broth, water, rice vinegar, and miso paste, stirring vigorously to dissolve the paste. Add peanuts and cayenne.

In a blender or food processor blend ancho pepper and its liquid thoroughly; add to soup along with vegetables. Bring soup to a boil, reduce heat, and simmer for 15 minutes, or until vegetables are tender. Swizzle egg into soup, stir in brandy, and serve immediately.

SERVES 4

Winter wheat and deserted farm buildings under a dramatic sky near Ritzville in eastern Washington.

Breads

===

Pecan Rolls

Basic Sweet Dough
2 packages dry yeast
½ cup warm water
4 cups flour
½ cup sugar
1 teaspoon salt
¾ cup butter
½ cup milk, scalded and cooled
2 eggs, beaten
2 tablespoons butter, melted

Topping
¼ cup butter
½ cup firmly packed brown sugar
¼ cup light corn syrup
¼ cup pecan halves

Filling
½ cup firmly packed brown sugar
1 tablespoon cinnamon
½ cup chopped pecans
2 tablespoons butter, melted

To prepare dough: Dissolve yeast in warm water. In a large bowl mix flour, sugar, and salt, and cut in butter. Combine milk, eggs, and yeast mixture, add to dry ingredients, and mix. Brush with melted butter, cover, and chill overnight.

Preheat oven to 375 degrees.

To prepare topping: Combine butter, brown sugar, and corn syrup in a saucepan. Bring to a boil and pour into a 9-x-13-inch pan or divide into 36 muffin-pan sections. Sprinkle with pecan halves. (Although this is now on the bottom, rolls will be inverted and this will become the topping.)

To prepare filling: Combine first 3 ingredients. Roll half of the chilled dough to measure about 18 x 12 inches and spread half of filling mixture onto this piece. Roll from long side, cut into 1-inch slices, and place cut side up in muffin cups or pan. Repeat with other half of dough and brush all with melted butter.

Bake for 15 to 20 minutes. Invert immediately onto foil and cool.

YIELD: 36 ROLLS

Easter Egg Cinnamon Braid

Basic Dough for Rolls
¾ cup milk
½ cup sugar
2 teaspoons salt
½ cup butter
½ cup warm water
2 packages dry yeast
1 egg
4 cups flour

Filling
¼ cup butter, melted
½ cup firmly packed brown sugar
1 cup raisins
2 teaspoons cinnamon
3 to 5 dyed uncooked eggs

Icing
1 cup powdered sugar
½ teaspoon vanilla extract
1 to 2 tablespoons milk

To prepare dough: Scald milk. Stir in sugar, salt, and butter and cool to lukewarm. Measure water in a warm bowl and add yeast to dissolve. Stir in milk mixture, egg, and half the flour, then the remaining flour to make a soft dough. Cover tightly with waxed paper and refrigerate at least 2 hours, or up to 3 days.

When ready to shape, remove bread from refrigerator and knead gently 8 to 10 times. Roll out on a lightly floured board to a 15-x-27-inch rectangle.

Preheat oven to 350 degrees.

To prepare filling: Mix butter with sugar, raisins, and cinnamon and spread on dough. Roll up lengthwise to make a 27-inch roll. Using a sharp knife, carefully cut lengthwise into 3 parts, pressing in any raisins that are loose. Braid the 3 strands very loosely, place in a circle on a lightly greased baking sheet, and pinch ends to seal. Nestle dyed uncooked eggs in dough strands (eggs will cook as bread bakes). Cover and let rise until doubled in bulk, about 1 hour.

Bake the bread 30 to 45 minutes, until lightly browned. Remove from oven and cool on baking sheet for 5 minutes; then carefully slide braid onto rack.

To prepare icing: Combine ingredients, mixing to desired consistency. While bread is still warm, drizzle with icing.

SERVES 8 TO 10

Buttermilk Cinnamon Rolls

Dough
2 packages dry yeast
¼ cup warm water
1½ cups buttermilk
3 tablespoons sugar
1 teaspoon salt
½ teaspoon soda

½ cup vegetable oil
4½ cups flour

Topping
½ cup butter, melted
1¼ cups firmly packed brown sugar
1½ teaspoons cinnamon

To prepare dough: Dissolve yeast in warm water. Heat buttermilk until warm. Stir in sugar, salt, soda, oil, flour and yeast until mixed. Knead 15 times. Cover and let rise 15 minutes. Roll dough into rectangle approximately 10 x 18 inches.

To prepare topping: Combine ingredients and spread on dough. Roll up rectangle, cut into 1-inch pieces, and place cut side up in buttered 9-x-18-inch pan. Let rise 30 minutes.

Preheat oven to 400 degrees. Bake rolls for 10 to 15 minutes — until lightly browned. Cool slightly and serve.

YIELD: ABOUT 18 ROLLS

Note: Half of recipe will easily fit in an 8-x-8-inch pan.

Pineapple Divine

Dough
⅔ cup milk
1 tablespoon sugar
1 package dry yeast
¼ cup warm water
4 egg yolks
1 cup butter
4 cups flour
½ teaspoon salt

Pineapple Filling
1 20-ounce can crushed pineapple
1 20-ounce can chunk pineapple
3 tablespoons cornstarch
¼ teaspoon salt
1 to 2 tablespoons lemon juice
¾ cup sugar
1 egg, beaten

Icing
1 cup powdered sugar
1 to 2 tablespoons milk

Lightly grease a 17-x-11-x-1-inch jelly roll or broiler pan.

To prepare filling: Drain pineapple. In a saucepan, bring ingredients to a boil, stirring constantly. Let cool while preparing dough.

To prepare dough: Scald the milk. Stir in sugar until dissolved and cool to lukewarm. Dissolve yeast in the warm water, then add milk mixture and egg yolks. In a separate bowl, cut butter into flour and add salt. Add the milk mixture to flour and stir.

Place dough on floured board and knead into a ball for about 10 minutes. Divide dough into 2 equal parts. Roll out half of dough to fill bottom of pan. Spread filling over dough to within ½ inch of edge. Roll out other half and place on top of filling. Let rise until doubled in bulk in a warm, draft-free place for about 1 hour.

Preheat oven to 350 degrees. Bake coffee cake 30 minutes or until top springs back when pressed lightly in the center.

To prepare icing: Combine powdered sugar with milk until frosting consistency is reached.

Cool cake slightly and spread with icing. Serve warm. (May be reheated.)

SERVES 12 TO 18

Swedish Kringle

Dough
¾ cup butter
1½ cups flour
6 tablespoons ice water

Filling
½ cup butter
1 cup water
1 cup flour

3 eggs
1 teaspoon almond extract

Icing
1 cup powdered sugar
½ teaspoon almond extract
1 teaspoon butter
1 to 2 tablespoons cream

Preheat oven to 325 degrees.

To prepare dough: Cut butter into flour until mixture reaches the consistency of oatmeal. Add ice water, a tablespoon at a time, mixing with a fork until dough forms a ball. Place on baking sheet. Pat into 2 long strips, 3 inches wide and about 12 inches long.

To prepare filling: Combine butter and water and bring to a boil. Remove from heat and add flour, mixing well. Add eggs, 1 at a time, beating after each addition, and add almond extract. Spread onto strips of dough and bake kringle for 45 to 60 minutes. Remove from oven and cool.

To prepare icing: Beat together icing ingredients and frost the kringle.

YIELD: 2 LONG STRIPS, EACH SERVING 8 TO 10

Variation: For a special holiday treat, sprinkle slivered almonds and sliced candied cherries over the kringle immediately after frosting.

Blueberry Crunch Coffee Cake

Batter
1 cup flour
1½ teaspoons baking powder
½ teaspoon salt
⅓ cup sugar
1 egg, well beaten
⅓ cup vegetable oil
½ cup milk

1 tablespoon lemon juice
1 cup fresh or frozen blueberries

Topping
¼ cup flour
⅓ cup sugar
1 teaspoon cinnamon
2 tablespoons butter
½ cup chopped walnuts

Preheat oven to 375 degrees. Butter an 8-x-8-inch pan.

To prepare batter: Combine flour, baking powder, salt, and sugar; make a well. Beat together egg, vegetable oil, milk, and lemon juice and add to well in dry mixture. Mix until smooth. Pour into prepared pan and sprinkle with blueberries.

To prepare topping: Mix ingredients together until crumbly and sprinkle over berries. Bake cake for 40 minutes, cool slightly and cut into squares. Serve warm or cold.

YIELD: 9 SQUARES

Cranberry Coffee Cake

Batter
½ cup margarine (butter doesn't work with this recipe)
1 cup sugar
2 eggs
1 teaspoon baking powder

2 cups sifted flour
½ teaspoon salt
1 cup sour cream
1 teaspoon almond extract
¼ cup sliced almonds or walnuts

Filling

1 7-ounce can whole-berry cranberry
    sauce

Glaze

¾ cup powdered sugar
2 tablespoons warm water
½ teaspoon almond extract

Preheat oven to 350 degrees. Butter and flour an 8-cup tube pan.

To prepare batter: Cream margarine and sugar. Add eggs 1 at a time, beating well after each addition. Stir in sifted dry ingredients alternately with sour cream. Add almond extract and half of the nuts. Pour half of the batter into pan. Spread cranberry sauce in middle of batter, being careful not to let sauce touch the pan. Cover with remaining batter. Bake for 55 minutes. Remove to rack and cool in pan.

To prepare glaze: Combine ingredients, spread over top of coffee cake, and sprinkle with remaining nuts.

YIELD: 1 LARGE RING SERVING 10 TO 12

Strawberry-Rhubarb Coffee Cake

Batter

3 cups flour
1 cup sugar
1 teaspoon baking soda
1 teaspoon salt
1 teaspoon baking powder
1 cup butter
1 cup buttermilk
2 eggs, slightly beaten
1 teaspoon vanilla extract

Rhubarb Filling

3 cups fresh or 1 13-ounce package
    frozen unsweetened rhubarb
1 16-ounce package frozen sliced
    sweetened strawberries
2 tablespoons lemon juice
1 cup sugar
⅓ cup cornstarch

Topping

¾ cup sugar
½ cup flour
¼ cup butter

Preheat oven to 350 degrees. Butter a 9-x-13-inch pan.

To prepare filling: Cut rhubarb in 1-inch pieces and combine with strawberries in saucepan. Simmer, covered, about 5 minutes. Add lemon juice. Combine sugar and cornstarch and add to strawberry mixture. Cook and stir 4 to 5 minutes until thickened and set aside to cool.

To prepare batter: Combine flour, sugar, soda, salt, and baking powder. Cut in butter until batter becomes fine crumbs. Beat together buttermilk, eggs, and vanilla and add to dry ingredients. Stir just to moisten. Spread half of batter in pan. Spread cooled filling over batter, then spoon remaining batter in mounds on top of filling.

To prepare topping: Combine ingredients until crumbly and sprinkle over batter.

Bake 40 to 45 minutes and allow to cool. Cut into squares and serve with a fork.

YIELD: 12 TO 16 LARGE SQUARES

Lemon-Walnut Bread

Batter

1½ cups butter
3 cups sugar
6 eggs
4½ cups sifted flour
½ teaspoon soda
½ teaspoon salt

1½ cups buttermilk
1½ cups chopped walnuts
finely minced zest of 2 lemons

Glaze

juice of 4 lemons
1½ cups sugar

Preheat oven to 325 degrees. Butter and flour 3 9-x-5-inch loaf pans.

Cream together butter and sugar. Beat in eggs 1 at a time. Sift flour with soda and salt and add alternately with buttermilk, beating well. Add walnuts and lemon zest and pour into the prepared pans. Bake for 1 hour, cool 5 minutes, and remove from pan to cooling rack.

To prepare glaze: Mix lemon juice and sugar in saucepan while loaves are baking and stir over low heat until sugar is dissolved. While loaves are still warm, pierce tops and spoon glaze over them. Cool thoroughly before slicing.

YIELD: 3 LOAVES, EACH LOAF SERVING 8 TO 10

Raspberry Strudel

Dough

1 cup butter
2 cups flour
½ teaspoon salt
1 cup sour cream

Filling

1¼ cups raspberry jam
1 cup coconut
⅔ cup chopped almonds

To prepare dough: Combine butter, flour, and salt by cutting together. Add sour cream and refrigerate overnight.

Preheat oven to 350 degrees and grease 2 baking sheets.

Combine filling ingredients. Roll dough into 2 10-x-15-inch sections. Spread each section with filling and roll lengthwise. Placed on greased baking sheets, seam side down. Bake 50 minutes. Cool 5 to 10 minutes and cut in narrow slices.

SERVES 8 TO 10

Variation: Substitute apricot jam and walnuts for raspberry jam and almonds. Or use blackberry jam and almonds.

Cinnamon Crown Rolls

Dough
2 packages dry yeast
¼ cup warm water
¾ cup milk
½ cup butter
½ cup sugar
1½ teaspoons salt
2 eggs, well beaten
4½ cups white flour

2 tablespoons butter, melted
¾ cup sugar
1 teaspoon cinnamon
1 cup heavy cream

Syrup
⅓ cup butter
½ cup firmly packed brown sugar
1 tablespoon corn syrup

To prepare dough: Soften yeast in warm water. Heat milk, and combine with butter, sugar, and salt and add to softened yeast mixture. Add eggs, then flour, to form a soft dough. Knead on lightly floured surface until smooth and elastic—about 10 minutes. Place in lightly greased bowl, turning to grease entire surface of dough. Cover with damp cloth and let rise in a warm place until doubled in bulk—1 to 2 hours. After it has doubled, punch down, cover, and let rise 10 more minutes.

To prepare syrup: Slightly melt butter, brown sugar, and corn syrup in a small pan. Spread this in bottom of a 9-inch tube pan.

Mix sugar and cinnamon. Shape dough into 1½-inch balls and roll in melted butter, then in cinnamon-sugar mixture. Arrange on top of syrup in tube pan. Sprinkle any remaining cinnamon-sugar on top of balls. Let rise again, covered, until doubled—about ½ to 1 hour.

Preheat oven to 350 degrees. Pour 1 teaspoon heavy cream over each ball and bake for 30 to 40 minutes. Invert pan immediately.

YIELD: 16 TO 18 ROLLS

Pecan Popovers

Dough	Lemon-Honey Butter
2 eggs	6 tablespoons butter, softened
1 cup milk	6 tablespoons honey
½ teaspoon salt	¾ to 1 teaspoon finely minced zest of
1 cup flour	lemon
¼ cup finely chopped pecans	

Preheat oven to 425 degrees. Grease 6 5- to 6-ounce custard cups.

To prepare popovers: With a wire whisk, beat together eggs, milk, and salt. Add flour and beat just until smooth, being careful not to overbeat. Stir in the pecans and pour into custard cups. Bake until puffed and golden brown—30 to 35 minutes. Remove from cups and serve immediately.

To prepare lemon-honey butter: Stir together the butter, honey, and zest and spread on warm popovers.

YIELD: 6 POPOVERS

Corn Bread Supreme

1 cup butter	½ cup grated mild Cheddar cheese
1 cup sugar	1 cup flour
4 eggs	1 cup yellow cornmeal
1 16½-ounce can creamed corn	4 teaspoons baking powder
½ cup grated jack cheese	¼ teaspoon salt

Preheat oven to 350 degrees. Lightly butter a 9-x-13-inch pan.

Cream the butter and sugar. Add the eggs, 1 at a time, beating after each addition. Stir in the creamed corn and the cheeses. Sift the dry ingredients together and stir into batter mixture. Pour into prepared pan. Bake 30 minutes, or until bread is lightly browned on top and springs back to touch. Cut into squares and serve warm.

SERVES 10

Buttermilk Scones

Scones are a Northwest favorite. This recipe comes from Robin Woodward, whose restaurant, The Surrogate Hostess, is located in one of

Seattle's oldest residential neighborhoods. Also a charcuterie and catering service, the restaurant does a thriving business in pastries that are eaten with equal relish by students of the parochial school across the street and residents of pillared, early 1900s mansions.

7¼ cups flour
1 tablespoon baking soda
1½ teaspoons salt
1 tablespoon cream of tartar

1 cup plus 2 tablespoons cold butter,
   cut into small pieces
2¾ cups buttermilk
1 cup currants (optional)

Preheat oven to 450 degrees.

Blend flour, soda, salt, and cream of tartar in a large bowl. Cut in butter until mixture resembles cornmeal. Add buttermilk and currants and mix lightly with a fork until moistened.

Remove dough to lightly floured board and gently knead to complete mixing. Divide in half and shape each half into a fairly smooth circle, approximately ¾ inch thick at center. Do not over-work. Cut each circle into 8 wedges, place on ungreased cookie sheet, and bake for 10 to 15 minutes.

At the side of each baked scone, slice halfway through from point and fill with butter and jam.

YIELD: 16 LARGE SCONES

Note: Can be frozen, unfilled, after baking.

Nut Muffins

½ cup butter
1 cup firmly packed brown sugar
1 egg
1 cup milk

½ teaspoon soda
1 teaspoon vanilla extract
2 scant cups flour
½ cup walnuts or pecans, chopped

Grease muffin tins. Mix ingredients together in order listed and, if possible, fill tins the night before muffins are to be baked. Tins should be almost full. (Do not use paper liners.)

Preheat oven to 400 degrees. Bake for 30 minutes.

YIELD: 12 LARGE MUFFINS OR 36 SMALL ONES

Pumpkin-Raisin Muffins

1½ cups flour
½ cup sugar
2 teaspoons baking powder
¾ teaspoon salt
½ teaspoon cinnamon
½ teaspoon nutmeg
¼ cup butter

½ cup raisins
½ cup milk
1 egg, beaten
½ cup cooked mashed pumpkin
    or canned pumpkin
1 tablespoon sugar

Preheat oven to 400 degrees. Grease 12 muffin tins.

Sift together first 6 ingredients. Cut in butter and add raisins. In another bowl combine milk, egg, and pumpkin and add to raisin mixture. Pour into prepared tins, filling two-thirds full. (Do not use paper liners.) Sprinkle ¼ teaspoon sugar over the top of each muffin. Bake for 18 to 20 minutes.

YIELD: 12 MUFFINS

Ragamuffins

BRAN MUFFINS

2 cups boiling water
5 teaspoons soda
1 cup butter
2 cups sugar
4 eggs
4 cups All-Bran cereal

2 cups 40% Bran Flakes
2 cups dates or raisins
1 cup nuts (optional)
1 quart buttermilk
5 cups flour sifted with 1 tablespoon
    salt

Mix boiling water with soda and cool. Cream butter, sugar, eggs, and soda-water mixture. Add cereals, dates, and nuts. Beat in buttermilk alternately with flour mixture.

Pour batter into airtight containers and store in refrigerator (where mixture will keep for weeks). When ready to bake, preheat oven to 400 degrees. Do not stir the batter. Pour into greased muffin tins and bake for 20 minutes.

YIELD: 4 DOZEN MUFFINS

Wenatchee Apple Bread

Batter

2 cups sifted flour
½ teaspoon baking soda
1 teaspoon baking powder
1 teaspoon salt
½ teaspoon allspice
½ teaspoon nutmeg
1 teaspoon cinnamon
¾ cup butter, melted
⅔ cup sugar
3 eggs, beaten

¼ cup applesauce
1 cup peeled and diced apples
⅓ cup sour cream
¼ cup chopped walnuts
⅓ cup raisins

Topping

¼ cup applesauce
¼ cup firmly packed brown sugar
¼ teaspoon cinnamon

Preheat oven to 375 degrees. Butter a 9-x-5-inch loaf pan.

To prepare batter: Sift dry ingredients together and set aside. Combine butter and sugar until well blended, stir in eggs a little at a time, and add applesauce, diced apples, sour cream, nuts, and raisins. Stir in flour mixture, mix well, and pour into prepared pan.

To prepare topping: Mix ingredients in a small bowl and spread on top of batter. Bake bread for 50 minutes and cool on wire rack.

YIELD: 1 LOAF

Whole-Wheat Bread

2 packages dry yeast
½ cup warm water
⅓ cup honey
3 tablespoons butter
½ cup lukewarm milk
1¾ cups warm water

3½ to 4½ cups white flour
1 tablespoon salt
2 cups unsifted whole-wheat flour
3 tablespoons 100 percent bran
melted butter (optional)

Grease 2 9-x-5-inch loaf pans.

Dissolve yeast in ½ cup warm water. In another bowl, combine honey, butter, milk, and 1¾ cups water. Add dissolved yeast. In a large bowl combine salt with 2 cups white flour, stirring well. Add yeast mixture. Add 1 cup whole-wheat flour. Beat until elastic and thick. Add bran and remaining whole-wheat flour and stir. Add enough white flour to make dough leave sides of bowl. Turn onto floured board and knead at least 10 minutes. Cover and let rise until almost doubled in bulk—approximately 2 hours. Punch down, shape into 2 loaves, and place in prepared pans, turning dough so tops will be greased with the grease in pan. Let rise until doubled.

Preheat oven to 400 degrees. Brush loaf tops with melted butter before baking if a softer crust is desired. Bake 30 to 40 minutes, or until loaf sounds hollow when tapped. Remove from pans and cool.

YIELD: 2 LOAVES

Faux Croissants

1 package dry yeast	1 egg
1 cup warm water	5 cups flour
¾ cup evaporated milk	¼ cup butter, melted and cooled
1½ teaspoons salt	1 cup butter, cold
⅓ cup sugar	1 egg, beaten with 1 tablespoon water

Soften yeast in warm water. Add milk, salt, sugar, egg, and 1 cup of flour. Beat until smooth. Add melted cooled butter. In another bowl, cut the cold butter into remaining flour until mixture looks like small peas. Pour yeast mixture over the flour mixture and mix with a spoon until all flour is blended. (Since this dough should not be handled, do not roll it into a ball.) Cover, and refrigerate 5 hours, or up to 4 days.

Remove dough from refrigerator and knead 6 to 8 times, then divide into quarters. When working with 1 part, refrigerate others until ready to use. On floured board, roll a quarter into a large circle, about 12 inches in diameter or larger. With a sharp knife, divide circle into 8 wedges. Roll each wedge toward the center. Place wedges point down, approximately 2 inches apart, on baking sheet. (You will need 3 to 4 baking sheets.) Repeat process for other 3 parts of dough. Cover with a light towel and let rise in a warm, draft-free place. Let rise about 2 hours, or until doubled in bulk.

Preheat oven to 325 degrees. Brush each roll with egg beaten with water. Bake 20 to 25 minutes, or until lightly browned.

YIELD: 32 ROLLS

Icebox Rolls

½ cup sugar	1 package dry yeast
½ cup butter	6 cups flour
2 teaspoons salt	¼ cup butter, melted, to brush on top
2 cups boiling water	

Combine sugar, butter, salt, and boiling water in a bowl and cool until warm. Add yeast and 1 cup flour and beat for 2 minutes with electric mixer. Add 1 more cup flour and beat another 2 minutes. Add remaining flour, by hand if necessary. Do not knead. Form into a ball and place in a greased bowl. Cover well with a weighted plate and chill in refrigerator overnight.

Lightly grease muffin tins or shallow pans.

Cut dough in halves or quarters and roll out approximately ¼ inch below), cut small rounds approximately 2 inches in diameter. Press finger across middle of roll to crease and brush with butter. Fold over to make a half-round. Place half-rounds close together in shallow pan, or put 2 together in a single section of a muffin tin. Finish rolling and cutting all the dough and brush tops again with melted butter. Cover with a light towel and let rise 2 to 2½ hours.

Preheat oven to 425 degrees. Bake rolls 10 to 12 minutes.

YIELD: 4 TO 5 DOZEN PARKER HOUSE ROLLS

Other shapes: Place 3 balls, each the size of a small walnut, in a muffin cup. Or place a 2-inch ball in each section of a muffin tin.

Whole-Wheat Refrigerator Rolls

1¾ cups milk
½ cup sugar
1 tablespoon salt
3 tablespoons butter
2 packages dry yeast
½ cup warm water
3 to 3½ cups unsifted whole-wheat flour

1 cup rye flour or more rye flour combined with less whole wheat flour to make same rye-whole-wheat total
3 cups sifted white flour
2 eggs, beaten
3 tablespoons cracked wheat

Grease 4 baking sheets.

Scald milk. Add sugar, salt, and butter and cool to warm. Sprinkle yeast on warm water and stir to dissolve.

In the large bowl of an electric mixer, combine milk mixture, 1 cup whole-wheat flour, and 1 cup white flour. Beat well for 2 minutes at medium speed. Add yeast mixture and eggs. Alternately stir in rye flour and remaining whole-wheat and white flour, until dough leaves sides of bowl. Place ball of dough in a greased bowl, turning to grease top. Refrigerate, covered, for 4 hours or up to 5 days.

Remove dough from refrigerator 2 hours before shaping. Punch down, turn out on floured board, and knead slightly. Divide into 4 parts. Cut each part into 8 to 12 pieces and roll each piece in hands to make a ball. Place each ball on a greased baking sheet. Cover and let rise 1½ hours in warm place.

Preheat oven to 400 degrees. Bake rolls for 15 to 20 minutes. Lower heat slightly if rolls are browning too fast on the bottom.

YIELD: 3 TO 4 DOZEN ROLLS

Cheddar Crown Loaf

2 packages dry yeast
½ cup lukewarm water
1¾ cups lukewarm milk
3 tablespoons sugar
2 teaspoons salt
7 tablespoons butter, melted

1½ to 2 cups shredded sharp Cheddar
    cheese
5½ to 7 cups flour
¼ teaspoon caraway seeds
1 egg, beaten

Carefully butter a tube pan.

Dissolve yeast in warm water. In a large bowl, mix milk, sugar, salt, and 3 tablespoons melted butter. Add yeast, cheese, and 2 cups flour. Stir well. Add as much of remaining flour as necessary to make a workable dough. Turn out on lightly floured board and knead 10 minutes. Return to bowl, punch down, and cover. Let rise in a warm place about 2 hours. Punch down and knead for 2 minutes.

Divide dough in half and cut each half into 16 equal pieces. Shape pieces into smooth balls, roll in the remaining melted butter and place 16 balls in prepared tube pan. Sprinkle half of caraway seeds on top. Repeat with remaining 16 balls and sprinkle with remaining seeds. You now have 2 layers of 16 balls. Let rise in a warm place until doubled in bulk.

Preheat oven to 375 degrees. Brush egg over top of warm bread and bake 30 to 40 minutes, or until bread is browned and sounds hollow when tapped. Remove from pan and cool on rack.

SERVES 12 TO 16

Crusty French Bread

1 tablespoon dry yeast	1 tablespoon salt
2½ cups warm water	7 cups flour
2 tablespoons sugar	1 egg white, beaten

Dissolve yeast in warm water. Add sugar and salt and stir in flour, a cup at a time. Knead until smooth, approximately 10 minutes, on lightly floured board. Cover with a wet tea towel and let rise in a warm place for 1½ hours.

Have enough boiling water ready to be 2 inches deep in a 9-x-13-inch pan. Punch bread down, knead a couple of times, and divide into 4 parts. Knead and stretch each part into a strip the length of a cookie sheet or a double French-bread pan made of iron. Place 2 strips on a cookie sheet or 2 strips in each of 2 double French-bread pans, and brush with beaten egg white.

Place bread on center rack in cold oven. Turn oven to 400 degrees. Put pan of boiling water in bottom of oven or on lower rack. Bake bread 30 minutes or until golden brown. Cool on racks.

YIELD: 4 LOAVES

Toppings for French Bread

Camembert Spread

6 ounces Camembert cheese	½ teaspoon basil
¾ cup butter	¾ teaspoon onion salt

Combine ingredients in saucepan and heat until cheese is melted.

Slice a loaf of French bread in half lengthwise, then slice vertically into serving-size pieces. Place bottom half on large piece of foil and spread the Camembert mixture on it, then cover with top half. Spread remaining mixture over crust. (This can be made ahead to this point and refrigerated for up to a day.) Close foil and bake topped bread 20 minutes at 325 degrees. Turn back foil and bake 5 minutes more. Serve hot.

SERVES 8 TO 10

Savory Spread
¾ cup butter
¼ teaspoon salt
¼ teaspoon paprika

¼ teaspoon savory
½ teaspoon thyme
dash cayenne

Combine ingredients, slice loaf of French bread in half lengthwise, and cover cut side of each half evenly with spread. Reassemble loaf and wrap in foil. Refrigerate overnight. Bake at 300 degrees for 20 minutes.

SERVES 8 TO 10

Herb Spread
¼ cup butter
½ cup grated onion

2 tablespoons minced parsley
2 tablespoons prepared mustard
2 tablespoons sesame seeds

Combine ingredients, slice loaf of French bread in half lengthwise, and cover cut side of each half evenly with spread. Place on cookie sheets and bake at 350 degrees for 12 minutes. Slice and serve.

SERVES 8 TO 10

Pita

POCKET BREAD

4½ cups white flour
1 package dry yeast
2 teaspoons sugar

1½ teaspoons salt
1¾ cups water
2 tablespoons vegetable oil

In a large bowl, thoroughly mix 2 cups flour, yeast, sugar, and salt. Heat water and oil until warm. Add to flour mixture and blend with electric beater at low speed until mixture is moistened, then blend at medium speed for 3 minutes. Stir in remaining flour by hand and knead until smooth and elastic—about 10 minutes. Cover with plastic wrap and let rest 20 minutes. Punch down dough and divide into 12 equal parts, shaping each part into a ball. Cover again and let rise for 30 minutes.

Preheat oven to 500 degrees. Roll each ball into a 6-inch circle, leaving middle as the thickest part and the edges thinner. Place 3 circles at a time directly on oven rack (it doesn't matter if they hang down a little between the rungs). Bake until puffed (the puff is the hollow space) and tops begin to brown—about 3 minutes. Cool. Do not stack until cooled. Serve warm with butter, or halve and add fillings.

YIELD: 12 PITA

Swedish Spice-Rye Bread

This has a strong anise flavor, making it good with cheeses on an hors d'oeuvres tray or with ham for sandwiches.

1 package dry yeast
¼ cup warm water
1 teaspoon fennel seed
1 teaspoon anise seed
12 ounces beer, at room temperature
¼ cup molasses

⅓ cup sugar
1 teaspoon salt
2 tablespoons vegetable oil
2½ cups sifted rye flour
2½ cups sifted white flour, or more if needed

In a large bowl, dissolve yeast in warm water. Let stand 5 minutes. Stir in fennel, anise, beer, molasses, sugar, salt, and oil and mix well. Gradually add rye flour, beating thoroughly after each addition, then gradually add white flour, forming a soft dough. Turn out onto floured board and knead until dough is smooth—about 10 minutes. Place in a well-greased bowl, cover with a damp cloth and let rise in a warm place until doubled in bulk—1 to 2 hours.

Butter and flour 2 round cake pans 8 inches in diameter. Punch down dough and shape into 2 round loaves. Place in prepared pans, cover, and let rise until doubled again.

Preheat oven to 375 degrees. Bake bread for 45 minutes or until it sounds hollow when tapped. Remove from oven and brush tops with butter. Cool, but serve freshly baked.

YIELD: 2 ROUND LOAVES

Note: Bread does not freeze well.

Parmesan Flatbread

12 to 16 Pita (pocket breads) (page 80)
1 cup butter, melted and cooled

½ pound Parmesan, finely grated
paprika

Split each pita horizontally into 2 rounds. Spread each round with melted butter, covering entire surface. Sprinkle liberally with Parmesan and add paprika for color. Cut each circle into quarters. Place on cookie sheet and broil until bubbly. (Watch carefully as these broil quickly.) Serve hot or put into a large plastic bag and freeze. These will still be crisp when defrosted.

SERVES 20

Sausage-filled Italian Bread

Dough
3 to 3¼ cups flour
¼ cup sugar
½ teaspoon salt
1 package dry yeast
¼ cup butter, softened
⅔ cup hot water
2 eggs

Filling
¾ pound Italian-style pork sausage
¼ cup minced parsley
¼ cup grated Parmesan cheese
3 green onions, chopped
½ teaspoon basil
½ teaspoon oregano
1 cup grated mozzarella cheese
½ cup sliced cherry tomatoes, drained

To prepare dough: Mix 1 cup flour, sugar, salt, and yeast in a large mixer bowl. Add butter and hot water and beat 2 minutes with mixer at lowest speed. Add 1 egg and ½ cup flour and beat at high speed for 2 more minutes. Add remaining flour by hand to make a soft dough.

Turn dough onto a lightly floured board; knead 10 minutes, until smooth and elastic. Place in greased bowl, turning dough to grease top. Cover and let rise in a warm place for about 1 hour, until doubled.

To prepare filling: When dough is almost doubled, brown the sausage and drain off all fat. Add all remaining ingredients except mozzarella and tomatoes and stir.

Butter a 9-inch spring-form pan. Punch down dough and halve. Roll out 1 half into a 9-inch circle and place in bottom of prepared pan. Place filling on top, spreading to edge. Roll out other half of dough into 9-inch circle and cut in 6 to 8 wedges. Place drained tomatoes and mozzarella on top of filling, then lay wedges on top, with points meeting in the center. Pinch outer edges of dough to seal. Cover and let rise again for about an hour.

Preheat oven to 350 degrees. Beat second egg and brush on top of dough. Bake bread on lower rack of oven for 35 to 40 minutes. Remove from oven and cool on a rack, then remove rim of pan. Bread may be served warm or at room temperature. To reheat, wrap in foil and heat for 40 minutes in 350-degree oven.

YIELD: 6 TO 8 SERVINGS

The internationally ranked University of Washington crew during a morning workout. The UW is recognized for its academic as well as its athletic achievements.

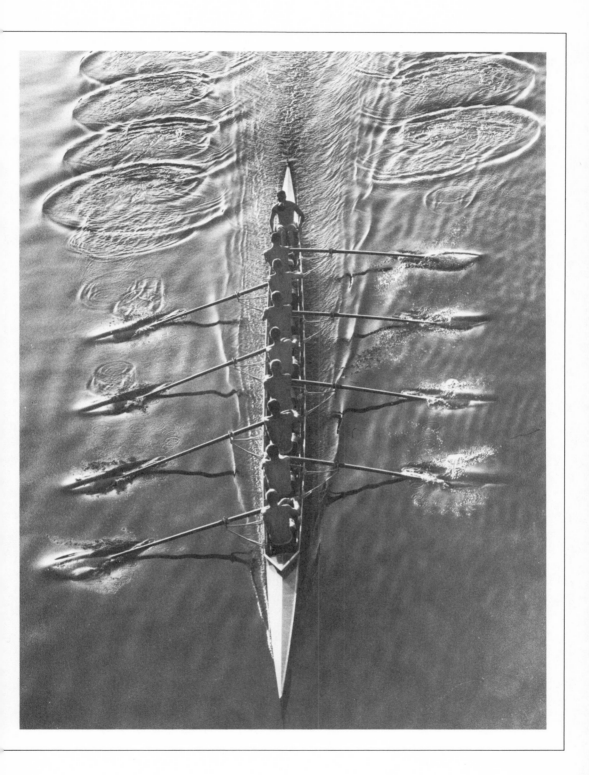

Salads

❖❖

Raspberry Mandarin Mold

2 10-ounce packages frozen raspberries, thawed, and liquid
1 6-ounce package raspberry-flavored
  gelatin
2 cups boiling water
¼ cup lemon juice

4 11-ounce cans mandarin orange
  segments, drained
lettuce leaves
orange or mandarin orange segments
  for garnish

Lightly oil an 8-cup mold. Drain raspberries thoroughly, reserving liquid. Measure liquid, add enough cold water to measure 1½ cups, and set aside.

Dissolve gelatin in boiling water and add reserved liquid and lemon juice. Chill until partially set. Stir in raspberries and mandarin orange segments. Pour into prepared mold and chill until firm. Unmold on a bed of lettuce leaves and garnish with orange segments.

SERVES 10 TO 12

Blueberry Salad Mold

1 3-ounce package lemon-flavored
  gelatin
1 cup boiling water
11 ounces cream cheese at room
  temperature

1 cup sour cream
3 cups boiling water
1 6-ounce package lemon-flavored
  gelatin
4 cups fresh or frozen blueberries

Lightly oil a 10-cup mold or bundt pan.

Dissolve the package of gelatin in 1 cup boiling water and cool slightly. Mix gelatin, cream cheese, and sour cream in a blender or food processor until smooth, pour into the prepared mold or bundt pan, and chill until barely firm.

Dissolve the 6-ounce package of gelatin in 3 cups boiling water and cool. Add blueberries, pour mixture on top of chilled cheese mixture, and chill until firm. Unmold salad on a chilled platter.

SERVES 10 TO 12

Fresh Cranberry Salad

2 cups raw cranberries
¾ cup sugar
3 cups miniature marshmallows
2 cups diced, unpeeled, red apples
½ cup seedless grapes

½ cup chopped walnuts
1 cup heavy cream, whipped
¼ teaspoon salt
Bibb or limestone lettuce

Chop cranberries in blender or food processor, add sugar, and stir in marshmallows. Chill overnight.

Mix apples, grapes, nuts, and salt with cranberry mixture. Fold in whipped cream. Chill until ready to serve. Serve in bowl lined with lettuce leaves.

SERVES 4

Frozen Waldorf Salad

1 8-ounce can crushed pineapple and
    liquid
2 eggs, slightly beaten
½ cup sugar
lemon juice
⅛ teaspoon salt
½ cup mayonnaise
2½ cups diced, unpeeled Red Delicious
    apples

⅔ cup diced celery
½ cup coarsely chopped walnuts
½ cup miniature marshmallows
½ cup heavy cream, chilled
Red Delicious apple wedges, unpeeled
    and cored, for garnish
juice of ½ lemon
¼ cup water

Drain pineapple and set aside, reserving the syrup. In a saucepan, mix together eggs, sugar, lemon juice, salt, and pineapple syrup, and simmer over low heat, stirring constantly, until slightly thickened—about 20 minutes. Cool. Fold in mayonnaise.

Combine pineapple, apples, celery, nuts, and marshmallows, and mix well. Whip the cream in a chilled bowl, fold into egg-mayonnaise mixture, and pour over fruit. Toss lightly to mix thoroughly; then pour into 8-inch-square ungreased pan or 6-cup mold. Freeze 3 to 4 hours.

Unmold on chilled platter. Surround salad with apple wedges dipped in lemon juice mixed with water.

SERVES 8

Confetti Overnight Salad

1 pound broccoli, cut into flowerets
1 head cauliflower, cut into flowerets
4 green onions, chopped
4 medium carrots, cut into ¼-inch
    diagonal slices
8 slices bacon, cooked, drained, and
    crumbled
parsley for garnish

Dressing
½ cup mayonnaise
⅓ cup tarragon wine vinegar
⅓ cup vegetable oil
⅓ cup sugar

Combine dressing ingredients and blend. Pour over salad vegetables and bacon, toss, and refrigerate overnight. Drain off surplus dressing before serving. Garnish with parsley.

SERVES 4 TO 6

Marinated Zucchini Salad

1 medium zucchini, sliced thin
1 16-ounce can baby whole carrots,
    drained, or 2 cups blanched 2-inch
    slices of French carrots
1 14-ounce can hearts of palm, drained
    and cut into thick slices, or
    1 15-ounce can artichoke hearts
    (not marinated), drained and
    halved
2 ounces blue cheese, crumbled
Boston or limestone lettuce leaves

Dressing
⅔ cup vegetable oil
¼ cup white wine vinegar
1 large clove garlic, minced
1 teaspoon sugar
¾ teaspoon dry mustard
¾ teaspoon salt
freshly ground pepper to taste

Place zucchini, carrots, and hearts of palm in shallow dish. Combine dressing ingredients and pour over vegetables. Chill overnight. To serve, drain vegetables and spoon onto lettuce leaves arranged on 8 individual plates. Top each with cheese.

SERVES 8

Broccoli Salad

4 cups chopped fresh broccoli
3 ounces cream cheese at room
   temperature
1 tablespoon unflavored gelatin
1¼ cups chicken consommé
1 tablespoon lemon juice
1 cup mayonnaise
2 hard-cooked eggs, chopped
1 dash nutmeg
1 dash lemon pepper

Dressing
2 tablespoons minced green onion
2 tablespoons lemon juice
2 tablespoons white wine vinegar
8 ounces sour cream
½ cup mayonnaise
¼ teaspoon tarragon, crushed

Lightly oil a 6-cup mold.

Blanch broccoli. Spread cream cheese over hot broccoli. Soak gelatin in ½ cup of cold consommé Heat remaining consommé and add to gelatin to dissolve. Add lemon juice, mayonnaise, eggs, nutmeg, and lemon pepper to gelatin, then pour mixture into prepared mold and refrigerate until firm.

Combine dressing ingredients, whisk until blended, and refrigerate. Unmold salad on a chilled platter and pass dressing separately.

SERVES 12

Green Pea Salad

2 10-ounce packages frozen tiny peas,
   thawed
½ cup chopped celery
2 green onions, chopped
10 slices bacon, cooked, drained, and
   crumbled
⅓ cup salted sunflower seeds or
   cashews

Boston or Bibb lettuce leaves
Parmesan cheese

Dressing
½ cup sour cream
½ cup mayonnaise

Toss together peas, celery, onion, bacon, and sunflower seeds. Combine dressing ingredients and blend. Toss salad with dressing and spoon onto lettuce leaves on individual plates. Sprinkle with cheese.

SERVES 6 TO 8

Okra Salad

1 cup okra, sliced and cooked, or
   1 9-ounce package frozen okra,
   cooked
2 tomatoes, quartered, or 1 cup cherry
   tomatoes, halved
1 teaspoon lemon juice
½ teaspoon salt

½ teaspoon chili powder
¼ teaspoon white pepper
1 teaspoon chopped parsley
lettuce leaves
1 hard-cooked egg, chopped, for
   garnish

Combine okra and tomatoes, and chill. Toss with lemon juice, salt, chili powder, pepper, and parsley. Serve on lettuce leaves and garnish with egg.

SERVES 4

Washington Salad

4 cups grated carrots
4 cups grated sharp Cheddar cheese
4 cups chopped celery
4 cups fresh, tiny shrimp
1 cup chopped green onion

2 cups mayonnaise
1 1½-ounce can shoestring potatoes, or
   1 3-ounce can chow mein noodles
lettuce leaves
chopped parsley for garnish

Toss together carrots, cheese, celery, shrimp, green onions, and mayonnaise and refrigerate overnight. Sprinkle shoestring potatoes over salad just before serving. Serve on a bed of lettuce and garnish with parsley.

SERVES 10 TO 12

Dandelion Salade Brasserie

This salad comes from one of Seattle's best French restaurants, the Brasserie Pittsbourg, which is located on the former site of a public bathhouse, a few steps from a turn-of-the-century glass pergola in the heart of the city's oldest business area.

4 cups loosely packed dandelion
    greens
3 slices bacon, cut in ¼-inch pieces
2 hard-cooked eggs, chopped
1 medium potato, boiled and finely
    chopped

Dressing
1 clove garlic, minced
½ teaspoon salt
freshly ground pepper to taste
1 teaspoon Dijon-style mustard
1 tablespoon wine vinegar
1½ teaspoons peanut oil

Wash and clean whole dandelion carefully, remove root, stem and blossom, and shake greens dry. Sauté bacon until lightly cooked but not crisp. Drain and keep warm. Reserve drippings. Combine dressing ingredients in small bowl and blend with a whisk. Toss together greens, bacon, chopped eggs, and potatoes. Pour dressing and hot bacon drippings over the mixture, toss, and serve immediately.

SERVES 4

Note: Dandelions are best when tender—during fall or at the end of winter.

Vegetables Vinaigrette

2 avocados
½ pound fresh button mushrooms
lemon juice
2 cups cherry tomatoes
½ pound fresh bean sprouts
1 6-ounce can pitted medium black
    olives
1 15½-ounce can garbanzo beans

Dressing
2 tablespoons lemon juice
3 tablespoons olive oil
3 tablespoons vegetable oil
½ teaspoon salt
1 teaspoon freshly ground pepper
1 medium clove garlic, minced
½ teaspoon Dijon-style mustard
¼ teaspoon sugar
1 egg yolk

Peel and cube avocados, add mushrooms, and sprinkle with lemon juice. Add remaining salad ingredients. In a separate bowl, combine dressing ingredients and blend, adding egg yolk last. Toss with salad and chill.

SERVES 8 TO 10

Variation: Add ½ pound small cooked shrimp.

Green Beans Vinaigrette

2 pounds fresh green beans
chopped tomato and chopped parsley
    for garnish

Dressing
3 green onions (including tops),
    chopped
1 garlic clove, minced
⅓ cup vegetable oil

⅓ cup wine vinegar
3 tablespoons lemon juice
1 teaspoon salt
1 teaspoon Dijon-style mustard
1 teaspoon basil, crushed
½ teaspoon oregano, crushed
½ teaspoon marjoram, crushed
⅓ teaspoon freshly ground pepper

Combine dressing ingredients and blend.

    Wash beans, snapping off the ends and removing any strings. Steam beans for 10 minutes or until tender but slightly crisp. Immediately rinse beans with cold water and drain well. Place in a shallow bowl or dish, top with dressing, cover, and chill at least 2 hours, stirring several times. Serve in a glass bowl, garnished with chopped tomato and parsley.

SERVES 6

Molded Gazpacho

3 tablespoons unflavored gelatin
2 18-ounce cans tomato juice
1 medium clove garlic, minced
⅓ cup red wine
½ teaspoon salt
1 dash Tabasco sauce
2 large tomatoes, peeled, seeded, and
    chopped
1 medium zucchini, chopped
1 green bell pepper, chopped

1 large cucumber, peeled and chopped
½ cup chopped green onion (including
    tops)
1 2-ounce jar pimientos
¼ cup sliced ripe olives
lemon juice to taste
red-leaf lettuce leaves
3 large avocados, peeled and sliced,
    for garnish

Lightly oil a 10-cup ring mold.

    Soften gelatin in ½ cup tomato juice. In a large saucepan, combine garlic, remaining tomato juice, wine, salt, and Tabasco, and heat just to boiling. Add gelatin and stir until dissolved. Add tomatoes, zucchini, green pepper, cucumber, green onions, pimiento, olives, and lemon juice. Pour into prepared ring mold and refrigerate until firm. Unmold on a bed of lettuce and garnish with avocado slices.

SERVES 12 TO 14

Tomato Aspic

1 16-ounce can seasoned stewed
   tomatoes
1 3-ounce package lemon-flavored
   gelatin
½ to 1 cup water
1 avocado, peeled and chopped
2 stalks celery, chopped
parsley or red-leaf lettuce for garnish

Dressing
½ cup mayonnaise
½ cup sour cream
⅓ cup chili sauce
½ small Bermuda or red onion, grated
1 teaspoon lemon juice
½ teaspoon prepared horseradish
⅛ teaspoon Tabasco
salt to taste

Heat tomatoes. Add gelatin and stir until dissolved. Remove from heat and add water, avocado, and celery. Pour into a 4-cup mold and chill until set.

Blend dressing ingredients just before serving. Unmold salad and pour on dressing. Garnish with parsley or lettuce leaves.

SERVES 4

Mushroom Salad

1 head Boston or Bibb lettuce
½ pound fresh mushrooms, sliced

Dressing

⅓ cup olive oil
1 tablespoon lemon juice
2 tablespoons wine vinegar

½ cup chopped parsley
½ teaspoon sugar
½ teaspoon basil
⅛ teaspoon garlic powder
¼ teaspoon salt
½ teaspoon coarsely ground pepper

Tear lettuce into medium-size pieces and place in bowl with mushrooms. Combine dressing ingredients and blend. Toss salad with dressing just before serving.

SERVES 4

Note: If salad is partially prepared in advance, mushrooms can be sliced into salad dressing to prevent them from browning.

Kent Valley Apple Slaw

3 cups thin-sliced green cabbage
1 medium carrot, shredded
1 unpeeled apple, cored and coarsely
    grated
½ cup diced green bell pepper
½ red onion, sliced
lettuce leaves
apple wedges for garnish

Dressing
¼ cup cider vinegar
3 tablespoons sugar
2 tablespoons vegetable oil
¼ teaspoon garlic salt
¼ teaspoon celery seed

Combine cabbage, carrot, apple, green pepper, and onion. Blend dressing. Toss salad with dressing and refrigerate until chilled. Serve on individual plates, a lettuce leaf per serving, and garnish with apple wedges.

SERVES 6 TO 8

Egg and Olive Mold

2 tablespoons unflavored gelatin
½ cup cold water
1 cup boiling water
¾ cup mayonnaise
1 clove garlic, minced
10 hard-cooked eggs, coarsely
    chopped

1 green bell pepper, diced
1 medium onion, chopped
1 4½-ounce can chopped green olives
1 teaspoon salt
lettuce leaves

Lightly oil a 6-cup mold.

Soften gelatin in cold water, then add boiling water to dissolve. Stir in all remaining ingredients except lettuce. (Do not use a blender or a food processor to chop or dice the eggs, green pepper, or onion because the results would be too small and mushy.) Pour mixture into mold and chill until firm. Unmold on a bed of lettuce leaves and serve on a chilled platter.

SERVES 8 TO 10

Variation: Garnished with parsley and surrounded with crackers, this salad may be served for brunch or as an appetizer for dinner.

Endive and Watercress Salad

2 large heads Belgian endive
1 cup tightly packed watercress leaves
½ cup crumbled feta cheese
¼ cup chopped pecans

3 tablespoons vegetable oil
1 tablespoon lemon juice
¼ teaspoon salt
⅛ teaspoon pepper

Trim off root end of endive, removing discolored leaves. Rinse, dry, and cut into julienne strips. Arrange endive and watercress on salad plates and top with cheese and pecans. Combine oil, lemon juice, salt, and pepper, and pour over salad.

SERVES 4

Mozzarella–Tomato Salad

3 large firm tomatoes, in ⅛-inch slices
¼ pound mozzarella cheese, in ⅛-inch
    slices (cut at the deli)
fresh basil leaves or curly endive
1 tablespoon minced fresh basil or
    1½ teaspoons dried basil

Dressing
½ cup vegetable oil
⅛ cup red wine vinegar
2 tablespoons Dijon-style mustard
1 tablespoon dried parsley
salt and freshly ground pepper to taste

Trim the mozzarella slices into the same shape as the tomato slices and alternate and overlap on a bed of basil or endive leaves on a long, narrow platter. Combine the dressing ingredients, blend, and pour over tomatoes and mozzarella. Sprinkle on the basil.

SERVES 6 TO 8

Endive, Mushroom, and Cucumber Salad

6 large heads Belgian endive
1 pound mushrooms
1 tablespoon lemon juice
1 quart water
2 cucumbers, peeled and sliced thin
2 tablespoons finely chopped parsley

Dressing
2½ tablespoons tarragon wine vinegar
¼ cup vegetable oil
½ teaspoon coarse salt
½ teaspoon coarsely ground pepper
2 tablespoons finely chopped shallots

Trim off root end of endive, removing any discolored leaves. Rinse, dry, and cut into julienne strips. Clean mushrooms in water to which lemon juice has been added, trim stems, and slice thin (do not use a food processor). Combine dressing ingredients and blend. Place endive, mushrooms, cucumbers, and parsley in a chilled bowl and toss with dressing just before serving.

SERVES 6

Condiment Salad

2 bunches fresh spinach (about 1
   pound)
1 medium head red cabbage, sliced
   thin

½ teaspoon Worcestershire sauce
½ teaspoon sugar
½ teaspoon salt
1 clove garlic, minced

Dressing
1¾ cups vegetable oil
¼ cup olive oil
¼ cup wine vinegar
¼ cup water
1½ teaspoons lemon juice
¾ teaspoon Dijon-style mustard

Condiments
toasted slivered almonds
orange segments
golden raisins
currants
chopped figs
chopped green onions

Tear spinach into bite-size pieces and add cabbage. Combine dressing ingredients and blend. Chill dressing and greens separately for 4 hours before serving. Serve salad with a cruet of dressing and pass the condiments.

SERVES 6 TO 8

Avocado and Orange Salad

2 oranges, peeled and in segments
2 large avocados, peeled and sliced
1 cup pecans
2 tablespoons butter
1 head iceberg lettuce
1 head Boston or Bibb lettuce

Dressing
1 cup vegetable oil
¼ cup wine vinegar
½ cup orange juice
¼ cup lemon juice
¼ cup sugar
½ teaspoon salt
½ teaspoon dry mustard
1 tablespoon grated onion

Combine dressing ingredients and blend. Marinate orange segments and avocado slices in dressing for 2 hours. Sauté pecans in butter. Tear lettuce into bite-size pieces. Toss oranges, avocado, lettuce, and pecans with enough dressing to coat lettuce.

SERVES 8

Variation: Substitute grapefruit and grapefruit juice for oranges and orange juice.

Seattle's Caesar Salad

1 medium clove garlic, minced
⅛ cup olive oil
1 medium head Boston or romaine
    lettuce or a combination of leaves
    from both
1 avocado, peeled and sliced thin
1 cup chopped green onions
½ pound bacon, cooked, drained, and
    crumbled
½ cup freshly grated Parmesan cheese

Dressing
½ cup lemon juice
½ cup olive oil
⅔ teaspoon freshly ground pepper
1 tablespoon finely chopped fresh
    mint
1 teaspoon crushed oregano
1 egg

Rub wooden salad bowl with garlic and olive oil and sprinkle with salt. Tear lettuce into bite-size pieces and place in bowl with avocado, green onions, and bacon. In a separate bowl combine dressing ingredients and blend. Toss salad with dressing, sprinkle with Parmesan, and toss again lightly.

SERVES 6

Armando Salad

1 clove garlic
1 head romaine lettuce
½ pound bacon, cooked, drained, and
    crumbled
lemon juice
¼ cup coarsely grated Parmesan
    cheese
croutons
freshly ground pepper

Dressing
3 tablespoons sour cream
3 tablespoons olive oil
3 tablespoons wine vinegar
1 egg
2 teaspoons mixed salad herbs (such
    as oregano, basil, parsley, thyme)

Rub wooden salad bowl with garlic, reserving garlic for dressing. Tear lettuce into bite-size pieces and place with bacon in the salad bowl. Crush the garlic and blend with dressing ingredients. Add croutons to salad and toss with dressing. Sprinkle with lemon juice and Parmesan and toss again lightly.

SERVES 6

Spinach Salad with Chutney

2 bunches fresh spinach (about 1 pound)
6 mushrooms, sliced
1 8-ounce can water chestnuts, drained and sliced
6 slices bacon, cooked, drained, and crumbled
½ cup shredded Gruyère cheese
¼ cup thin–sliced red onion

Dressing
¼ cup wine vinegar
4 tablespoons fruit-based chutney with liquid
1 clove garlic, minced
2 tablespoons Dijon-style mustard
2 tablespoons sugar
½ cup vegetable oil
salt and freshly ground pepper

Tear spinach into bite-sized pieces and add mushrooms, water chestnuts, bacon, cheese, and onion. In a blender or food processor mix vinegar, liquid from chutney, garlic, mustard, and sugar until smooth. Slowly add oil and process until thick and creamy. Chop the chutney coarsely. Add chutney to dressing, then season to taste with salt and pepper. Toss salad with dressing. Dressing may be refrigerated, but bring to room temperature before serving.

SERVES 4 TO 6

Watercress–Walnut Salad

2 cups watercress leaves, tightly packed
½ cup walnut halves, lightly toasted
1 tablespoon minced chives

Dressing
1½ tablespoons walnut or vegetable oil
1¼ teaspoons wine vinegar
¼ teaspoon Dijon-style mustard
salt and freshly ground pepper to taste

Place watercress leaves, walnut halves, and chives in a bowl. In another bowl, combine and blend dressing ingredients. Just prior to serving, toss the salad with the dressing, lightly coating the salad.

SERVES 3 TO 4

Three-Leaf Salad

1 head romaine lettuce
1 head red–leaf lettuce
1 bunch spinach (about ½ pound)
2 cups canned mandarin orange
    segments, drained
1½ cups crumbled feta cheese
½ pound bacon, cooked, drained, and
    crumbled
½ medium red onion, sliced in rings

Dressing
¼ cup sugar
1 teaspoon grated onion
1 teaspoon dry mustard
1 teaspoon salt
⅓ cup cider vinegar
1 cup vegetable oil
1 teaspoon poppy seeds
1 teaspoon sesame seeds

Combine lettuce and spinach leaves, orange segments, cheese, bacon, and red onion slices. In another bowl, combine sugar, grated onion, mustard, salt, and vinegar and blend with a whisk. Add oil gradually, blending well. Stir in poppy seeds and sesame seeds and toss salad with dressing.

SERVES 8

Sweet-and-Sour Spinach Salad

2 bunches spinach (about 1 pound)
12 mushrooms, sliced thin
¾ cup cooked and crumbed bacon

Dressing
4 egg yolks
1 teaspoon dry mustard

1 teaspoon salt
¼ teaspoon ground white pepper
2 tablespoons lemon juice
¼ cup sugar
½ cup vegetable oil
3 tablespoons red wine vinegar

Tear spinach into bite-size pieces. In a large bowl, combine spinach, mushrooms, and bacon. Beat egg yolks in a small bowl until light and lemon-colored, then add mustard, salt, pepper, and lemon juice and blend well. Add sugar and oil, whisk until thickened, and blend in vinegar. Toss salad with dressing.

SERVES 8

Crunchy Green Salad

2 cups torn lettuce leaves
½ cup thin–sliced Bermuda or red
    onion
2 tablespoons sliced green olives with
    pimiento
1 cup broccoli flowerets
¼ cup crumbled blue cheese

Dressing
¼ cup vegetable oil
2 tablespoons tarragon wine vinegar
¼ teaspoon sugar
¼ teaspoon salt
⅛ teaspoon paprika

Combine lettuce, onion, olives, and broccoli flowerets. Combine dressing ingredients and blend. Just before serving, toss salad with dressing and top with blue cheese.

SERVES 4

Jicama Salad

2 cups raw jicama, peeled and diced
1 green bell pepper, seeded and
    slivered
½ Walla Walla sweet or red onion,
    sliced thin
1 cup sliced or diced cucumber
1 tablespoon chopped pimiento

(optional)
salt and pepper to taste

Dressing
¼ cup olive oil
2 tablespoons red wine vinegar
½ teaspoon oregano, crumbled

Combine jicama, green pepper, onion, cucumber, and pimiento. Add salt and pepper. Pour olive oil and vinegar over vegetables, add oregano, and mix lightly. Refrigerate several hours or overnight, stirring occasionally.

SERVES 4 TO 6

Note: This salad particularly complements a Mexican entrée.

Mandarin–Spinach Salad

2 large bunches spinach leaves (about
    1½ pounds)
5 mandarin oranges, peeled and sliced
    thin

Dressing
1 cup heavy cream, whipped
2 tablespoons orange liqueur
½ cup finely chopped green onion
    tops

Combine dressing ingredients and blend. Pour over greens and orange slices.

SERVES 8

Note: This is a refreshing salad to make when mandarin oranges are available. If fresh mandarins are not available, substitute fresh orange sections, halved.

Greek Salad

4 cups torn Boston or Bibb lettuce
2 cups unpeeled new potatoes, cooked and sliced
2 cups cherry tomatoes
1 cup sliced radishes
¼ cup chopped green onions
¼ cup coarsely chopped parsley
½ cup crumbled feta cheese

1 cup pitted ripe or Greek olives, halved
Dressing
¼ cup vegetable oil
2 tablespoons white vinegar
½ teaspoon oregano, crushed
½ teaspoon salt
¼ teaspoon pepper

Arrange lettuce over bottom of large salad bowl. Place potatoes, tomatoes, radishes, green onions, parsley, and feta on lettuce and arrange olives around edge. Combine oil, vinegar, oregano, salt, and pepper in small jar. Cover and shake vigorously until thoroughly mixed. Just before serving, pour over salad and toss lightly.

SERVES 6

Sunchoke Salad with Mayonnaise Sauce

1 pound sunchokes (Jerusalem artichokes)
2 hard-cooked egg whites
1 red bell pepper
1 dill pickle
12 medium-size green olives
12 pickled cocktail onions
1 celery stalk
1 10-ounce package frozen green peas, thawed
salt and pepper to taste

Mayonnaise Sauce
2 hard-cooked egg yolks
2 tablespoons lemon juice
1 tablespoon vegetable oil
¼ cup mayonnaise
¼ cup sour cream
2 tablespoons Dijon-style mustard
salt and pepper to taste

Clean sunchokes and boil 15 minutes, then peel. Chop sunchokes, egg whites, red pepper, pickle, olives, onions, and celery and combine with peas. Add salt and pepper. Prepare sauce by mashing yolks and gradually adding lemon juice and oil, stirring with a whisk until well blended. Blend in remaining ingredients. Pour over salad, toss, and chill several hours.

SERVES 6

Scallop Salad

½ cup dry white wine
¼ cup water
1 onion, sliced
3 sprigs parsley
¼ teaspoon tarragon

1½ pounds sea or bay scallops
½ pound whole small mushrooms
12 green olives, rinsed, drained, and
    sliced
mayonnaise

Combine wine, water, onion, parsley, and tarragon in skillet. Bring to a boil, reduce heat, add scallops, and simmer: 2 to 3 minutes for sea scallops, 1½ minutes for bay scallops. Cool scallops in broth and drain.

Rinse mushrooms, break off stems, and steam stems and caps for 2 to 3 minutes, depending on size. Drain. Combine scallops, mushrooms, olives, and just enough mayonnaise to moisten. Chill at least 2 hours for flavors to blend. Remove from refrigerator 10 minutes before serving.

SERVES 4

Mussel–Rice Salad

1 cup cooked long-grain rice
1 pound fresh mussels in shells
1 cup dry vermouth
1 teaspoon salt
1 tablespoon lemon juice
¼ cup shredded green bell pepper
2 tablespoons minced onions
2 tablespoons French Dressing
1 cup diced raw cauliflower
⅓ cup mayonnaise
pepper to taste

French Dressing
½ teaspoon salt
½ teaspoon pepper
½ teaspoon paprika
1 teaspoon dry mustard
1 tablespoon sugar
1 tablespoon Worcestershire sauce
3 tablespoons catsup
1 cup vegetable oil
¼ cup vinegar

Steam mussels in vermouth until shells open—approximately 10
minutes. Cool and remove from shells. Discard vermouth.

To prepare dressing: Mix dry ingredients and add Worcestershire,
catsup, and vinegar. Beat well. Add oil gradually, beating constantly.
Toss dressing and mussels together and refrigerate overnight.

SERVES 5 TO 6

Molded Vegetable Seafood Salad

2 tablespoons unflavored gelatin
¼ cup cold water
1 10¾-ounce can condensed tomato
    soup, undiluted
6 ounces cream cheese at room
    temperature

½ cup chopped celery
½ cup chopped green bell pepper
½ cup chopped onion
1 pound cooked crabmeat or shrimp
    or a combination of both
1 cup mayonnaise

Lightly oil a 6-cup mold.

Soak gelatin in cold water for 5 minutes. Heat soup to the boiling
point, add gelatin and cream cheese, and beat until frothy. Stir in
celery, green pepper, onion, and crab or shrimp. Fold in mayonnaise,
then pour into prepared mold. Refrigerate until firm.

SERVES 8

Shrimp Salad

1 head iceberg lettuce, shredded
5 to 6 green onions, chopped
1 3-ounce package ramen (Japanese
    noodles), without the seasoning
    included in package
4 tablespoons butter
2 tablespoons sesame seeds
⅓ cup sliced almonds
½ pound tiny cooked shrimp

Dressing
¼ cup vegetable oil
¼ cup vinegar
2 tablespoons sugar
1 teaspoon salt
½ teaspoon pepper

Place lettuce and onions in a bowl. In a separate bowl, combine dressing ingredients and blend. (Salad may be prepared ahead to this
point.) Break up noodles and sauté in butter. Add sesame seeds and almonds, and sauté until seeds and almonds are toasted, stirring con-

stantly. Add noodle mixture and shrimp to salad bowl and toss salad with dressing. Serve immediately.

SERVES 4

Pasta Salad with Spinach Pesto

2 red bell peppers, cut in julienne
    strips or, if unavailable, a large jar
    pimientos, drained
1 16-ounce package rotelle (corkscrew-
    shaped) pasta
2 10-ounce packages frozen peas,
    thawed
2 7-ounce cans tuna packed in oil,
    drained

Spinach Pesto
1 10-ounce package frozen spinach,
    thawed and squeezed to remove
    liquid
1 cup chopped parsley
⅔ cup Parmesan cheese
½ cup walnut pieces
4 flat anchovy fillets
3 to 4 cloves garlic
3 tablespoons basil
1 teaspoon salt
¼ teaspoon ground fennel seed
juice of ½ lemon
1 cup olive oil

Blanch the red peppers for 30 seconds and drain. Plunge into ice water to stop further cooking and drain well. Boil the pasta until *al dente*. Drain and rinse.

To prepare pesto: Blend all ingredients except oil until mixture is smooth, using the steel blade of a food processor. With the motor running, add olive oil in a stream.

In a large bowl, combine the pasta with pesto, peas, tuna, and red peppers. Add salt and pepper to taste. Chill the salad, covered, for at least 1 hour or overnight.

SERVES 8 TO 10

Note: The pesto, refrigerated, keeps well for a few days.

Potato and Sausage Salad

1 pound uncooked pork sausage (plain or garlic; fresh or smoked; French, Italian, or Polish)
3 pounds firm boiling potatoes cut in ¼-inch slices
¼ cup chicken stock
¼ cup white wine vinegar

2 teaspoons salt
1 tablespoons Dijon-style mustard
⅔ cup olive oil
2 tablespoons thin–sliced green onions, including tops
¼ cup chopped parsley
freshly ground pepper to taste

Pierce sausage with fork and fry until brown. Drain and cool. Cook potato slices in boiling salted water 12 to 15 minutes until barely tender (do not overcook). Drain and transfer to large bowl. Heat chicken stock and pour over potatoes, toss gently, and let stand until absorbed.

In a small bowl, combine vinegar, salt, and mustard. Add to potatoes and gently toss again. Let stand to absorb seasoning. Pour olive oil over potatoes and sprinkle in green onions and parsley. Toss to coat potatoes with oil and herbs. Cut sausage into bite-size pieces, removing casing if necessary. Toss with potatoes or arrange on top.

SERVES 4 TO 6

Armenian Salad

1 cup uncooked bulgur
6 tablespoons vegetable oil
2 tablespoons white wine vinegar
2 tablespoons diced green bell pepper
¼ cup chopped chives
¼ cup diced celery
12 cured-in-oil (Greek-style) olives, pitted and halved

1½ pounds tiny cooked shrimp
12 cherry tomatoes, halved
¼ cup mayonnaise or 2 tablespoons mayonnaise combined with 2 tablespoons plain yogurt
salad greens

Cover the bulgur with hot water and allow to stand for about 30 minutes—until liquid is absorbed and grains are tender. Combine oil and vinegar and pour over bulgur. Refrigerate at least 1 hour, or overnight, so that flavors blend. Mix with green pepper, chives, celery, olives, shrimp, and tomatoes. Carefully mix in mayonnaise and serve on salad greens.

SERVES 8

Hood Canal Shrimp Salad

2 cups cooked rice
20 green olives, sliced
½ cup raw cauliflower, broken into
    flowerets
2 to 4 green onions, chopped

½ cup chopped green bell pepper
½ cup mayonnaise
1 teaspoon lemon juice
1 cup medium-size cooked shrimp

Combine all ingredients except shrimp and marinate overnight. Just before serving add shrimp and toss well. Serve in lettuce cups.

SERVES 4

Fiesta Rice Salad

1 tablespoon vegetable oil
1 tablespoon butter
3 medium cloves garlic, minced
1 small onion, chopped
1 cup uncooked pearl rice
¼ cup white wine
2 cups water
1 green bell pepper, chopped
2 to 3 carrots, sliced thin
2 tablespoons chopped parsley

3 green onions, chopped
1 cup large pitted black olives, sliced
salt and pepper to taste
parsley for garnish

Dressing
4 to 6 tablespoons red wine vinegar
2 tablespoons olive oil
1 teaspoon oregano, crushed
1 inch anchovy paste

Sauté garlic and onion in vegetable oil and butter. Add rice and wine and cook for 2 minutes, stirring constantly. Add ½ cup of the water and cook until it is absorbed, then add remaining water and other salad ingredients. Cover and simmer 10 to 12 minutes. Cool.

To prepare dressing: Whisk ingredients together until blended and stir into rice mixture. Serve salad in a glass bowl or shape in a buttered ring mold and unmold on a platter. Garnish with parsley.

SERVES 6 TO 8

Rice–Artichoke Salad

1 cup uncooked long-grain rice
2 cups chicken broth
¼ cup chopped green bell pepper
¼ cup chopped green onion
¼ cup sliced green pimiento-stuffed
    olives
1 6-ounce jar marinated artichoke
    hearts, drained and chopped

lemon wedges and parsley sprigs for
    garnish

Dressing
½ cup mayonnaise
½ cup unflavored yogurt
½ teaspoon dill
salt and pepper to taste

Wash uncooked rice several times until water runs clear. Cook rice in chicken broth until dry and fluffy. Cool. Add green pepper, onion, olives, and artichokes.

To prepare dressing: Combine dressing ingredients and blend. Toss with salad and chill until ready to serve. Garnish with lemon wedges and parsley.

SERVES 6 TO 8

Rising Sun Chicken Salad

1 whole chicken (approximately
    3 pounds)
2 English cucumbers, sliced thin
1 3.85-ounce package cellophane
    noodles (in Asian stores or
    specialty shops these are
    harusame or saifun)

Dressing
4 tablespoons soy sauce
3 tablespoons sesame oil
4 tablespoons rice vinegar

In a covered saucepan, simmer chicken in water to cover until tender—approximately 45 minutes. Skin, bone, and shred chicken. Add cucumbers and refrigerate.

Combine dressing ingredients and blend. Boil noodles according to directions on package. When noodles are transparent, rinse in cold water and drain. Toss chicken, cucumbers, and noodles with dressing.

SERVES 4

Note: For a more pronounced flavor, marinate chicken and cucumber in dressing for 30 minutes before mixing with noodles.

Chicken-Asparagus Salad

1 chicken, quartered
2 cups fresh asparagus, sliced
    diagonally
1 large stalk celery, sliced diagonally
1 2-ounce jar pimientos, drained
2 green onions, both tops and bottoms,
    chopped

Dressing
⅓ cup mayonnaise
1 teaspoon basil, crushed
1 teaspoon sugar
3 tablespoons capers with juice
salt and pepper

In a covered saucepan, simmer chicken in water to cover until tender—approximately 45 minutes. Skin, bone, and cube chicken, then chill. Blanch asparagus for 2 minutes and immediately rinse under cold water and drain.

    Combine dressing ingredients and blend. Combine chicken, celery, pimiento, asparagus, and green onion, and toss with dressing.

SERVES 4 TO 6

Chinese Chicken Salad

2 whole chicken breasts
1 head lettuce, shredded
4 green onions, including tops,
    chopped
4 tablespoons blanched almonds,
    chopped
2 ounces rice sticks (in Asian stores or
    specialty shops these are maifun)
peanut oil for frying rice sticks

Dressing
¼ cup peanut oil
6 tablespoons rice vinegar
¼ cup toasted sesame seeds
¼ cup sugar
4 teaspoons freshly ground pepper

Bake chicken, or simmer in chicken broth, until tender. Skin, bone, and shred. Combine chicken, lettuce, onions, and almonds. Combine dressing ingredients and blend.

    Fry rice sticks in very hot oil according to package directions. The sticks should puff up immediately—if they do not, discard and start over with hotter oil. Toss salad and rice sticks with dressing immediately before serving.

SERVES 4

Chicken Chutney Salad

5 cups diced cooked chicken or turkey
1 cup sliced water chestnuts
1 cup sliced celery
2 cups pineapple tidbits, well drained
½ cup sliced green olives
1 3-ounce can chow mein noodles

Dressing
1 cup sour cream
1 cup mayonnaise
¼ cup chopped Major Grey-type
   chutney
1 teaspoon curry powder

Combine chicken, water chestnuts, celery, pineapple, and olives. In another bowl, combine dressing ingredients and blend. Toss chicken mixture and noodles with dressing.

SERVES 4 TO 5

Hawaiian Chicken Salad

1 large whole chicken breast
½ cup sliced onion
¼ cup chopped celery leaves
salt and pepper to taste
1 15¼-ounce can pineapple tidbits,
   drained
¾ cup diced celery
½ cup flaked coconut

1 tablespoon grated onion
½ pound fresh bean sprouts

Dressing
1 cup mayonnaise
1 tablespoon lemon juice
½ to ¾ teaspoon curry powder
¾ teaspoon salt
½ teaspoon pepper

In water to cover, simmer chicken until tender with onions, celery leaves, salt, and pepper—approximately 45 minutes. Skin, bone, and cube chicken, and chill. Discard vegetables.

Combine chicken, pineapple, celery, coconut, onion, and bean sprouts. In a separate bowl, combine dressing ingredients and blend. Toss salad with dressing and chill for 24 hours.

SERVES 6

Indian Curry Salad

2 cups cooked, cubed chicken
1 large tart green apple, pared, cored,
   and diced

1 16-ounce can dark red kidney beans,
   rinsed and drained
1 cup diced celery

1 green onion, minced
red–leaf lettuce leaves

Dressing
¼ cup mayonnaise
¼ cup unflavored yogurt
1 teaspoon lemon juice
½ teaspoon curry powder

½ teaspoon salt

Condiments
sliced bananas
toasted coconut
salted peanuts
sour cream
raisins

Combine chicken, apple, kidney beans, celery, and onion. In a separate bowl, combine dressing ingredients and blend. Toss salad with
dressing and serve in a bowl lined with red–leaf lettuce. Pass condiments separately.

SERVES 6

Scallop–Linguine Salad

4 ounces freshly made spinach or egg
   linguine
3 cloves garlic, minced
3 tablespoons butter
2 tablespoons olive oil
½ pound fresh scallops (whole bay
   scallops or halved sea scallops)
1 medium zucchini, cut into ¼-inch
   slices and halved
1 pound fresh spinach broken into
   bite-size pieces, with a few large
   leaves reserved to line bowl

1 large tomato, seeded and diced
1 tablespoon chopped fresh dill or
   ½ teaspoon dried
1 teaspoon fresh or ½ teaspoon dried
   thyme
2 tablespoons lemon juice
½ lemon, cut into paper-thin slices,
   halved
salt and freshly ground pepper to taste

Cook pasta in rapidly boiling salted water until *al dente*. Drain and
chill. In large pan, sauté garlic in oil and butter for 2 minutes. Add
scallops and sauté *until they are barely white*—2 to 3 minutes. Remove
and drain on paper towels. Leave oil mixture in pan to cool to room
temperature, then gently mix pasta and scallops with oil and stir in remaining ingredients. Transfer to spinach-lined bowl and serve.

SERVES 4

Pasta and Chicken Salad

One of Seattle's earliest identifiable ethnic areas was Italian—Rainier Valley, known at one time as Garlic Gulch. Today, Italian specialty shops and homemade pasta (not to mention garlic) command attention from all self-respecting chefs, and Nancy Varriale, who teaches cooking and specializes in Italian foods, finds that this recipe is one that her students most want to master.

2 whole chicken breasts
1 cup salted chicken stock
¼ cup dry white wine
¾ pound pasta bows or medium-sized conchiglie
1 cup chopped provolone cheese
1 cup coarsely chopped cooked green beans
1 cup cherry tomatoes, halved
1 cup coarsely chopped celery
4 green onions, coarsely chopped
½ cup coarsely chopped pitted black olives
¼ cup toasted pine nuts or blanched almonds

salt to taste
lettuce leaves
1 cantaloupe for garnish
2 thin slices prosciutto cut in julienne strips for garnish

Garlic Mayonnaise
2 whole eggs
2 egg yolks
4 cloves garlic
½ cup lemon juice
2 teaspoons Dijon-style mustard
2 cups corn oil
salt and pepper to taste
dash of dry mustard

Gently cook chicken breasts in broth and wine for 15 minutes and let cool in broth. Skin, bone, and chop coarsely. Cook pasta in rapidly boiling salted water until *al dente*. Drain and cool.

To prepare mayonnaise: Mix eggs, yolks, garlic, lemon juice, prepared mustard, salt, and pepper in blender or food processor. With motor running, slowly drizzle in oil to make a thin sauce.

Set aside 1 tablespoon of each vegetable for garnish. Mix all remaining salad ingredients in a large bowl. Add mayonnaise to taste, and toss gently. (There will be extra mayonnaise. Add, as necessary, if salad is kept for several days.) Salt to taste.

To serve, place salad on a platter lined with lettuce and sprinkle reserved vegetables over salad for garnish. Surround with thin-sliced melon and arrange prosciutto on top.

SERVES 6 TO 8

Calamari Salad

1 pound squid
1 cup vermouth
2 pimientos, sliced
2 stalks celery, sliced
1 green bell pepper, sliced
1 bunch spinach (about ½ pound)
1 head green lettuce

Dressing
⅔ cup vegetable oil
¼ cup tarragon wine vinegar
2 cloves garlic, minced
1 teaspoon sugar
¾ teaspoon salt
¾ teaspoon dry mustard
dash of freshly ground pepper

Wash squid and clean according to directions on page 183. Slice body crosswise into ¼-inch strips, forming rings, place in saucepan, and cover with vermouth. Bring to a boil and poach for 30 seconds, until rings just become rigid. Mix dressing ingredients and combine in a bowl with squid, pimiento, celery, and green pepper. Marinate 8 hours. Wash spinach, slice into thin strips, mound on lettuce leaves, and top with marinated squid.

SERVES 6

Note: Scallops may be substituted for squid.

Prosciutto–Pasta Salad

16 ounces spaghetti twists or bow ties (farfalle), cooked
2 6-ounce jars marinated artichoke hearts, quartered, (marinade reserved for dressing)
1 8½-ounce can artichoke hearts (not marinated), drained and quartered
1 8-ounce can pitted black olives, sliced
8 ounces prosciutto, sliced thin and cut in julienne strips

2 cups frozen tiny peas, thawed and drained

Dressing
1 cup minced chives or green onions, both tops and bottoms
¼ cup lemon juice
⅛ cup olive oil
2 tablespoons minced fresh oregano or 1 tablespoon dried oregano
1 teaspoon garlic salt
salt and freshly ground pepper to taste

Combine salad ingredients in a large serving bowl.

To prepare dressing: Combine ingredients, add reserved artichoke marinade, and mix well. Pour over salad and toss gently. Serve at room temperature.

SERVES 10 TO 12

Tortellini Salad

14 ounces dried cheese tortellini
⅓ cup olive oil
¼ cup garlic-flavored red wine vinegar
2 tablespoons Worcestershire sauce
3 tablespoons Dijon-style mustard
1½ teaspoons coarsely ground pepper
1 large clove garlic, minced
2 tablespoons sugar
2 teaspoons salt
2 dashes Tabasco sauce

1 cup thin-sliced celery
1 cup chopped green onions, both tops
    and bottoms
1 cup mushrooms, sliced thin
1 cup aged Cheddar cheese, crumbled
    into small pieces
⅓ cup chopped pimiento (optional)
2 tablespoons minced Italian or
    regular parsley

In a large pot, cook tortellini in boiling water until *al dente*. Drain and rinse in cold water. Transfer to a medium-size bowl and toss thoroughly with olive oil.

In another medium-size bowl mix vinegar, Worcestershire, mustard, pepper, garlic, sugar, salt, and Tabasco, blending well. Add celery, green onions, mushrooms, cheese, and pimiento and mix well again. Combine with tortellini in a large bowl. Toss well and marinate 8 to 24 hours in the refrigerator, tossing frequently.

Three hours before serving, remove salad from the refrigerator and toss occasionally. Serve at room temperature, garnished with parsley.

SERVES 6

Wild Rice Salad

½ pound fresh mushrooms, sliced thin
juice of 1 large lemon
½ pound wild rice, cooked and
    drained
4 green onions, sliced thin, both white
    and green parts
1 red bell pepper, coarsely chopped
salt and pepper to taste
2 cups frozen tiny peas, thawed and
    drained

Dressing
12 medium cloves garlic, minced
2 teaspoons Dijon-style mustard
1 teaspoon coarse salt
½ teaspoon freshly ground pepper
¼ cup champagne vinegar
½ cup vegetable oil
1 teaspoon finely chopped fresh
    tarragon or ¼ teaspoon dried
    tarragon
¼ teaspoon sugar

Combine mushrooms and lemon juice in a large bowl. Add rice, onion, and red pepper.

To prepare dressing: Combine ingredients and mix well. Add to rice mixture and toss lightly, seasoning with salt and pepper. Toss in peas 1 hour before serving and serve at room temperature.

SERVES 10 TO 12

Note: This is lovely served in cored tomatoes for individual servings.

Vinaigrette Dressing

1 medium clove garlic
½ teaspoon Pommery-style mustard
   (available at specialty stores)
½ teaspoon Dijon-style mustard

1 teaspoon lemon juice
1 teaspoon white wine vinegar
⅓ cup olive oil

Mix all ingredients in blender or food processor.

YIELD: ½ CUP

Emerald City Dressing

½ cup mayonnaise
2 tablespoons milk
2 anchovy fillets, minced
1 tablespoon tarragon wine vinegar

1½ tablespoons lemon juice
1 cup chopped parsley
2 tablespoons minced fresh chives

Combine all ingredients in food processor or blender until creamy and uniform in texture.

YIELD: ¾ CUP

Roquefort Dressing

2 cups mayonnaise
1 cup sour cream
¼ cup wine vinegar
¼ cup chopped parsley or fresh dill

½ teaspoon dry mustard
1 medium clove garlic, minced
2 ounces crumbled Roquefort cheese

Blend all ingredients except Roquefort with wire whisk until creamy. Add Roquefort and stir well.

YIELD: ABOUT 3 CUPS

Mushroom Dressing

6 large mushroom caps
1 tablespoon lemon juice
2 teaspoons sugar
salt and pepper to taste
4 green onions, both tops and bottoms,
    chopped fine

2 tablespoons sour cream
6 tablespoons vegetable oil
2 tablespoons cider vinegar
1 medium clove garlic, minced

Slice mushroom caps wafer-thin and sprinkle with lemon juice, sugar, salt, pepper, and green onions. Stir in sour cream. In another bowl, mix together oil, vinegar, and garlic, and stir into the mushroom mixture. Refrigerate 1 to 6 hours.

YIELD: ABOUT 1 CUP

Garlic-Caper Dressing

¼ cup lemon juice
¾ cup olive oil
1 teaspoon salt
1 teaspoon freshly ground pepper

1 tablespoon capers
6 cloves garlic, halved
dash Worcestershire sauce

Combine ingredients and blend thoroughly in food processor or blender.

YIELD: ABOUT 1 CUP

Fruit Dressing

1 cup sugar
2 tablespoons flour or 1½ tablespoons
    cornstarch

2 eggs, slightly beaten
1 cup pineapple juice
1 cup heavy cream

Thoroughly mix sugar and flour. In a medium saucepan, heat this mixture with eggs and pineapple juice, stirring constantly. Cook until mixture comes to a low boil. Cool, then place in an airtight container and refrigerate. When ready to serve, whip cream and fold in refrigerated mixture. Serve with tossed or molded fruit salads.

YIELD: ABOUT 3 CUPS

Sailors enjoy a brisk wind on opening day of the yachting season as yachts parade through the Montlake Cut to Lake Washington. Boats are decorated with flags—and more—for the occasion.

Eggs, Cheese Dishes, & Brunches

Oatmeal-Buttermilk Pancakes

2 cups rolled oats
2¼ cups buttermilk
½ cup white or whole wheat flour
1 teaspoon baking soda
1 teaspoon baking powder
1 teaspoon salt

3 tablespoons firmly packed brown
　sugar
4 eggs, beaten
3 tablespoons vegetable oil
⅓ cup coarsely chopped pecans

Soak oats in buttermilk 5 to 10 minutes. Sift together the dry ingredients and add to them the buttermilk mixture, beaten eggs, and oil. Fold in nuts.

Preheat griddle to hot.

Cook on lightly greased griddle until bubbles begin to appear, turn, and cook briefly. Serve topped with syrup, yogurt and cinnamon, or applesauce.

SERVES 4

Cottage Cheese Pancakes

1 cup cottage cheese	½ cup flour
2 tablespoons vegetable oil	¼ teaspoon salt
6 eggs	½ teaspoon vanilla

Preheat griddle to hot.

Place all ingredients in blender and mix until smooth. Cook on lightly greased griddle until bubbles begin to appear. Turn, cook briefly, and serve topped with powdered sugar, fruit butter, honey, or fresh berries.

SERVES 4

Swedish Pancakes

3 eggs	butter for frying and spreading
½ cup flour	lingonberry or strawberry jam
½ cup milk	for filling
pinch of salt	

Preheat 8-inch skillet or crêpe pan to hot (400 degrees).

Mix eggs, flour, milk, and salt until well blended. Melt butter in a hot pan and wipe with paper towel, leaving a thin film of butter. To make a large and very thin pancake, pour in enough batter to cover bottom of pan. Cook until the sheen is off the top of the batter, then turn and cook the other side briefly. Butter each pancake, spread with jam, and roll up. You can be rolling a pancake while the next is cooking. Repeat until all the batter is used.

SERVES 2

Dutch Baby

3 eggs	¼ cup butter
¾ cup flour	2 tablespoons powdered sugar
¾ cup milk	juice of ½ lemon

Preheat oven to 425 degrees.

Put eggs in blender, beat about a minute, then gradually add flour and milk. Continue mixing about 30 seconds. Put butter in 2- to

3-quart baking pan or oven-proof skillet, and place in oven to melt butter. Pour the batter over the hot melted butter and bake 20 to 35 minutes, or until puffy and brown. Remove pancake from oven, sprinkle with sugar and lemon juice, and return to oven for 2 to 3 minutes, until pancake is glazed.

SERVES 2 TO 4

Variations: In place of sugar and lemon juice, the pancake may be topped with any of the following: 2 tablespoons raisins plumped in ¼ cup rum; 1 tablespoon powdered sugar; sliced apples sautéed in butter; chopped bacon and sliced avocado; Kasseri cheese and peach slices.

Aebleskivers

These Scandinavian pancake balls are particularly appropriate; Seattle, along with Minneapolis, claims the largest Scandinavian population in North America. Danes, Norwegians, Swedes, and Finns settled the Puget Sound area because it provided work in familiar industries—fishing, boatbuilding, and lumber—as well as islands and fjords that reminded them of home. In some parts of Ballard, the Scandinavian section of Seattle, wonderful pastries like aebleskivers are easier to buy than hamburger buns.

2 eggs, separated
2 tablespoons sugar
2 cups flour
½ teaspoon salt
2 teaspoons baking powder
½ teaspoon baking soda
½ teaspoon cinnamon or ground
   cardamom

grated zest of ½ lemon
½ cup plus 2 tablespoons butter,
   melted
2¼ cups buttermilk or whole milk
powdered sugar
strawberry, raspberry, or apple jam

In a small bowl, beat egg yolks and sugar until thick and lemon-colored. In a second bowl, sift together flour, salt, baking powder, baking soda, and cinnamon or cardamom. Add lemon zest, yolk mixture, ¼ cup melted butter, and milk, beating until smooth. In another bowl, beat egg whites until stiff peaks form; carefully fold into yolk-flour mixture. (Mixture may be made ahead to this point and refrigerated overnight.)

Heat a seasoned *aebleskiver* pan over medium heat until drops of water sizzle when sprinkled in the pan. Brush each section of the pan with the remaining melted butter and fill each section about ¾ full with batter. In about 30 to 40 seconds, a thin shell will form on the bottom of each pancake ball. Using a slender skewer or a knitting needle, gently pull the shell up about halfway to allow the unbaked batter to flow out. Continue to rotate each pancake ball about every 30 seconds, pulling up the baked shell to let the remaining batter flow into the pan. When you have turned the shell about 4 times, a hollow ball should almost be formed; it will be complete when the ball is turned upside down to seal itself. Continue to rotate the balls until they are evenly browned. They are done when a skewer inserted in the center comes out clean. Use the skewer to lift the balls onto a plate.

Dust *aebleskivers* with powdered sugar, then break each in half and fill with jam. *Aebleskivers* are meant to be eaten by hand.

YIELD: 65 TO 70 SMALL AEBLESKIVERS

Note: Aebleskivers can be kept warm for up to 30 minutes in a bun warmer, or on a warming tray, or in a low oven.

Normandy French Toast

Custard Sauce

1 large apple, cored
1 tablespoon butter
1 tablespoon vegetable oil
¾ cup light cream
2 egg yolks
¼ cup sugar
1 teaspoon flour
½ teaspoon vanilla
2 tablespoons rum

French Toast

1 baguette of French bread
2 eggs
2 tablespoons sugar
2 cups milk
1 teaspoon vanilla
¼ teaspoon salt
¼ cup rum
butter
vegetable oil

Preheat oven to 350 degrees.

To prepare sauce: From thickest portion of apple, slice 10 very thin rings; peel and dice remaining apple. Sauté apple rings and diced apple in butter and oil until just softened, and set aside. Scald cream. Beat egg yolks, sugar, and flour until smooth and place in a saucepan. Add cream slowly to egg mixture, stirring constantly. Add vanilla and cook until thickened, then add rum and diced apples.

To prepare French toast: Slice bread diagonally into 10 1-inch-thick pieces. Make batter by combining the eggs, sugar, milk, vanilla, salt, and rum. Dip bread into batter and sauté each side in butter-oil mixture until golden brown. Remove from pan and cover each piece with 2 to 3 tablespoons of custard sauce and top with an apple ring.

SERVES 5 TO 10

Note: Both sauce and toast may be prepared in advance. In this case, warm the French toast on a cookie sheet in a 350-degree oven for 15 mintues. Add the warmed sauce, top with apple rings, and heat 5 minutes more.

Orange French Toast

8 eggs, beaten
grated zest of 1 orange
juice of 1 large orange (about ¾ cup)
8 1-inch-thick slices French bread

butter for frying
1 tablespoon cinnamon
½ cup sugar

Combine eggs, orange juice, and orange zest. Soak bread slices well in egg mixture and start to sauté slowly in butter. Meanwhile, mix together cinnamon and sugar, and sprinkle lightly over toast as it cooks. Turn, sprinkle with more cinnamon-sugar, and sauté until golden brown on both sides. Serve topped with butter and maple syrup.

SERVES 4 TO 8

Note: Oatmeal or other whole-grain breads may be substituted.

English Muffin Bread French Toast

1 cup light cream
1 egg
¼ teaspoon vanilla extract
1 tablespoon powdered sugar

¹/₈ teaspoon cinnamon
½ cup butter
⅓ loaf English muffin bread, sliced

Beat together cream, egg, vanilla, and powdered sugar. Add cinnamon and stir. Melt ¼ cup butter in a large frying pan over medium heat. Soak bread in liquid, then fry slowly, turning often until golden brown. As butter in pan is absorbed, replace it when adding more bread. Sprinkle toast with powdered sugar and serve with orange marmalade or gooseberry jam.

SERVES 2 TO 3

Ham and Cheese Sandwich Puff

2 cups ground ham (about 1 pound)
2 cups grated Swiss cheese (about ½ pound)
½ cup mayonnaise

1 teaspoon Dijon-style mustard
12 slices white bread, toasted
6 eggs
2 cups milk

Combine ham, cheese, mayonnaise, and mustard. Spread on 6 slices of toast. Place remaining slices on top to make 6 sandwiches and cut sandwiches diagonally into quarters. In a 9-x-13-inch baking pan, stand the quarters on edge, crust sides down. Beat together eggs and milk, and pour over the sandwiches. Cover and chill at least 4 hours or overnight. (Don't worry if egg mixture does not completely cover sandwiches.) When ready to cook, preheat oven to 325 degrees. Bake uncovered for 25 minutes, until the custard is set. Serve hot.

SERVES 6 TO 10

Scrambled Eggs with Smoked Salmon

8 eggs
2 tablespoons light cream
pinch of salt
freshly ground black pepper to taste
dash Tabasco sauce
1 to 1½ cups flaked Nova Scotia-style smoked salmon

3 tablespoons butter
triangles of wheat bread, sautéed in butter
½ cup cooked peas or 2 tablespoons minced chives
½ cup sour cream

Beat together the eggs and cream, and season with salt, pepper, and Tabasco. Continue beating until well blended, then fold in salmon. Heat butter in a 10-inch omelet pan or a heavy skillet. When butter starts to foam, add egg mixture and cook over medium heat for 2 to 3 minutes, stirring with a fork until eggs are set. Serve over sautéed bread triangles, garnish with peas or chives, and serve sour cream separately.

SERVES 4

Cheese and Mushroom Eggs in Lemon Sauce

Eggs	Sauce
1 pound mushrooms	5 tablespoons butter
7 tablespoons butter	6 tablespoons flour
2 tablespoons minced shallots or green onions	2 cups milk
salt and pepper to taste	1 cup heavy cream
12 to 16 eggs	salt and pepper to taste

½ cup freshly grated Parmesan
    cheese, or mixture of Parmesan,
    Cheddar, and Swiss cheese
	¼ teaspoon lemon juice

parsley for garnish	

Wash, trim and slice mushrooms; sauté 5 to 6 minutes in 4 tablespoons butter. Add shallots or green onions and sauté over medium heat 1 to 2 minutes. Season with salt and pepper and set aside.

To prepare sauce: Melt 5 tablespoons butter in saucepan. Blend in flour and cook, stirring constantly, for 5 minutes. Remove from heat and beat in milk with a wire whisk. Beat in cream, salt, and pepper, and simmer 4 to 5 minutes. Beat in lemon juice, cover, and keep warm.

Preheat broiler and lightly butter a 9-x-13-inch glass baking dish.

To prepare eggs: Scramble the eggs in 3 tablespoons butter over low heat until soft and creamy and not quite done. Spoon a thin layer of sauce into the bottom of the prepared baking dish; sprinkle with 2 tablespoons cheese and spread half of the eggs over the cheese. Fold 1 cup sauce into mushrooms, and spoon mixture over eggs. Sprinkle with 3 tablespoons cheese, cover with remaining eggs and sauce, and sprinkle with remaining cheese. Dot with butter.

Place dish 1 inch below the broiler element for 1 minute, or until top of eggs is lightly browned. Garnish with parsley and serve immediately.

SERVES 6 TO 10

Avocado Omelet

Sauce	3 large tomatoes, peeled, seeded, and
4 slices bacon	chopped
1 small onion, finely chopped	¼ teaspoon salt

½ teaspoon pepper
2 avocados, peeled and mashed
    (reserve a few slices for garnish)

Omelet
2 tablespoons butter

6 eggs
⅓ cup milk
½ teaspoon salt
freshly ground pepper to taste
1 avocado, peeled and diced

To prepare sauce: Cook and crumble the bacon. Drain half the grease from the pan; sauté onion and tomatoes in the remaining grease until onion is soft. Add salt and pepper, remove from heat, and add crumbled bacon and mashed avocados. Cover and keep warm.

    To prepare omelet: Melt butter in a medium or large skillet over low heat until butter sizzles. Beat together eggs, milk, salt, and pepper, and pour into skillet. Cook slowly over low heat, lifting omelet to let liquid eggs flow under the cooked portion, until eggs are set. Spoon diced avocado across center, fold sides over the avocado, and place on platter. Pour sauce over omelet and garnish with avocado slices.

SERVES 4

Baked Eggs with Herbs

1 teaspoon chopped shallots or
    green onions
¼ cup butter
1 teaspoon lemon juice
¾ cup grated Swiss cheese
4 eggs

salt and pepper to taste
pinch of basil or thyme or dill or
    marjoram
½ cup sour cream
2 tablespoons heavy cream
2 tablespoons sherry

Preheat oven to 325 degrees.

    Sauté shallots or onions in butter until golden. Add lemon juice, then spoon about 2 teaspoons shallot mixture and ¼ cup cheese into each of 2 ramekins or small casseroles. Break 2 eggs into each ramekin and season with salt, pepper, and a pinch of herb. Whisk together the sour cream, cream, and sherry. Pour mixture over the eggs and top with remaining cheese and shallots. Place ramekins in a pan containing 1 inch simmering water and bake for 15 to 25 minutes, or until the cheese is melted and the eggs are as firm as you like them.

SERVES 2

Baked Eggs San Juan

Sofrito (sauce)
2 tablespoons olive oil
½ cup chopped onions
1 tablespoon minced garlic
1 small red bell pepper, seeded and
    chopped
½ cup finely diced lean smoked ham,
    seranno ham, or prosciutto
1 chorizo sausage, in ½-inch slices
2 medium tomatoes, skinned, seeded,
    and chopped fine
1 tablespoon chopped parsley
1 small bay leaf

⅛ to ¼ teaspoon freshly ground
    pepper
⅓ cup water
salt to taste

Eggs
1 teaspoon olive oil
6 eggs
½ cup cooked peas
6 3- to 4-inch-long asparagus tips,
    cooked
6 to 8 pimiento strips
3 tablespoons sherry

To prepare sofrito: In a heavy 10- to 12-inch skillet, heat oil over moderate heat. Add the onions, garlic, and red pepper, and sauté, stirring frequently, for 5 minutes, until soft but not brown. Stir in remaining ingredients and bring to a boil. Cook briskly, uncovered, until most of the liquid has evaporated and mixture is thick. Cool slightly, taste, and add up to ¼ teaspoon of salt. Remove bay leaf before serving the sofrito.

Preheat oven to 400 degrees. Coat bottom and sides of a 9-x-9-x-2-inch baking dish with olive oil.

To prepare eggs: Spread sofrito evenly in baking dish. Break eggs into dish, arranging them in a circle on top of the sauce. Put peas in 3 or 4 mounds on the sauce and arrange asparagus tips over the peas in parallel rows. Place pimiento strips on top; sprinkle with sherry, cover, and bake for 20 minutes, or until an opaque film has formed over the yolks and the whites are firm. Serve at once, accompanied by fresh warm French bread or soft tortillas and butter.

SERVES 6 FOR BRUNCH, 3 FOR DINNER

Stuffed Eggs in Cheese Sauce

Eggs
6 hard-cooked eggs
½ cup chopped green onions
⅓ cup mushrooms, chopped and
    sautéed in butter

1 teaspoon Worcestershire sauce
½ cup grated Cheddar cheese
3 English muffins, halved, toasted,
    and buttered

Cheese Sauce
¼ cup butter
¼ cup flour

2 cups milk
1 cup grated Cheddar cheese
6 slices bacon, cooked and crumbled

Preheat oven to 350 degrees.

To prepare sauce: Melt butter; add flour and stir until smooth. Cook over low heat 5 minutes, stirring constantly. Slowly add milk, blend well, and continue cooking and stirring until thick. Add cheese and stir until melted, then add bacon. Set aside.

To prepare eggs: Cut hard-cooked eggs in half lengthwise and remove yolks. Mash yolks with fork and mix with ¼ cup cheese sauce. Add green onions, mushrooms, and Worcestershire to yolk mixture. Fill the egg-white halves with this mixture, place eggs in an 8-x-8-inch baking dish and cover with remaining cheese sauce. Top with remaining grated cheese and bake for 20 minutes. Serve immediately on English muffins.

SERVES 6

Spinach–Broccoli Fritatta

3 ounces sesame crackers
½ cup milk
1 large head broccoli (about ½ pound)
1 bunch spinach (about ¾ pound)
1 medium onion, chopped
¼ pound mushrooms or olives, sliced

2 small cloves garlic, minced
2 to 4 tablespoons olive oil
¼ pound feta cheese
1 cup cottage cheese
½ cup freshly grated Parmesan cheese
6 eggs

Preheat oven to 375 degrees. Oil a 9-x-13-inch baking dish.

Crush crackers and soak in milk. Steam broccoli until barely tender. Wash spinach and steam until tender but still bright green; cool spinach and thoroughly squeeze out the liquid. Finely chop spinach and broccoli together. Sauté onion, mushrooms, and garlic in olive oil over low heat until all the liquid is evaporated and vegetables are tender. Combine with broccoli, spinach, and the cracker-and-milk mixture, and stir in the cheeses (ingredients may be refrigerated at this point). Beat eggs and add to vegetable mixture, pour into prepared baking dish, and bake for about 30 minutes.

SERVES 4 TO 6

Italian Sausage and Mushroom Quiche

½ pound mushrooms, sliced
1 tablespoon butter
4 eggs
1½ cups evaporated milk
¼ teaspoon salt
1½ cups grated Cheddar cheese

1 tablespoon flour
½ pound Italian sausage, casing
    removed
partially baked 9-inch pie shell
1 egg white
2 tablespoons chopped parsley

Preheat oven to 375 degrees.

Sauté mushrooms in butter. Beat eggs; stir in milk and salt. Dust cheese with flour. Cook, drain, and crumble sausage. Brush pastry with egg white. Place a layer each of cheese, mushrooms, and sausage in pie shell; pour in egg–milk mixture and sprinkle parsley on top. Bake 35 to 40 minutes, or until knife inserted in center comes out clean. Cool for 15 minutes before serving.

SERVES 6

Asparagus-Leek Quiche

12 to 14 asparagus spears
¼ cup butter
2 cups chopped leeks, tops and
    bottoms
1½ teaspoons crushed dried basil
    or 1 tablespoon chopped fresh
    basil
2 teaspoons salt

freshly ground white pepper to taste
partially baked 10-inch pie shell
1¾ cups grated Swiss or Gruyère
    cheese
4 eggs
2 cups heavy cream or 1 cup light
    cream and 1 cup heavy cream
dash of nutmeg

Preheat oven to 400 degrees.

Trim tough portions from asparagus spears and cut off asparagus tips in 3½- to 4-inch pieces. Blanch tips for 2 to 3 minutes—until tender but slightly crisp—and set aside. Chop remaining stalks to equal 1¼ cups. Melt butter in medium frying pan, add chopped asparagus and leeks, and sauté about 8 minutes, or until pieces are tender. Add basil, 1 teaspoon salt, and pepper; sauté 1 to 2 minutes more. Spoon asparagus–leek mixture into partially baked pie shell and sprinkle evenly with cheese.

Combine eggs, cream, 1 teaspoon salt, and nutmeg and mix well. Pour slowly over mixture in pie shell and bake for 30 minutes. Remove from oven, arrange asparagus tips in spoke-like fashion on top of quiche, and return quiche to oven for about 20 minutes more, or until golden and set in center. Cool slightly and cut into wedges.

SERVES 8 TO 10

French Fondue Seattle Style

2 cups chicken broth or 1 cup chicken
    broth and 1 cup dry white wine
2 cloves garlic, minced
¾ pound Gruyère cheese, grated (do
    not substitute other cheeses)
3 tablespoons cornstarch
3 tablespoons dry sherry (optional)

2 to 6 tablespoons heavy cream
2 tablespoons butter
freshly ground pepper to taste
dash of nutmeg
1 baguette of French bread, cut into
    1½-inch cubes

Pour broth and garlic into saucepan and boil briskly until liquid is reduced to 1½ cups. Strain into a fondue pot, discarding garlic. Place grated cheese in a paper bag and shake with cornstarch to coat well. Bring broth almost to a boil and add cheese a handful at a time, stirring after each addition, until cheese has melted. When all the cheese has melted, and with the mixture almost boiling, add sherry and cream a tablespoon at a time; stir until mixture is smooth, then stir in butter and seasonings. Serve with bread cubes for dunking.

SERVES 4 TO 6

Pennsylvania-Dutch Tomatoes

8 ripe, firm tomatoes
½ cup flour
½ cup butter
½ cup firmly packed brown sugar

1 cup heavy cream
salt and freshly ground pepper to taste
16 slices cooked bacon

Peel tomatoes, cut into thick slices, and press both sides into flour, coating well. Melt butter in skillet over medium heat; add tomatoes and start to sauté. As tomatoes brown, sprinkle the tops heavily with brown sugar. Turn carefully, and when just browned on both sides, add cream and let tomatoes simmer 3 to 4 minutes. Transfer to a hot platter and serve garnished with bacon.

SERVES 8

Eggs Benedict with Mushrooms

1 English muffin, halved and lightly
    toasted
2 slices ham, lightly sautéed
4 medium-size mushrooms, sliced and
    sautéed in butter

2 eggs, poached
4 tablespoons Hollandaise Sauce
    (following recipe)

Place muffin halves on plate, cut side up. Put a slice of ham on each, an egg, and the mushroom slices. Top with Hollandaise Sauce.

SERVES 2

Hollandaise Sauce

3 egg yolks
2 tablespoons lemon juice
¼ teaspoon salt

dash Tabasco sauce
½ cup butter, melted, clarified,
    and hot

Put egg yolks, lemon juice, salt, and Tabasco into a blender or a food processor. Process for 2 seconds; then, while still processing, very slowly—drop by drop—pour hot, bubbling butter into yolk mixture.

YIELD: ¾ CUP

Note: If not used immediately, the sauce may be kept warm over very warm, but not boiling, water. It may also be frozen and warmed over hot water, being beaten as it warms.

Irresistible Eggs Hussarde

1 Holland rusk or ½ English muffin,
    toasted
1 slice ham, lightly sautéed
2 tablespoons Marchand de Vin Sauce
    (following recipe)

1 slice tomato, lightly sautéed
1 egg, poached
¼ cup Hollandaise Sauce (preceding
    recipe)
dash of paprika

Place ham on rusk. Cover with Marchand de Vin Sauce, top with tomato, and then the egg. Cover with Hollandaise Sauce and sprinkle with paprika for a dish that looks like eggs Benedict but is richer and more flavorful.

SERVES 1

Marchand de Vin Sauce

⅓ cup finely chopped mushrooms
⅓ cup minced ham
⅓ cup finely chopped shallots
½ cup finely chopped onion
2 tablespoons minced garlic
¾ cup butter

2 tablespoons flour
½ teaspoon salt
⅛ teaspoon pepper
dash cayenne
¾ cup beef stock
½ cup red wine

Lightly sauté mushrooms, ham, shallots, onion, and garlic in the butter. When onion is soft and golden, add flour, salt, pepper, and cayenne. Brown well, cooking gently for 5 to 10 minutes. Blend in stock and wine, and simmer over low heat for 35 to 45 minutes.

YIELD: ABOUT 2 CUPS

Breakfast Egg Casserole

This hearty dish is particularly good for a crowd.

6 tablespoons butter
6 tablespoons flour
4 cups milk
2 tablespoons white wine
⅛ teaspoon marjoram
salt and pepper to taste
¼ cup minced parsley
3 to 4 drops Worcestershire sauce

1½ pounds link sausage
1 dozen hard-cooked eggs, quartered
½ pound mushrooms, quartered
½ pound sharp Cheddar cheese in
    ½-inch cubes
1 cup dry bread crumbs
½ cup grated Cheddar cheese

Preheat oven to 325 degrees. In a saucepan, cook together butter and flour over medium heat until bubbly, about 5 minutes. Beat in milk with a wire whisk and continue to cook over low heat, until thick. Stir in wine, marjoram, salt, pepper, parsley, and Worcestershire and remove from heat. Cut sausage into large pieces and brown. Evenly distribute eggs, mushrooms, and cheese cubes in a 9-x-13-inch baking dish and cover with sauce. Mix bread crumbs with grated cheese, top casserole with mixture, and bake uncovered for 1 hour.

SERVES 8 TO 10

Note: May be made the day ahead, covered, and refrigerated.

Paskha

A traditional Russian spread of sweetened cream cheese.

¼ cup raisins
¼ cup rum or brandy
1 pound cream cheese, softened
¼ cup butter, softened
1 cup sifted powdered sugar

2 egg yolks
1 teaspoon vanilla extract
zest of 1 lemon
½ cup toasted slivered almonds

Soak raisins in rum or brandy overnight.

Beat together the cream cheese and butter. Gradually beat in powdered sugar, then beat in egg yolks and vanilla until well blended. Fold in raisins, excess rum or brandy, lemon zest, and almonds. Place mixture in an attractive serving dish or in a mold that has been lined with cheesecloth. (A clean flower pot works well as a mold.) Cover and chill overnight. To unmold, loosen cheesecloth and invert on a serving dish. Decorate pashka with flower blossoms, and serve with slices of coffee cake, sweet bread, or sliced fresh fruit.

Crêpes

1⅓ cups flour
1⅓ cups milk

2 eggs
6 tablespoons melted butter

Mix ingredients together with a whisk or in a blender. Cover and let stand at least 1 hour. (If it is to stand longer, refrigerate.) Batter should be very light.

In a 6- to 8-inch skillet, melt a little butter and wipe with paper towel to leave a thin film. Pour 2 to 3 tablespoons of batter into pan; quickly tilt pan in all directions to cover pan bottom with a thin layer of batter. If the first crêpe is too heavy, beat up to ⅓ cup more milk into batter. Cook crêpe until edges are browned and it becomes loose from pan. Turn with a spatula and cook the other side for a few seconds. Remove from the pan and stack on a plate or tray, placing waxed paper between crêpes. After a few crêpes have been cooked, you may not need to butter the pan again.

To fill, place a crêpe, browned side down, on a plate. Spoon filling along the center of the crêpe. Fold 1 side over, covering most of the filling, then fold over the opposite side, overlapping the first side. Arrange in a serving dish with the seam side down.

YIELD: 16 TO 20 CRÊPES

Crêpes St. Jacques

1½ teaspoons minced shallots or
   green onions
1 clove garlic, minced
2 tablespoons butter
⅔ cup bay scallops or halved sea
   scallops
⅔ cup crabmeat
⅓ cup dry white wine
salt and pepper to taste

2 tablespoons butter
2½ tablespoons flour
1 cup milk
1 egg yolk
¼ cup heavy cream
¼ cup grated Swiss cheese
2 tablespoons lemon juice
8 6- to 8-inch crêpes (preceding recipe)

Preheat oven to 350 degrees. Butter a 9-x-13-inch baking dish.

Lightly sauté shallots and garlic in butter. Add scallops and sauté over low heat for 5 minutes. Add crabmeat and sauté another 2 minutes. Add wine, salt, and pepper; simmer 1 minute, then boil until most of the liquid has evaporated. Set aside.

In a saucepan, stir together the butter and flour and cook over medium heat until bubbly, about 5 minutes. Beat in milk with a whisk, and cook until the sauce is thickened. Add salt and pepper. Beat together egg yolk and cream in a small bowl. Gradually beat in a few tablespoons of the hot sauce, then add cream mixture to the remaining sauce. Boil about 1 minute, stirring constantly. Sauce will be thick. Fold in scallop and crab mixture, Swiss cheese, and lemon juice. Divide equally among the crêpes, roll crêpes, place seam side down in prepared baking dish, and bake for 20 minutes.

SERVES 4

Variations: Serve with Hollandaise Sauce. Or use any combination of shrimp, crab, scallops, and lobster in place of the scallops and crab.

Ham and Asparagus Crêpes

16 to 24 thin asparagus spears
8 paper-thin slices Westphalian ham or
   prosciutto

8 6- to 8-inch crêpes (facing page)
2 cups Hollandaise Sauce (page 128)

Preheat oven to 350 degrees. Butter a 9-x-13-inch baking dish.

Stream asparagus about 6 minutes—until tender but slightly crisp. Place a slice of ham and 2 or 3 asparagus spears on each crêpe, and trim the asparagus to the width of the crêpe. Roll the crêpes, place seam side down in prepared baking dish, and bake for 10 to 15 minutes, or until hot. Serve with Hollandaise Sauce.

SERVES 3 TO 4

Note: If fresh asparagus is not available, use frozen spears rather than canned ones. Defrost but do not precook.

Spinach and Mushroom Crêpes

2 pounds fresh spinach (about 4 bunches)	¼ teaspoon grated lemon zest
5 tablespoons butter	1½ cups mushrooms, sliced
salt and pepper to taste	½ cup grated Swiss cheese
pinch of nutmeg	6 6- to 8-inch crêpes (page 130)
	¼ cup freshly grated Parmesan cheese

Preheat oven to 350 degrees. Butter an 8-x-8-inch baking dish. Wash spinach well, remove stems, and steam until limp but still bright green. Drain, squeeze dry, and chop. Heat 2 tablespoons butter to bubbling. Add spinach and cook to remove any remaining water—2 to 3 minutes. Season with salt, pepper, nutmeg, and lemon zest.

In a separate skillet, sauté mushrooms in remaining butter, then combine with spinach and Swiss cheese. Spoon mixture onto crêpes, roll crêpes and place seam side down in prepared baking dish. Sprinkle with Parmesan and bake for 15 to 20 minutes.

SERVES 6

Variation: Substitute diced ham for the sautéed mushrooms.

Chicken Crêpes

¼ cup butter	1 cup chicken broth
1 clove garlic, minced	¼ teaspoon salt
½ cup sliced mushrooms	1 egg yolk
1¼ cups diced cooked chicken	¼ cup heavy cream
⅓ cup dry white wine	¼ cup grated Swiss cheese
1 tablespoon minced parsley	8 6- to 8-inch crêpes (page 130)
2½ tablespoons flour	

Preheat oven to 350 degrees. Butter a 9-x-13-inch baking dish.

Melt 2 tablespoons butter in a large skillet; sauté garlic and mushrooms until mushrooms are soft. Add chicken and wine, simmer 1 minute, then boil to evaporate most of the liquid. Stir in parsley and set aside.

In a separate pan, cook remaining butter and flour over medium heat until bubbly. Beat in the broth with a whisk, cook until sauce is thickened, and add salt. Beat together egg yolk and cream in a small bowl. Gradually beat in a few tablespoons of the hot sauce, then add cream mixture to remaining sauce. Boil about 1 minute, stirring constantly. The sauce will be thick. Fold in chicken mixture and Swiss cheese and divide equally among crêpes. Roll crêpes, place seam side down in prepared baking dish, and bake for 20 minutes.

SERVES 4

Variations: Omit the garlic and add 1 teaspoon curry powder to the butter-flour mixture before adding broth. Or omit the garlic and add to the chicken mixture the following ingredients:

4 slices bacon, cooked and crumbled
¼ cup sliced water chestnuts
1 small onion, chopped and lightly sautéed

½ cup cooked chopped spinach, drained and squeezed dry

Chicken and Spinach Crêpes

8 whole chicken breasts
1 whole onion, peeled
2 stalks celery
1 pound bacon
1 onion, sliced
6 ounces mushrooms, sliced
2 10-ounce packages frozen spinach, thawed and well drained
16 ounces cream cheese, at room temperature

1 8-ounce can sliced water chestnuts
½ cup freshly grated Parmesan cheese
2 tablespoons minced parsley
white pepper to taste
30 to 36 6- to 8-inch crêpes (page 130)
2 cups White Sauce (page 22)
2 tablespoons dry sherry

Preheat oven to 350 degrees. Butter 2 9-x-13-inch baking dishes.

Poach chicken breasts with onion and celery in water to cover. Cool chicken, remove bones, and cut meat into bite-size pieces. Fry bacon until crisp and drain off all but 2 tablespoons of fat. Crumble bacon. Sauté sliced onion for 2 minutes in bacon fat, adding mushrooms at the last minute.

Combine chicken, bacon, sautéed onion, mushrooms, spinach, cream cheese, water chestnuts, and Parmesan; mix well and add parsley and pepper. Spread 3 to 4 tablespoons of chicken mixture over half of each crêpe and roll. Arrange seam side down in prepared baking dishes and bake for 20 minutes. Serve with White Sauce thinned with sherry.

SERVES 12 TO 15

Apple and Sausage Crêpes

4 apples, peeled, cored, and sliced
2 tablespoons butter
¼ cup sugar
1 tablespoon cinnamon

16 link sausages, cooked
8 6- to 8-inch crêpes (page 130)
juice of 1 lemon

Preheat oven to 350 degrees. Butter a 9-x-13-inch baking dish.

Sauté apple slices in butter for 5 to 7 minutes, until soft but not mushy. Mix together sugar and cinnamon. Place 2 sausages and several apple slices on each crêpe. Sprinkle with lemon juice and sugar-cinnamon mixture. Roll crêpes and place seam side down in prepared baking dish. (Filled crêpes may be prepared ahead to this point and refrigerated.) Bake for 10 to 15 minutes, or until hot. Serve with maple syrup.

SERVES 4

Cheese Blintzes with Sour Cherry Sauce

12 to 18 6- to 8-inch crêpes (page 130)
½ cup sour cream

Filling
8 ounces cream cheese, softened
1 pound ricotta cheese
1 egg
¼ cup sugar
1 teaspoon vanilla extract

Sour Cherry Sauce
½ cup sugar
1 tablespoon cornstarch
1 16-ounce can pitted sour cherries
   and liquid
1 tablespoon kirsch (optional)
¼ to ½ teaspoon almond extract

To prepare filling: Beat cheeses together until smooth. Add egg, sugar, and vanilla, and beat well. Spoon about 2 tablespoons of filling into the center of each crêpe and fold top and bottom of each crêpe, then sides, over filling. (The blintzes may be frozen or refrigerated at this point. Thoroughly thaw before cooking.) To cook, fry seam side down in butter until brown; turn carefully and brown the other side. Serve warm with Sour Cherry Sauce and sour cream.

To prepare sauce: Combine sugar and cornstarch in a saucepan. Add kirsch and juice from cherries and heat to boiling, stirring constantly. Cook until thickened, then add almond extract and cherries and remove from heat.

SERVES 6

Roulade

Béchamel Sauce
½ cup butter
⅔ cup flour
3 cups milk
½ teaspoon salt
¼ teaspoon pepper
large pinch nutmeg

Filling
¼ cup minced shallots or green onions
¼ cup butter
3 to 4 cups steamed broccoli, chopped spinach, sautéed mushrooms, shellfish, or ham

salt and pepper to taste
2 cups Béchamel Sauce
¼ cup grated Swiss cheese
milk (optional)

Roulade
2 cups Béchamel Sauce
6 large eggs, separated
1 cup grated Swiss cheese
¼ teaspoon cream of tartar
⅛ teaspoon salt
½ cup toasted and buttered white bread crumbs

Butter an 11-x-17-inch jelly roll pan and line it with waxed paper, leaving a 2-inch overhang at each end. Butter the paper, then dust it with flour and shake out the excess.

To prepare sauce: Combine the butter and flour and cook over medium heat until bubbly—about 5 minutes. Beat in milk with a wire whisk until blended, then cook over medium heat, stirring constantly, until sauce comes to a boil and thickens. Beat in seasonings with a whisk.

To prepare filling: Sauté shallots in butter. Stir in vegetables, mushrooms, shellfish, or ham, cook briefly, and season to taste. Stir in 2 cups of the Béchamel Sauce and cheese, adding milk if necessary to make the mixture spreadable. Keep warm over low heat or in a double boiler.

Preheat oven to 425 degrees.

To prepare roulade: In a bowl, combine the remaining Béchamel

Sauce with egg yolks and cheese, mixing well. In another bowl beat the egg whites together with cream of tartar and salt until the whites hold a peak. Mix a quarter of the whites into the sauce-yolk mixture, then fold into the remaining whites. (This mixture will remain stiff for up to an hour.) Spread the roulade mixture evenly into the prepared jelly roll pan, and bake 12 to 15 minutes. Mixture will puff and shrink slightly from the pan edges. The roulade must be set, but do not let it get too dry.

Remove roulade, still on waxed paper, from oven; sprinkle top with 6 tablespoons of bread crumbs, unmold onto a tray covered with waxed paper, and let rest for 5 minutes. Remove the waxed paper that lined the jelly roll pan. (You may freeze the roulade at this point. To reheat it, cover and bake for a few minutes in a 300-degree oven.) Just before serving, spread hot filling over warm roulade. Roll up from 1 of the long sides, using the waxed paper to help roll. Slide onto a serving dish, seam side down. Sprinkle with remaining bread crumbs, slice, and serve immediately.

Variations: Use other fillings such as ham and mushrooms, spinach and mushrooms, or your own specialty.

SERVES 8 TO 10

Cheese Soufflé

3 tablespoons plus 1 teaspoon butter
1 tablespoon freshly grated Parmesan
cheese
3 tablespoons flour
1 cup milk
½ teaspoon salt
⅛ teaspoon pepper
pinch of cayenne
pinch of nutmeg
4 egg yolks
5 egg whites
pinch of salt
¼ cup grated Swiss cheese or
combination of Swiss and
Parmesan

Preheat oven to 375 degrees. Butter a 6-cup soufflé dish with 1 teaspoon butter and sprinkle with Parmesan.

Melt the remaining butter over medium heat and stir in flour, cooking about 5 minutes or until bubbly. Beat in the milk with a wire whisk, stirring until the mixture is thickened. Stir in the seasonings and remove pan from heat immediately. Beat in the egg yolks one at a time with the whisk. (The soufflé may be prepared ahead of time to this point.)

Beat egg whites with salt until stiff. Stir a quarter of the beaten egg whites into the sauce, stir in the cheese, and fold in the remaining egg whites. Spoon mixture into the prepared dish and bake for 25 to 30 minutes—until the top is browned and the soufflé has risen about 2 inches above the top of the mold. Serve immediately.

SERVES 4

Broccoli Soufflé

¼ cup plus 1 teaspoon butter	1 cup milk
1 tablespoon freshly grated Parmesan cheese	½ teaspoon salt
	⅛ teaspoon pepper
¾ cup chopped broccoli	4 egg yolks
1 tablespoon minced green onion	5 egg whites
½ teaspoon chopped zest of lemon	pinch of salt
3 tablespoons flour	½ cup grated Swiss cheese

Preheat oven to 375 degrees. Butter a 6-cup soufflé dish with 1 teaspoon butter and sprinkle with Parmesan.

Steam broccoli until tender but slightly crisp. Melt 1 tablespoon butter and sauté green onions for a few minutes; add broccoli and stir just until moisture has evaporated. Remove from heat, add lemon zest, and set aside. Melt remaining butter, add flour, and cook over medium heat until bubbly—about 5 minutes. Beat in milk with a wire whisk, stirring until mixture is thickened. Beat in salt and pepper, remove from heat, and immediately beat in the egg yolks 1 at a time, still using the whisk. Stir in the broccoli mixture. (The soufflé may be prepared ahead of time to this point.)

Beat egg whites with a pinch of salt until stiff. Stir a quarter of the beaten egg whites into broccoli sauce, then stir in the Swiss cheese. Fold in remaining egg whites and spoon mixture into prepared soufflé dish. Bake for about 30 minutes—until the top is browned and the soufflé has risen about 2 inches above the top of the dish. Serve immediately.

SERVES 4

Variations: Add ¼ cup chopped mushrooms, sautéed in a little butter, along with the broccoli. Or use chopped spinach or asparagus in place of the broccoli.

Salmon Soufflé with Dill Sauce

Soufflé

3 tablespoons plus 1 teaspoon butter
1 tablespoon freshly grated Parmesan
     cheese
2 tablespoons green onions
3 tablespoons flour
1 cup milk
½ teaspoon oregano
½ teaspoon salt
⅛ teaspoon pepper
1 tablespoon tomato paste
4 egg yolks
¼ cup flaked cooked or canned
     salmon

½ cup grated Swiss cheese
5 egg whites
pinch of salt

Dill Sauce

½ cup mayonnaise
½ cup sour cream
1 teaspoon Dijon-style mustard
⅛ teaspoon salt
1 teaspoon tarragon wine vinegar
1 teaspoon dill

To prepare sauce: Combine all ingredients and mix well. Let stand at least 30 minutes to allow the flavors to combine.

Preheat oven to 375 degrees. Butter a 6-cup soufflé dish with 1 teaspoon butter and sprinkle with Parmesan.

To prepare soufflé: Melt remaining butter and sauté onions over medium heat about 1 minute. Stir in flour and cook until bubbly—about 5 minutes. Beat in milk with a wire whisk, stirring until mixture is thickened. Stir in seasonings and tomato paste and remove pan from heat. With the whisk, immediately beat in the egg yolks 1 at a time, then stir in the salmon and cheese. (The soufflé may be prepared ahead of time to this point.)

Beat egg whites with salt until stiff. Stir a quarter of the beaten egg whites into the sauce, fold in remaining egg whites, and spoon mixture into the prepared soufflé dish. Bake about 30 minutes—until the top is browned and the soufflé has risen about 2 inches above the top of the dish. Serve immediately with Dill Sauce.

SERVES 4

Variation: Crab or chopped shrimp may be substituted for the salmon; if making either substitution, eliminate the tomato paste and oregano.

The beauty of Elliott Bay belies the fact that the port of Seattle is one of the world's busiest. Here a Washington State ferry passes in front of Harbor Island and Mount Rainier en route from Bainbridge Island to Seattle.

Pasta and Grains

❖❖

Marinara Sauce

¼ cup olive oil
2 large cloves garlic, pressed
1 large onion, minced
2 4-inch sprigs fresh or 1 teaspoon
    dried rosemary
2 3-inch sprigs fresh or 1 teaspoon
    dried oregano

2 3-inch sprigs fresh or 1 teaspoon
    dried thyme
1 tablespoon minced fresh basil
2 15-ounce cans tomato sauce
¼ cup water

Heat olive oil in a large skillet; add garlic and onion and sauté until transparent. Remove stems from fresh herbs. Add herbs, tomato sauce, and water to skillet and simmer 30 to 40 minutes.

YIELD: 4 TO 4½ CUPS

Spaghetti Sauce with Peppers and Sausage

3 tablespoons olive oil
3 cloves garlic, sliced
2 28-ounce cans whole peeled
    tomatoes and liquid
4 1-inch sprigs fresh rosemary
2 teaspoons oregano

2 medium red bell peppers, sliced thin
2 medium green bell peppers, sliced
    thin
2 pounds fine-quality hot Italian
    sausage

Heat olive oil in skillet and add garlic; discard garlic after it starts to brown. Drain tomatoes, reserving juice, and add tomatoes to skillet, breaking them apart with a spoon. Simmer mixture until tomatoes are soft and almost liquid—about 15 minutes. Add rosemary, oregano, and peppers. Meanwhile, brown sausage in another skillet, and crumble. Add sausage and reserved tomato juice to sauce, cover, and simmer for 3 hours; do not take shortcuts on timing.

SERVES 6

World's Greatest Spaghetti Sauce

1 tablespoon vegetable oil
2 pounds very lean ground beef
1 clove garlic, pressed
1 large white onion, chopped
1 tablespoon minced parsley
1 28-ounce can whole tomatoes
1 15-ounce can tomato sauce
2 6-ounce cans tomato paste

1 cup water
1½ tablespoons salt
2 tablespoons oregano
2 tablespoons thyme
2 tablespoons basil
½ pound mushrooms, sliced
1 teaspoon sugar
1 bay leaf

Heat oil in a skillet and add meat, garlic, and onion, and brown. Add remaining ingredients, cover, and simmer about 2½ hours. Remove bay leaf before serving.

YIELD: 8 CUPS

Rosemary–Tomato Sauce

¼ cup olive oil
4 cups peeled, diced tomatoes
1 cup sliced mushrooms

1 3-inch sprig fresh or ¾ tablespoon
dried rosemary

Heat olive oil in a saucepan. Add tomatoes, mushrooms, and rosemary, and simmer until tomatoes are soft and of a sauce consistency. Remove rosemary before serving.

YIELD: ABOUT 5 CUPS

Pesto Genoa Style

½ cup pine nuts
¼ cup fresh basil
1 cup spinach leaves, chopped
2 teaspoons finely minced garlic
¼ cup freshly grated Romano or
    Parmesan cheese

6 tablespoons butter, softened
½ cup olive oil
¼ teaspoon salt
⅛ teaspoon freshly ground pepper

With a mortar and pestle, mash the pine nuts, basil, spinach, and garlic into a smooth paste. Slowly stir in the cheese and softened butter. Add the olive oil a little at a time, stirring constantly. Season with salt and freshly ground pepper.

YIELD: 2 CUPS

Note: This may be prepared in a blender, but mix all the ingredients together before blending. Pesto can be frozen.

Dungeness Crab Special

½ cup butter
3 large cloves garlic, minced
¼ cup chopped chives, into ½-inch
    pieces
½ pound Dungeness crabmeat
6 to 7 tablespoons freshly grated
    Mizithra or Parmesan cheese

12 cherry tomatoes, halved
1 tablespoon vegetable oil
½ pound fresh spinach spaghettini,
    fettuccine, or other thin noodles

Melt butter in a large skillet; add garlic and sauté for 1 to 2 minutes, not allowing garlic to brown. Add 3 tablespoons chives, crabmeat, and ¼ cup cheese and toss. Gently stir in the tomato halves and allow to warm through. Add oil and pasta to rapidly boiling salted water and cook until pasta is *al dente*; drain and place in a warm serving bowl. Combine pasta and sauce, tossing gently but thoroughly. Sprinkle remaining chives and cheese on top and serve immediately.

SERVES 2 TO 4

Fettuccine with Caviar Sauce

1 cup sour cream
2 egg yolks at room temperature
1 tablespoon the finest possible vodka
¼ cup freshly grated Parmesan cheese
1 to 2 tablespoons minced parsley

3 teaspoons minced chives
freshly ground black pepper to taste
1 tablespoon vegetable oil
1 pound fresh fettuccine
2 ounces caviar

Blend sour cream into egg yolks; add vodka and Parmesan, and mix until smooth. Add parsley, chives, and pepper. Add oil and pasta to rapidly boiling salted water and cook until pasta is *al dente*. Drain and transfer to a warm serving bowl. Add sour-cream sauce and caviar, and toss very gently;. Add more Parmesan and pepper if desired.

SERVES 4 TO 8

Prawns–Spaghettini Milano

4 medium cloves garlic
½ cup plus 2 tablespoons butter
1 cup loosely packed parsley
1 tablespoon vegetable oil
1 pound fresh spaghettini

1 pound fresh medium shrimp
   (approximately 30), washed,
   shelled, and deveined
¼ cup freshly grated Parmesan cheese
salt and freshly ground pepper to taste

Place garlic, ½ cup butter, and parsley in a food processor, and process to a thick paste (which can be stored for several days). Add oil and spaghettini to rapidly boiling salted water and cook until pasta is *al dente*. When spaghettini is nearly cooked, melt garlic-butter mixture in a frying pan. Add shrimp and sauté until pink (do not overcook or shrimp will become tough). Drain pasta and place in a warm serving bowl. Add 2 tablespoons butter, Parmesan, salt, and pepper; toss gently. Add shrimp, toss again, and serve.

SERVES 4

Scallop-and-Broccoli Fettuccine

1 pound broccoli flowerets
½ cup butter
4 cloves garlic, minced
1 pound scallops, halved
1 small red bell pepper, diced
   (optional)

1 tablespoon vegetable oil
1 pound fresh spinach fettuccine
1 cup freshly grated Parmesan cheese
salt and freshly ground pepper to taste

Steam broccoli until tender but slightly crisp. Rinse with cold water and set aside. Melt butter in a large skillet; add garlic and sauté over low heat about 10 minutes. Add scallops and red pepper and sauté until scallops are just white. Add broccoli and stir.

Add oil and fettuccine to rapidly boiling salted water and cook until pasta is *al dente*. Drain and place in a warm serving bowl. Add about ½ cup Parmesan and toss gently. Then add broccoli, scallops, all pan juices, and remaining cheese. Toss together gently, add salt and pepper and serve immediately.

SERVES 4

Fettuccine with Smoked Salmon

¼ cup butter
⅔ cup minced onion
4 ounces cream cheese, cubed
2 cups heavy cream
dash of Tabasco sauce
1 tablespoon vegetable oil

1 pound fettuccine
freshly ground pepper to taste
8 ounces lightly smoked Nova Scotia-
    style salmon, diced
2 tablespoons minced parsley

Melt butter, add onion, and sauté over medium heat for about 3 minutes. Add cream cheese and stir until melted, then add cream and Tabasco. Keep warm. Add oil and pasta to rapidly boiling salted water and cook until pasta is *al dente*. Drain and place in a warm serving bowl; add sauce and pepper, and toss gently. Add smoked salmon and parsley, toss once more, and serve.

SERVES 4

Note: This is a first course; it is too rich to serve as a main dish.

Ravioli Supreme

Pasta
2¼ cups sifted unbleached flour
3 eggs
¼ cup water
2 tablespoons vegetable oil

Sausage-and-Veal Filling: Step 1
4 bunches spinach
6 tablespoons butter
1 cup ricotta cheese
⅛ teaspoon freshly grated nutmeg
salt to taste
⅛ teaspoon freshly ground pepper
1 cup freshly grated Parmesan cheese
2 eggs, lightly beaten

Sausage-and-Veal Filling: Step 2
2 tablespoons butter
1 medium onion, minced
4 Italian sausages, casings removed,
    crumbled (approximately 2 cups
    of sausage)
2 cups ground veal
spinach filling (step 1, above)
salt and freshly ground pepper to taste

Sauce
½ cup butter
3 cups heavy cream
¼ cup grated Parmesan cheese

Ingredients for Assembly
1 egg white, lightly beaten
1 tablespoon oil
1½ cups freshly grated Parmesan
    cheese

To prepare pasta: Place flour in a large mixing bowl; add eggs, water, and 2 tablespoons of oil, and stir. Knead on a floured surface for approximately 5 minutes or process in a food processor until ingredients are thoroughly blended. (The dough will be quite stiff.) Cover with a towel and let stand for about 30 minutes.

To prepare filling, step 1: Wash spinach, remove stems, dry leaves thoroughly, and chop fine. Melt butter and sauté spinach approximately 2 minutes. Press out all liquid, add ricotta, and cook for 2 minutes more, then remove from heat. Add nutmeg, salt, pepper, and Parmesan, and stir well. Cool 5 to 10 minutes, add lightly beaten eggs, and mix thoroughly.

To prepare filling, step 2: Melt butter in skillet, add onion, and sauté until transparent. Add sausage and veal and cook until browned, draining off fat once during cooking. When meat is well browned, drain thoroughly, chop fine, and add to spinach mixture (step 1). Add salt and pepper and mix well. (Filling can be made in advance and stored 1 or 2 days.)

To prepare sauce: Melt butter and add cream and Parmesan. Heat thoroughly and set aside, keeping warm.

To assemble ravioli: Divide dough in half, covering half with a towel. Working quickly, spread the other half on a lightly floured surface and roll to a ⅛-inch-thick sheet. Brush with egg white and place approximately 1 heaping teaspoon of sausage-and-veal filling every 2 inches. Roll out second sheet of dough and place over the first. Press between mounds of filling to close squares, then cut between mounds. (Ravioli may be frozen at this point; see note.) Drop ravioli, 1 at a time, into rapidly boiling salted water to which oil has been added. Cook until pasta is *al dente* and drain. Put half the sauce into a warm serving bowl, add the cooked ravioli, and cover with remaining sauce. Sprinkle with Parmesan and serve. See note, next page.

SERVES 8

Note: The filling can also be used with manicotti. To freeze filled ravioli, place on a floured cookie sheet, freeze, and wrap tightly in plastic bags. When ready to cook, do not defrost.

Manicotti

Wrappers

2 cups flour
2 cups water
4 eggs
salt to taste
oil for frying

Cheese Filling

1 bunch fresh spinach (about ½
    pound)
2 cups freshly grated Parmesan cheese
8 ounces mozzarella cheese, chilled
    and grated
2½ cups ricotta cheese
freshly ground pepper to taste
4 cups Marinara Sauce (page 140)

To prepare wrappers: Place ingredients in a large food processor or blender and process for 5 seconds. Scrape down the sides of the bowl and process for 10 seconds more. Set batter aside at room temperature for 1 hour.

Pour 1 tablespoon oil into a 6- or 7-inch crêpe pan or skillet; heat over high heat until oil smokes. Quickly remove from heat and wipe out the pan with a paper towel, leaving a film of hot oil on the pan. Return to high heat for 5 seconds, then pour ⅛ cup of batter into pan; tilt the pan to distribute the batter evenly over the bottom. Cook for about 30 seconds, turn, and cook the other side for about 10 seconds, or until wrapper is a light, speckled brown. Repeat with remaining batter. If wrappers begin to stick, repeat oiling procedure. As they cook, transfer wrappers to a plate, separating them with waxed paper. The wrappers may be made up to 24 hours in advance, covered with plastic wrap, and refrigerated until ready to fill. You should have 16 to 18 wrappers.

To prepare filling: Wash and carefully dry spinach leaves, chop fine, and measure out ¾ cup, setting aside remainder for another use. In a large mixing bowl, combine spinach with 1¾ cups Parmesan, mozzarella, ricotta, and pepper, and stir to mix.

Preheat oven to 350 degrees.

Cover the bottoms of 2 7-×-11-inch glass baking dishes with a thin layer of Marinara Sauce. Place 2 heaping tablespoons of filling on the lower third of each wrapper, roll up, and arrange seam side down in the baking dishes. Pour remaining sauce over the manicotti and sprinkle with reserved Parmesan. (At this point the manicotti may be refrigerated overnight.) Bake for 20 minutes, or until cheese melts and sauce bubbles.

SERVES 6 TO 8

Conchiglie with Ricotta, Spinach, and Prosciutto

1 cup fresh chopped spinach or
  1 10-ounce package frozen
  chopped spinach
1 tablespoon vegetable oil
1 pound jumbo conchiglie (seashell)
  pasta
1 pound ricotta cheese
½ pound mozzarella cheese, finely
  grated

1 cup freshly grated Parmesan cheese
4 ounces prosciutto, sliced thin and
  diced
3 eggs, lightly beaten
¼ teaspoon salt
freshly ground pepper to taste
4 cups Marinara Sauce (page 140)
¼ cup freshly grated Parmesan cheese
2 tablespoons minced parsley

Wash and dry spinach; if using frozen spinach, defrost and squeeze dry. Chop fine. Add oil and pasta to rapidly boiling salted water and cook until pasta is *al dente*. Drain and return to pot; add cold water and set aside until ready to use.

Preheat oven to 350 degrees.

While pasta is cooking, thoroughly mix together all remaining ingredients except last 3 in a large mixing bowl. Pour 1 cup of sauce into the bottom of a 9-×-13-inch glass baking dish or any large, shallow ovenproof pasta platter. Fill each cooked shell about half full and press edges to close. Arrange shells seam side up in baking dish and pour sauce over and around them. (Conchiglie may be refrigerated at this point.) Cover the baking dish with foil and bake 30 minutes. Remove foil, sprinkle with Parmesan and parsley, and serve.

SERVES 6 TO 8

Note: This pasta dish travels well, and is especially suitable for pot-lucks or for having on hand on a busy weekend. It can be served as a main course in a buffet or as an accompaniment for roasted meat or chicken. It can be frozen or made up to 2 days ahead and refrigerated.

Lasagne Bolognese

An elegant and unusual lasagne—another contribution from caterer/cooking teacher Nancy Varriale.

Meat Sauce

1 large carrot, shredded
1 stalk celery, minced
1 large onion, minced
1 tablespoon vegetable oil
1½ pounds ground beef
½ pound unseasoned ground pork
½ cup dry red wine
¼ cup chopped parsley
2 cloves garlic, pressed
1½ cups beef broth
3 tablespoons olive oil
2 tablespoons tomato paste
1½ cups plum tomatoes, drained and
*   chopped*
salt and pepper to taste

Sauce Bolognese

6 tablespoons butter
½ cup flour
3 cups milk
salt and nutmeg to taste

Pasta and Filling

½ pound mozzarella or Monterey
*   jack cheese, grated*
1 cup freshly grated Parmesan cheese
½ pound fresh mushrooms, sliced
¼ cup butter
¼ cup white wine
2 sheets fresh 16-inch spinach lasagne
*   or 1 8-ounce box spinach lasagne*

To prepare meat sauce: Lightly sauté carrot, celery, and onion in oil. Add beef and pork, and sauté 15 minutes. Drain fat from pan; then add red wine and cook over high heat until wine has evaporated. Add remaining ingredients and simmer, uncovered, for 1 hour or until very thick. Cool.

To prepare sauce bolognese: Melt butter and stir in flour; cook 3 to 5 minutes. Remove from heat and slowly pour in milk, beating with a whisk. Return to heat and cook, beating constantly, until sauce comes to a slow boil and thickens. Remove from heat; add salt and nutmeg.

Preheat oven to 350 degrees. Butter a 9- × -13-inch baking dish.

To prepare pasta and filling: Combine grated cheeses. Sauté mushrooms in butter and white wine. If using fresh pasta, do not precook. If using dried pasta, add pasta to boiling salted water to which 1 tablespoon oil has been added and cook for 1 to 2 minutes. Drain and rinse in cold water. Drain again and dry on a clean, damp cloth in a single layer.

Cover bottom of buttered dish with pasta, leaving 2 inches to hang over the edges. In order, and using *half* of each, put in a layer of meat sauce, sauce bolognese, cheeses, and mushrooms. Make a second layer of meat sauce and fold the pasta ends over meat sauce so it is completely covered. Top with the remaining sauce bolognese, cheeses, and mushrooms. Bake uncovered for 25 to 30 minutes; if using fresh pasta, cover the pan tightly with foil, removing it to let the lasagne brown for the last 10 minutes. Cool 15 minutes before cutting and serving.

SERVES 8

Note: This dish is truly marvelous with fresh pasta, but it tends to be a little dry if noodles are from a box.

Lasagne Blanco con Gambas

2 14-ounce cans artichoke hearts (not marinated)
1 tablespoon vegetable oil
3 sheets fresh lasagne pasta or 8 ounces lasagne noodles (preferably spinach noodles)
1 pound fresh prawns, cooked, shelled, and deveined
1½ cups natural white Cheddar cheese, grated

Cream Sauce
¼ cup butter

2 tablespoons grated onion
¼ cup flour
1 teaspoon salt
⅛ teaspoon white pepper
1½ teaspoons chicken bouillon or stock
2 cups light cream

Filling
2 cups ricotta cheese
2 eggs, lightly beaten
½ cup freshly grated Parmesan cheese

Preheat oven to 350 degrees. Butter a 9- × -13-inch baking dish.

Drain artichoke hearts and cut large pieces into quarters. Set aside. Add oil and lasagne to rapidly boiling salted water and cook until lasagne is *al dente*. Rinse in cold water, drain, and set aside. If using fresh pasta, do not precook.

To prepare sauce: Melt butter over low heat. Add onion and sauté until tender. Blend in flour, salt, pepper, and bouillon to make a *roux*. Cook, stirring constantly, until *roux* bubbles for 2 minutes, and remove from heat. Meanwhile, heat light cream almost to boiling. Pour all at once into *roux*, stirring vigorously with a whisk to blend well. Bring to a boil over medium heat, cover, and set aside.

To prepare filling: Beat ricotta until smooth (about 3 seconds in a food processor). Stir in eggs and ¼ cup Parmesan, then combine with cream sauce.

Place about a third of the lasagne noodles in the bottom of the buttered baking dish. Spread with a third each of the artichoke hearts, the prawns, and filling. Sprinkle with a third of the white Cheddar. Repeat twice and top with remaining ¼ cup Parmesan. Bake for 40 minutes; let stand 10 minutes before serving.

SERVES 8 TO 10

Pasta with Tomato and Avocado

½ cup plus 1 tablespoon butter
2 4-inch sprigs fresh rosemary
5 cloves garlic, minced
2 cups cherry tomatoes, halved, at
    room temperature
1 cup peeled and diced avocado, at
    room temperature

⅔ cup (1 3½-ounce can) pitted black
    olives, drained and halved
1 tablespoon vegetable oil
½ pound fresh fettuccine
salt and pepper to taste
¼ cup freshly grated Parmesan cheese
    and more if desired for topping

Melt ½ cup butter in a skillet over low heat; add rosemary and garlic, sauté for several minutes, and remove rosemary. Add tomatoes, avocado, and olives and sauté, stirring, until warm. Set aside.

Add oil and fettuccine to rapidly boiling salted water and cook until pasta is *al dente*. Drain and toss pasta with salt, pepper, Parmesan, and remaining butter. Add the sauce and lightly toss again; serve immediately in a warm serving bowl. Additional Parmesan may be passed separately.

SERVES 4

Avocado Angel Wings

AVOCADO PASTA

3½ cups flour
¼ teaspoon salt
4 medium-size avocados, at room
    temperature
3 medium eggs
2 tablespoons water (optional)
1 tablespoon vegetable oil

salt and pepper to taste
2 tablespoons butter, softened
2 cups heavy cream
3 cloves garlic, pressed
6 to 7 tablespoons freshly grated
    Parmesan cheese
chopped walnuts for garnish (optional)

Combine flour and salt in a large mixing bowl. In another bowl, mash 1 avocado and add eggs, mixing well. Add avocado mixture to the flour and beat with an electric mixer until smooth, adding water if necessary. (Do not use a food processor for this step or pasta will become chewy.) Place the dough on a floured board and knead by hand 5 to 7 minutes (the dough will be soft). Using a pasta maker, roll dough into paper-thin sheets and cut into 1½-inch squares; separate layers with waxed paper and store in a freezer in covered containers if not to be used immediately.

Put frozen or unfrozen pasta into boiling salted water to which the vegetable oil has been added. Cook until pasta is *al dente* and drain; *do not rinse*. Put pasta back into saucepan and add salt, pepper, and butter, stirring lightly. Return to stove over low heat.

In a medium saucepan, heat cream and add garlic. Reserve ¼ cup of cream; add remaining cream and 2 to 3 tablespoons of Parmesan to noodles, and toss the pasta squares until well coated with sauce. Place pasta in a chafing dish or very hot serving bowl and garnish with remaining avocado cut into thick slices. Pour reserved cream over the avocados, sprinkle with remaining Parmesan and optional walnuts, and serve.

SERVES 6

Note: Don't reheat this dish, as it loses its flavor and tends to separate. Serve as a first course.

Orzo and Peas

The use of orzo, a tiny pasta resembling rice, results in a simple but interesting treatment of peas.

2 cloves garlic
1 tablespoon vegetable oil
1 cup orzo or rosa marina pasta
    (which is small)
1 10-ounce package frozen tiny peas
3 tablespoons butter

3 tablespoons freshly grated Parmesan
    cheese
⅛ pound prosciutto, sliced thin and
    cut into julienne strips
salt and freshly ground pepper to taste

Fill a 2- or 3-quart saucepan with water, add garlic and oil, and bring water to a boil. Add pasta and cook until *al dente*. Add peas and, when water returns to a boil, drain. Place in a warm serving bowl and remove the garlic. Toss pasta and peas with butter, Parmesan, and prosciutto, and season with salt and pepper.

SERVES 6 TO 8

Pasta Primavera

½ pound broccoli flowerets or
    asparagus tips
1 cup snow peas
½ cup butter
6 cloves garlic, minced
1 cup sliced mushrooms
1 red bell pepper, chopped
¼ cup minced fresh or 2 tablespoons
    dried basil

1 pint box cherry tomatoes, halved, at
    room temperature
4 ounces prosciutto, minced
1 tablespoon vegetable oil
¾ pound fresh egg or spinach
    fettuccine
3 large eggs
1 cup freshly grated Parmesan cheese
salt and pepper to taste

Blanch broccoli by adding to boiling water and cooking 4 to 5 minutes. Drain and rinse with cold water, and set aside. Blanch snow peas and set aside.

    Melt butter in skillet, add garlic, and sauté briefly. Add mushrooms, red pepper, broccoli, peas, and basil. When hot, add tomatoes and prosciutto, tossing lightly to heat through. Add oil and fettuccine to rapidly boiling salted water and cook until pasta is *al dente*; drain and transfer to a warm serving bowl. Combine eggs with ½ cup Parmesan and toss with the pasta, adding salt and pepper to taste. Serve immediately and pass the remaining grated cheese in a separate bowl.

SERVES 8 AS A SIDE DISH

Party Pasta

¼ cup olive oil
4 to 5 small zucchini, diced
2 onions, diced
9 cloves garlic, minced
1 teaspoon oregano, crushed
1 tablespoon vegetable oil
¾ pound fresh fettuccine, preferably
    spinach

½ cup butter
salt and pepper to taste
1 cup freshly grated Parmesan cheese
4 to 5 fresh tomatoes, cored, seeded,
    and diced
½ cup sliced black olives
½ cup minced parsley

Heat olive oil in a skillet; add zucchini, onions, and 4 cloves garlic and sauté until limp. Add oregano, mix well, and set aside.

Add oil and fettuccine to rapidly boiling salted water and cook until pasta is *al dente*. Drain and transfer to a warm serving bowl and add sautéed vegetables. Melt butter in a separate pan and sauté the remaining garlic; add salt and pepper to taste. Pour over pasta and vegetables, add ½ cup Parmesan, and toss. Arrange tomatoes, olives, and parsley in an attractive design on top. Garnish with remaining cheese and serve immediately.

SERVES 6 TO 8

Fettuccine alla Pentola

A re-creation of a dish served at the Roman restaurant La Pentola.

7 tablespoons butter
1 clove garlic, minced
2 tablespoons flour
¾ cup veal or chicken stock
2 cups light cream
1 teaspoon minced fresh or
    ½ teaspoon dried basil
3 egg yolks
½ teaspoon white pepper
2 tablespoons olive oil

¾ pound fresh fettuccine
1 bunch (about 2 cups) fresh spinach,
    coarsely chopped or processed
¼ pound prosciutto, sliced and cut in
    julienne strips
2 cups grated Gruyère or Swiss cheese
    (or a combination of both)
salt to taste
½ cup freshly grated Parmesan cheese

Melt ¼ cup butter in a medium saucepan; add garlic and sauté for 1 minute. Pour into an ovenproof serving dish and set aside to warm.

Melt remaining 3 tablespoons butter in same saucepan. Add flour and whisk over low heat until bubbly. Remove from heat, whisk in stock, then gradually whisk in cream; continue whisking over medium heat until thickened. Add basil. Whisk in egg yolks and pepper. Keep warm over low heat.

Add olive oil and fettuccine to boiling salted water and cook until pasta is *al dente*; drain but do not rinse. Transfer hot pasta to the serving dish containing butter and garlic and toss. Add spinach, prosciutto, and Gruyère or Swiss cheese, toss, add cream sauce, and toss again. (If Gruyère cheese has not melted, heat the dish for 10 to 15 minutes in a 350-degree oven.) Add salt to taste, sprinkle with Parmesan, and serve immediately. Avoid allowing dish to stand.

SERVES 4 TO 5

Variation: Substitute bacon or crab for prosciutto.

Fettuccine with Prosciutto and Peas

1 tablespoon olive oil
1 pound egg or spinach fettuccine
¼ pound butter
1¼ cups freshly grated Parmesan
  cheese
¾ cup heavy cream

1 egg, lightly beaten
2 ounces prosciutto, cut in julienne
  strips
1 cup tiny peas, blanched
salt and pepper to taste

Add olive oil and fettuccine to rapidly boiling salted water and cook until pasta is *al dente*. Drain thoroughly and set aside. Melt butter in a chafing dish or large skillet. Gradually add ¾ cup Parmesan, cream, and beaten egg; blend until slightly thickened. Add fettuccine, prosciutto, peas, salt, and pepper. Toss until fettuccine is coated evenly with sauce and serve on warm plates. Pass remaining Parmesan in a separate dish.

SERVES 4 TO 5

Fettuccine with Pancetta and Peppers

6 tablespoons butter
2 tablespoons olive oil
1 medium onion, chopped
½ pound pancetta (available in Italian
  specialty shops), sliced thin and
  diced
2 large red bell peppers, diced

2 large green bell peppers, diced
1 cup heavy cream
1 tablespoon vegetable oil
1 pound fresh fettuccine
1½ cups freshly grated Parmesan
  cheese
½ cup chopped parsley

Melt butter with oil in a skillet over medium heat and sauté onion until limp but not brown. Add pancetta and sauté lightly. Add diced peppers to the same pan, cooking until pancetta is limp but peppers are still crunchy. Add the cream and heat thoroughly. Add oil and fettuccine to rapidly boiling salted water, cook until pasta is *al dente*, and drain. To serve, pour a small amount of sauce into a heated serving bowl and add fettuccine, tossing well. Add remaining sauce and toss, then top with 1 cup Parmesan and toss again. Sprinkle with parsley and serve immediately, passing a separate bowl of the remaining cheese.

SERVES 4 TO 5

Chicken and Ham à la Pasta & Co.

One or two stones' throws away from the University of Washington, the first store of Pasta & Co. offers unusual pastas, sauces, olive oil, and appropriate serving and cooking utensils to any student or faculty member—not to mention neighborhood residents—who can't resist temptation.

1 whole chicken breast
½ cup white wine
1 cup chicken stock
1¼ cups light cream
2 egg yolks, lightly beaten
salt and pepper to taste
1 tablespoon vegetable oil
1 pound rigatoni or fresh fettuccine

¼ pound butter
2 cloves garlic, minced
¾ cup sliced mushrooms
1 cup cubed ham
½ cup freshly grated Parmesan cheese
¼ cup minced parsley
3 tablespons chives, cut into ½-inch
    pieces

Poach chicken breast in wine and stock for 15 minutes. Cool in broth and cut into cubes. In a medium saucepan, mix cream with egg yolks. Salt and pepper generously, and stir sauce over medium-low heat until it thickens.

Add oil and fettuccine to rapidly boiling salted water and cook until pasta is *al dente*. Drain and return to kettle. Meanwhile, melt butter and sauté garlic until limp. Add mushrooms and sauté until tender and slightly browned; add to fettuccine and toss well. Add the chicken, ham, and Parmesan, to pasta and stir until heated through and well coated. Add the parsley and chives, adjust the seasonings, and serve immediately in a warm serving bowl.

SERVES 4 TO 6

Turkey Tetrazzini

1 tablespoon vegetable oil
1 pound spaghetti

½ teaspoon salt
¼ teaspoon white pepper

Sauce

1 pound fresh mushrooms, sliced
1 clove garlic, minced
½ cup butter
⅓ cup freshly grated Parmesan cheese
⅓ cup freshly grated Cheddar cheese

Turkey

3 tablespoons butter
3 tablespoons flour
2 cups turkey or chicken broth
2 cups diced cooked turkey
⅓ cup sour cream

Add oil and spaghetti to rapidly boiling salted water and cook until pasta is *al dente*. Drain and set aside.

To prepare sauce: Sauté mushrooms and garlic in butter. Add the cheeses, salt, and pepper and stir until cheeses melt. Set aside.

To prepare turkey: Melt butter, stir in flour, and cook until bubbly. Add broth slowly and cook, stirring occasionally, until thickened. Add diced turkey.

Pour turkey mixture into cheese sauce and warm through (but do not boil because the sauce will separate). Stir in sour cream and serve immediately, spooning turkey mixture over individual servings of spaghetti.

SERVES 8 TO 10

Linguine with Gorgonzola, Pecorino, and Parmesan

1 tablespoon vegetable oil
1 pound linguine
3 tablespoons olive oil
2 small cloves garlic, minced
½ cup chopped Italian parsley
½ cup grated Italian Gorgonzola
　　cheese
¼ cup grated pecorino or Romano
　　cheese
¼ cup grated Parmesan cheese
salt and freshly ground black pepper
　　to taste

Add vegetable oil and linguine to rapidly boiling salted water and cook until pasta is *al dente*; drain. Meanwhile, heat olive oil in a large skillet, add garlic and half of the parsley, and sauté briefly. Set aside until pasta is cooked.

Place drained linguine in the skillet with the garlic and oil and toss to mix. Add the cheeses a little at a time, mix, and cook for 3 minutes. Add pepper to taste and salt if necessary. Sprinkle with remaining parsley and serve immediately.

SERVES 6

Note: If possible, use the strong Gorgonzola, Columbo Cremificato, rather than the milder Galbani–Dollecitti.

Fettuccine with Cream and Parmesan

1 tablespoon vegetable oil
10 ounces fettuccine
6 tablespoons butter
1 cup sour cream
1 cup heavy cream

1 cup freshly grated Parmesan cheese
dash of freshly grated nutmeg
salt and pepper to taste
2 tablespoons finely chopped chives

Add oil and fettuccine to boiling salted water and cook until pasta is *al dente*. Drain and set aside.

Melt butter in the pan used to cook the noodles, add sour cream, and stir over low heat approximately 2 minutes. Add heavy cream and cook slowly, stirring constantly, for approximately 5 minutes, being careful not to allow sauce to boil, because it will separate. Add Parmesan, nutmeg, salt, and pepper, and continue stirring over low heat until cheese is melted. Add the fettuccine and half of the chives. Heat thoroughly and serve in a warm serving bowl, garnishing with remaining chives.

SERVES 2 TO 4

Note: If sauce must be reheated, do not use a microwave oven.

Fettuccine with Fresh Tomatoes and Cheese Sauce

¼ cup olive oil
4 large cloves garlic, minced
4 cups peeled, diced tomatoes
2 3-inch sprigs fresh or
   1½ tablespoons dried rosemary
1 tablespoon vegetable oil
¼ pound fresh spinach fettuccine
¼ pound fresh egg fettuccine

½ cup freshly grated Mizithra or
   Parmesan cheese
3 tablespoons butter
salt and pepper to taste
2 tablespoons heavy cream
¼ cup freshly grated Parmesan cheese
   for garnish

Heat olive oil in skillet. Add garlic, tomatoes, and rosemary, and simmer approximately 30 minutes, or until tomatoes are consistency of tomato sauce.

Add vegetable oil and fettuccine to rapidly boiling salted water; cook until pasta is *al dente*. Drain, transfer to a warm serving bowl, and add Mizithra, butter, salt, and pepper. Toss gently until thoroughly mixed. Add cream to tomato mixture, add to pasta, and toss. Serve immediately, accompanied by a bowl of Parmesan.

SERVES 2

Fettuccine with Tomato-Prosciutto Sauce

3 tablespoons butter
2 cups skinned, diced tomatoes
¼ pound prosciutto, sliced thin, then
   cut in julienne strips
¾ cup freshly grated Parmesan cheese

2 tablespoons butter
salt and pepper to taste
1 tablespoon vegetable oil
1 pound fettuccine

Melt butter in skillet, add tomatoes, and simmer until soft and the consistency of tomato sauce. Add prosciutto and simmer 5 minutes more. (Do not overcook.)

Add oil and fettuccine to rapidly boiling salted water and cook until pasta is *al dente*. Drain and transfer to a warm serving bowl. Add ¼ cup Parmesan, butter, salt, and pepper to pasta; top with tomato sauce and toss lightly. Serve immediately, accompanied by a bowl of the remaining Parmesan.

SERVES 2 TO 4

Perciatelli with Tomatoes, Pancetta, and Hot Chilis

3 tablespoons butter
3 tablespoons vegetable oil
1 large yellow onion, chopped (about
   2 cups)
1 cup sliced mushrooms
½ pound pancetta (available in Italian
   specialty shops), sliced thin and cut
   in julienne strips
1 15-ounce can tomato sauce plus
   water to produce 2 cups liquid
1 14½-ounce can peeled Italian
   tomatoes, drained

3 dried hot chili peppers
½ teaspoon salt
1 tablespoon vegetable oil
¼ pound perciatelli, bucatini, or
   fettuccine
½ cup freshly grated Parmesan cheese
3 tablespoons freshly grated Romano
   cheese
3 tablespoons chopped parsley for
   garnish

In a large skillet, melt butter with oil and sauté onion and mushrooms until golden. Add pancetta and sauté briefly. Add watered tomato sauce, tomatoes, chili peppers, and salt. Cook, uncovered, about 25 minutes, or until the tomatoes and the cooking fats have separated. Set aside.

Add oil and perciatelli to rapidly boiling salted water and cook until pasta is *al dente*. Drain and transfer to a warm serving bowl. Add sauce and toss. Add 5 tablespoons Parmesan and the Romano, and toss again. Top with remaining Parmesan and chopped parsley, and serve immediately.

SERVES 4 TO 6

Rice for Indian Lamb Curry

1 cup rice
2 tablespoons butter
1 3-inch stick cinnamon
1/8 teaspoon turmeric
1/2 teaspoon mustard seeds

1/2 teaspoon cumin seeds
1 small onion, minced
2/3 cup raisins
2 ounces cashew nuts

Cook rice according to package directions and set aside. Melt butter in a skillet, add spices and onion, and sauté until onion is clear. Add raisins and cashews, mix well, and add to cooked rice. Stir well, remove cinnamon stick, and serve.

SERVES 4

Note: This rice has a subtle curry flavor and is meant to be served with Indian Lamb Curry (page 231). Double the spice measurements if rice is served with a less spicy main dish.

Saffron-Vermouth Pilaf

3/4 cup butter
1 cup sliced mushrooms
6 green onions, sliced
2 cups long-grain white rice
2 teaspoons salt

1/2 teaspoon white pepper
1/4 teaspoon mild saffron powder or
    1/16 to 1/8 teaspoon saffron threads
3 cups canned chicken broth
1/2 cup extra-dry vermouth

Melt butter in a large saucepan; add mushrooms and green onions and sauté until soft. Add rice, salt, pepper, and saffron, and stir until rice is coated with butter. Add broth and vermouth, cover pot tightly, and set over low heat to simmer for about 1 hour, or until all liquid is absorbed and rice is tender. (If more liquid is needed, add a mixture of ½ cup chicken broth and 1 to 2 tablespoons vermouth.) Serve hot.

SERVES 8

Rice with Walnuts and Currants

⅓ cup butter
1½ cups minced green onions
¾ cup currants
1½ teaspoons paprika
¼ teaspoon Tabasco sauce

4½ cups hot rice cooked in chicken
    broth and ½ cup white wine
1 cup chopped walnuts
1 teaspoon salt
½ teaspoon freshly ground pepper
½ cup minced parsley

Melt butter in a skillet; add green onions, currants, paprika, and Tabasco, and sauté lightly for 5 minutes, being careful not to let the onions brown. Add hot rice and walnuts and toss thoroughly with 2 forks. Season and toss with minced parsley just before serving.

SERVES 8

Wild Rice with Pecans and Mushrooms

½ pound wild rice
3 cups water
1½ teaspoons salt
1½ cups sliced mushrooms

½ cup butter
pepper (optional)
½ cup coarsely broken toasted pecans
chopped parsley for garnish

Soak rice overnight in water. Drain, wash well, and put in a medium saucepan. Cover with water, add salt, and bring to a boil. Reduce heat to low, cover, and cook about 1 hour, or until tender; drain if necessary. Sauté mushrooms in butter, add pepper, and pour over rice; add pecans, toss, and garnish with parsley before serving.

SERVES 8 TO 10

Variation: Substitute walnuts or cashews for pecans.

Wild Rice Casserole

½ pound wild rice
3 cups water
2 teaspoons salt
½ cup butter
¼ cup flour

2 cups light cream
8 ounces cream cheese, softened
½ teaspoon salt
2 cups sliced or small whole
　　mushrooms

Soak rice overnight in water. Drain, wash well, and put in a medium saucepan. Cover with water, add salt, and bring to a boil. Reduce heat to low, cover, and cook about 1 hour, or until tender. Drain if necessary and set aside.

Preheat oven to 350 degrees. Butter a 2-quart casserole.

Melt butter in a heavy skillet, add flour, and stir until mixture bubbles and forms a thick paste. Add cream very slowly, stirring constantly. Add cream cheese, stirring until it is melted and sauce is smooth, and add salt. Alternate layers of rice, raw mushrooms, and sauce, ending with a generous amount of sauce on top. Bake 30 minutes, or until casserole bubbles around edges and is golden brown on top.

SERVES 8 TO 10

Couscous Confetti

1½ cups water
2 teaspoons chicken stock base
　　(powdered seasoning for dissolv-
　　ing in water)
dash Tabasco sauce
1 cup couscous
5 tablespoons butter
1 teaspoon dill

1 clove garlic, minced
1 cup chopped red bell pepper
　　(optional)
8 small mushrooms, sliced thin
½ cup coarsely shredded carrots
½ cup chopped green onions
½ teaspoon salt

Mix water, stock base, and Tabasco in a medium saucepan, cover, and bring to a boil. Remove from heat and stir in couscous; cover tightly and allow to stand for 20 minutes. Meanwhile, in a large skillet, melt butter and add dill, garlic, pepper, mushrooms, and carrots. When these are slightly limp, add green onion and salt. Toss lightly, add couscous, and mix thoroughly. Serve immediately or keep warm over low heat for up to 30 minutes. Serve in a clear glass bowl.

SERVES 8

Early morning fog shrouds gillnetters and salmon trawlers in the harbor of La Conner, north of Seattle at the mouth of the Skagit River.

Seafood

HOW TO CHOOSE FISH

With years of experience behind him, Wayne Ludvigsen, kitchen manager of Ray's Boathouse, a restaurant specializing in seafood, offers a helpful guide for determining which fish is the freshest.

Try to find out what method was used to catch the fish. Ideally, it would be trolling, with a long line—the old-fashioned hook and line. This way, the fish is brought on board alive, and would be bled immediately to avoid hemorrhaging. But if the fish is netted, or dredged, it may have been battered and bruised by other fish in the net, and may die before reaching the boat. Dying before proper treatment causes the fish to release chemicals internally, resulting in soft meat and affecting the taste. Also, check to see how the fish was handled. There should be minimal scale loss.

The key is to use your senses—touch, sight and smell. The eyes of the fish should be neither red nor cloudy. When you handle the fish, the meat should bounce back and feel firm. When you smell the fish, there shouldn't be an offensive smell. And when the fish is cut, you shouldn't find any blood.

When fresh seafood is unavailable, don't necessarily rule out frozen fish. If a product has been fresh-frozen and properly handled, it can be good.

Trout Meunière

½ cup flour
½ teaspoon salt
freshly ground pepper to taste
5 ¾-pound trout
¼ cup butter

juice of ½ lemon
½ teaspoon chervil
½ teaspoon tarragon
½ teaspoon minced chives
½ teaspoon minced parsley

Mix together flour, salt, and pepper. Trim off fins and tail of fish. Wash fish and pat dry. Score trout once or twice on each side and roll in seasoned flour. Melt 2 tablespoons butter in a heavy frying pan. When it foams, add fish and cook approximately 6 minutes on each side, until golden brown. Place trout on a warm serving platter and keep warm.

Wipe out the frying pan. Add remaining butter and cook slowly to a nutty brown. Add lemon juice and herbs; pour foaming butter over the trout and serve.

SERVES 5

Trout Belin

4 ¾-pound trout, boned, with heads
    left on
¼ cup flour
½ teaspoon salt
freshly ground pepper to taste
7 tablespoons butter
1 large orange, sliced thin
2 tablespoons sugar
juice of 1 lemon
juice of 1 orange
1 tablespoon minced parsley
watercress for garnish

Stuffing
¾ pound fresh spinach or 1 10-ounce
    package frozen chopped spinach
1 tablespoon chopped parsley
1 teaspoon mixed herbs (chervil,
    tarragon, and minced chives)
salt and pepper to taste
4 green onions, finely chopped
3 tablespoons butter
½ pound mushrooms, very finely
    chopped

To prepare stuffing: Cook and drain spinach and squeeze dry. Chop spinach and mix with parsley, herbs, salt, and pepper. Sauté green onions in butter until soft. Add mushrooms and spinach mixture. Cook over low heat stirring occasionally until liquid has evaporated. Cool.

Fill cavity of each trout with stuffing; reshape and tie. Mix together flour, salt, and pepper. Coat fish carefully with seasoned flour. Trout may be set aside at this point for finishing later.

In a skillet, melt 3 tablespoons butter and sauté the trout over medium heat, about 4 to 5 minutes on each side, until fish are golden brown and flake when pressed with a fork. Remove to serving dish and keep warm.

Wipe out the skillet. Melt 1 tablespoon butter over medium-high heat and add orange slices. Sprinkle with sugar, turn oranges, and cook until golden and caramelized. Place 1 to 2 slices on each trout, or arrange them, overlapping, around side of dish. Wipe out pan again. Melt the remaining 3 tablespoons butter and cook to a nutty brown. Add lemon juice, orange juice, and parsley; pour the foaming sauce over fish. Garnish with watercress and serve.

SERVES 4

Baked Salmon, Northwest Style

1 6- to 7-pound whole salmon, cleaned
   and scaled
salt and freshly ground pepper to taste
1 cup diced jack cheese
1 cup diced celery

1 small onion, diced
2 tablespoons butter, melted
1 cup sour cream
8 ounces tomato sauce
1 small clove garlic, minced

Preheat oven to 350 degrees. Line large baking dish with aluminum foil.

Season fish inside and out with salt and pepper and place in prepared dish. Combine cheese, celery, and onion and stuff into fish cavity. Mix butter, sour cream, tomato sauce, and garlic and pour over top of fish. Cover with foil, if desired, and bake for 15 minutes per pound.

SERVES 6 TO 8

Barbecued Salmon, Delano Style

1 5- to 8-pound whole salmon, scaled
   and filleted
1 cup butter
1 to 2 bunches green onions, chopped
4 lemons, sliced
2 to 4 tablespoons soy sauce
1½ cups dry vermouth or dry white
   wine

Delano Sauce
1¼ cups tightly packed watercress
   leaves, with blossoms if available
dash of Tabasco sauce
1¼ cups tightly packed tender spinach
   leaves
¾ cup mayonnaise
¼ cup capers
2 teaspoons minced chives

Prepare coals in barbecue. The salmon will have additional flavor if hickory or alderwood chips, previously soaked in water, are added to the coals.

Lay the salmon in a tray of heavy-duty aluminum foil with sides crimped to a depth of at least 1 inch. Place ¼-inch-thick slices of butter over salmon. Cover the butter with green onions, cover the green onions with lemon slices, and lightly sprinkle on the soy sauce. Pour vermouth or wine over all.

Lay foil tray of salmon on the grill over the coals. Cover the fish with a foil tent larger than the tray, so the smoke can circulate around the fish, or cover the barbecue. Cook salmon until milky white substance appears and fish flakes when pressed with a fork. *Do not overcook.* Serve with Delano Sauce.

SERVES 8 TO 12

To prepare sauce: Place all ingredients in food processor or blender and blend until smooth and creamy. Chill for 1 hour or more.

YIELD: APPROXIMATELY 3 CUPS

Salmon Steamed on a Barbecue

1 6- to 7-pound whole salmon with head, tail, and fins removed
¼ to ½ cup butter, slivered
1 tomato, sliced

1 medium onion, sliced
1 lemon, sliced
½ teaspoon dill
½ teaspoon salt

Prepare coals in barbecue.

Clean cavity of fish and layer inside with butter, tomato, onion, and lemon. Sprinkle dill and salt over stuffing. Wrap salmon securely in heavy-duty foil and lay on grill over bed of hot coals. Cook 20 minutes, or until fish flakes when pressed with a fork.

SERVES 6 TO 8

Riptide Salmon Barbecue

1 cup vegetable oil
¼ cup brown sugar, firmly packed
juice of 3 lemons
1 tablespoon chopped fresh dill or 1 teaspoon dried dill

1 generous teaspoon Beau Monde seasoning
1 6- to 7-pound salmon, scaled and filleted

Combine oil, brown sugar, lemon juice, dill, and Beau Monde. Marinate fish in this mixture, meat side down, for 3 hours.

Prepare coals in barbecue.

Place fish in a tray of heavy-duty aluminum foil with sides crimped to a depth of 1 inch, and set the tray on a grill over hot charcoal coals. Cover loosely with additional foil or cover barbecue. Cook over coals until a milky white substance appears and fish flakes when pressed with fork. *Do not overcook.*

SERVES 4 TO 8

Cold Salmon Buffet

1 4- to 6-pound whole salmon, head
    and tail on
3 quarts strained Court Bouillon
    (page 190)
2 cucumbers, sliced thin
2 green olives for garnish
1 bunch parsley for garnish

Dill Glaze
1 cup mayonnaise
1 cup sour cream
½ teaspoon salt
1 teaspoon dill
½ teaspoon Dijon-style mustard
1 tablespoon unflavored gelatin
⅓ cup cold water

Wrap cleaned fish in cheesecloth and place on a rack in a poacher or a long pan. Add Court Bouillon to cover. Bring to a boil, reduce heat, and simmer 6 minutes per pound. Cool fish in the stock.

To prepare glaze: Combine mayonnaise, sour cream, salt, dill, and mustard, and set aside to bring to room temperature. Soak gelatin in water for 5 minutes, then dissolve over medium heat. Stir into dilled mayonnaise and cool slightly.

Remove fish from stock and carefully unwrap. Remove skin on top side from gills to tail. With a spatula, spread glaze on fish as you would frost a cake. Arrange the cucumbers on the fish, starting at the tail, overlapping them to resemble scales. Use olives for the eye and nose. Garnish with parsley.

SERVES 6 TO 10

Salmon Teriyaki

This is a favorite dish at a popular restaurant—Ray's Boathouse, which is situated between Seattle's largest marina and the Chittenden Locks, with a lively view of the city's boat traffic. Seafood is the restaurant specialty and Salmon Teriyaki is one of the most often requested dinners. You'll see why.

1 quart soy sauce
1 pound brown sugar

1 teaspoon dry mustard
2 cloves garlic, minced

1 tablespoon fresh ginger, minced
½ cup white wine
6 salmon fillets, about 8 ounces each,

or 1 whole 6- to 7-pound salmon,
    filleted
3 tablespoons toasted sesame seeds

Prepare the teriyaki marinade by combining all ingredients except salmon and sesame seeds. Place fillets in this mixture and allow to marinate 4 to 6 hours.

Remove salmon from marinade, put in a tray of heavy-duty aluminum foil, and place on a grill. Cover loosely and grill about 7 to 10 minutes or until milky white substance appears and fish flakes when pressed with a fork. *Do not overcook.* Top with sesame seeds and serve.

SERVES 6

Salmon Mousse

½ teaspoon salt
1½ tablespoons sugar
1 teaspoon dry mustard
¾ cup scalded milk
2 egg yolks
4 tablespoons cold water
¼ cup red wine vinegar
1½ tablespoons melted butter
¾ tablespoon unflavored gelatin
    (1 envelope)

1 pound cooked salmon, flaked
watercress leaves for garnish

Cucumber Sauce
1 small cucumber
salt
⅓ cup mayonnaise
⅔ cup sour cream
2 teaspoons dill
⅛ teaspoon freshly ground pepper

Prepare a 4-cup mold by coating liberally with mayonnaise.

Combine salt, sugar, and mustard with milk in a double boiler; cook over medium heat for 5 minutes, stirring constantly. Beat together egg yolks and 2 tablespoons cold water. Mix vinegar with butter and egg yolks. Stir in 2 tablespoons of the hot milk mixture, then add to remaining hot milk mixture. Cook 2 to 3 minutes, stirring constantly.

Soften gelatin in remaining 2 tablespoons of cold water. Add to mixture in double boiler and stir until gelatin is dissolved. Add salmon and turn into prepared mold. Chill several hours, or until firm. Unmold, garnish with watercress, and serve with Cucumber Sauce.

To prepare sauce: Peel cucumber, remove seeds, and chop well. Lightly salt, place cucumber in colander, and press to drain out bitter liquid. Combine with remaining ingredients and chill. This is best if prepared several hours before serving.

SERVES 6

Sockeye Salmon Terrine

1 tablespoon olive oil
1 bunch spinach (about ½ pound)
1 clove garlic
2 tablespoons lemon juice
1¼ pounds fresh sockeye or other
   salmon
½ pound Nova Scotia-style salmon

2 cups heavy cream, chilled
2 egg whites
1 teaspoon cayenne
¾ cup artichoke hearts, not marinated
Avocado Mayonnaise (page 192)
French bread

Preheat oven to 350 degrees. Lightly oil a ½-quart terrine, mold, or loaf tin. Set aside.

Wash spinach thoroughly and remove stems. Steam leaves until just barely cooked. Set aside on an absorbent cloth. Using metal blade of food processor, mince garlic in lemon juice. Add both fresh and smoked salmon and process until smooth. With machine running, slowly add cream, then egg whites; season with cayenne and blend well.

Spread one-third of salmon mixture in bottom of terrine. Layer half the spinach leaves to cover salmon evenly. Spread another third of salmon mixture on top of spinach. Press artichoke hearts into salmon in a line down the middle; layer remaining spinach on top. Spread remaining salmon over the spinach and cover tightly with lid or foil.

Place terrine in a shallow pan filled with 1½ inches of water; bake for 1 hour, checking occasionally to be sure water has not evaporated. Remove from oven and cool to room temperature, then chill overnight in refrigerator. Cut into ½-inch-thick slices and serve with Avocado Mayonnaise and French bread.

SERVES 16

Seattle Sole

1 pound crabmeat
5 tablespoons minced chives
5 tablespoons minced parsley
5 tablespoons butter, melted
¼ cup chopped celery
½ cup plus 2 tablespoons heavy cream
½ teaspoon salt
freshly ground pepper to taste
8 sole fillets (2 pounds)

3 tablespoons butter
3 tablespoons flour
¼ teaspoon salt
1½ cups milk
⅓ cup dry white wine
4 ounces grated Swiss cheese (1 cup)
½ teaspoon paprika
minced parsley for garnish

Preheat oven to 400 degrees.

Combine first 8 ingredients and spread over fillets. Roll fillets and place seam side down in a baking dish. In a saucepan, melt 3 table-spoons butter and blend in flour and salt. Cook slowly for about 2 minutes. Stir in milk and wine, and cook, stirring constantly, until mixture thickens. Pour sauce over fillets and bake for 15 minutes. Sprinkle with cheese, then bake 5 minutes longer, or until cheese is melted. Sprinkle with paprika and parsley, and serve.

SERVES 8

Petrale Sole Florentine

2 10-ounce packages frozen chopped
  spinach or equivalent amount of
  cooked fresh spinach
¼ cup butter
salt and freshly ground pepper to taste
2 pounds Petrale sole fillets
2 ounces freshly grated Parmesan
  cheese

Sauce
2 tablespoons butter
2 tablespoons flour
2 cups milk or light cream
½ teaspoon dill
¼ teaspoon lemon juice
salt and freshly ground pepper to taste
½ cup grated Cheddar cheese

Defrost spinach, if using frozen spinach, and squeeze dry. Melt 2 tablespoons butter in skillet; add spinach and sauté lightly. Add salt and pepper to taste. Remove from skillet, spread in a shallow, 9-x-13-inch casserole, and set aside.

Dry fillets with paper towels. Melt remaining butter in a skillet over medium heat, add sole, and cook 30 to 45 seconds on each side, just until fillets become opaque. Remove from skillet and lay cooked fillets on top of spinach. Sprinkle with a thin layer of Parmesan, reserving some as casserole topping.

To prepare sauce: Melt butter in the skillet used to cook the fish. Add flour, blend with a whisk, and cook over low heat for 2 minutes. Add the milk, stirring constantly, and cook slowly until sauce has thick-ened. Stir in dill, lemon juice, salt, pepper, and Cheddar. Pour some of the sauce over the sole and spinach, reserving the rest to serve sepa-rately. (May be prepared ahead to this point.) You may cover the dish and set it aside at this point.

Preheat oven to 350 degrees and bake uncovered for 15 minutes. Sprinkle with remaining Parmesan and place under broiler until brown. Warm remaining sauce and serve separately.

SERVES 6

Chinese Cod

1 clove garlic, minced
½ cup soy sauce
¼ cup sugar
2 tablespoons vegetable oil

¼ cup white wine
½ teaspoon grated fresh ginger
1½ pounds cod fillets
1 tablespoon sesame seeds

Combine garlic, soy sauce, sugar, oil, wine, and ginger. Marinate cod fillets in this mixture for ½ hour, but no longer. Broil fillets in foil-covered pan, 5 inches from heat, for 4 minutes. Baste, turn, and baste again. Cover with sesame seeds and broil 4 minutes more.

SERVES 6

Steamed Black Cod

1 to 2 pounds black cod fillets, skinned
3 green onions, chopped
2 teaspoons grated fresh ginger
⅛ teaspoon minced fresh dill

1 tablespoon soy sauce
1 tablespoon peanut oil
½ teaspoon sesame oil
1 clove garlic, minced

Place fish on ovenproof plate, cover with onions and ginger, and sprinkle with dill and soy sauce. Place plate of fish in a steamer on a tray ½ inch above water. Steam for 12 minutes and remove fish to warm serving platter.

While fish is steaming, heat peanut and sesame oil in a small skillet; add garlic and brown. Strain oil, drizzle it over fish, and serve fish immediately.

SERVES 4 TO 6

Johnny's Greek-style Fish Fillets

Rare is the Puget Sound community without a waterfront restaurant. Johnny's Dock, in Tacoma, overlooks the city waterway, which empties into Commencement Bay, scene of bustling port activity. Predictably, Johnny's Dock specializes in seafood, and one of the favorites, not so predictably, has a Greek accent.

1 tablespoon olive oil
3 to 4 pounds sea bass, red snapper,
   or halibut fillets

1 cup minced parsley
½ teaspoon salt
freshly ground pepper to taste

juice of 1 lemon
3 onions, thinly sliced
2 cloves garlic, minced
1 16-ounce can whole tomatoes,
    drained

1 cup white wine
1 cup clam broth
½ cup olive oil
3 to 4 fresh tomatoes, sliced
½ teaspoon oregano

Preheat oven to 350 degrees. Grease a 9-x-13-inch baking dish with olive oil.

Wash fish and pat dry. Spread half of the parsley on bottom of the baking dish. Lay the fish on the parsley, season with salt and pepper, and squeeze lemon over fish. Combine onions, garlic, remaining parsley, canned tomatoes, wine, and clam broth with ½ cup olive oil; mix and pour over fillets. Place the fresh tomato slices on top and sprinkle with oregano. Bake for 30 minutes, basting occasionally.

SERVES 6

Red Snapper à l'Orange

2 pounds red snapper fillets
3 tablespoons butter, melted
½ cup frozen orange juice concentrate
2 teaspoons zest of orange
1 teaspoon salt

dash nutmeg
freshly ground pepper to taste
watercress and orange slices for
    garnish

Preheat oven to 350 degrees. Butter a 9-x-13-inch baking dish.

Cut the snapper into serving-size pieces; wash and pat dry. Place fish skin side down in baking dish. Combine juice concentrate, orange peel, salt, nutmeg, and pepper and pour over fish. Bake for 25 minutes. Serve on a bed of watercress garnished with orange slices.

SERVES 6

Snapper Veracruz

4 red snapper fillets
½ cup mayonnaise
juice of 1 lemon
salt, pepper, and paprika to taste

1 red onion, sliced into thin rings
2 tablespoons minced parsley
½ teaspoon oregano

Preheat oven to 400 degrees.

Generously coat fillets with mayonnaise. Squeeze lemon over each fillet and season both sides with salt, pepper, and paprika. Cover bottom of a baking dish with half the onion rings and place fillets on top. Cover with remaining onion rings, sprinkle with parsley and oregano, and bake approximately 20 minutes or until fish flakes. *Do not overcook.*

SERVES 4

Sweet and Sour Snapper

1 pound red snapper, boned and cut
   into 1-inch cubes
1 egg, beaten
½ teaspoon salt
1 tablespoon dry sherry
⅓ cup flour
¼ cup cornstarch
6 cups oil for deep-frying

Sweet and Sour Sauce
2 tablespoons cornstarch
¼ cup water

1 20-ounce can pineapple chunks in
   heavy syrup (drain off and reserve
   syrup)
¼ cup rice vinegar
⅓ cup sugar
2 tablespoons soy sauce
2 ounces Chinese pickles (optional—
   available in Asian food shops)
1 green bell pepper, seeded and cut
   into chunks
1 large tomato, cut into wedges

Dry snapper with paper towel. Mix together egg, salt, and sherry. Dip fish in egg mixture, then roll in mixture of flour and cornstarch. Deep-fry fish in a wok over high heat. Drain on paper towels, transfer to serving dish, and keep warm in a 250-degree oven.

To prepare sauce: Mix together cornstarch and water, then combine with reserved pineapple syrup, vinegar, sugar, and soy sauce. Bring to a boil. Add pineapple chunks, pickles, and green pepper and cook for 2 minutes. Remove from heat, add tomato wedges, and pour around fish just before serving.

SERVES 4

Fish with Cheese, Danish Style

3 pounds halibut fillets
½ teaspoon salt
½ teaspoon freshly ground pepper
½ cup butter

1 cup grated Gorgonzola or blue
   cheese
2 tablespoons lemon juice
1 tablespoon minced parsley for
   garnish

Preheat broiler. Grease 9-x-13-inch metal baking dish (anything else will break).

Wash fish, pat dry, and place in prepared baking dish. Sprinkle with salt and pepper. In a heavy saucepan (or a double boiler, if saucepan isn't heavy), melt butter, add cheese and lemon juice, and stir until cheese is melted. Pour half of sauce over fish. Broil fish 3 minutes, turn over, add remaining sauce, and broil 3 minutes more. Remove to a heated platter and sprinkle with parsley.

SERVES 6

East Indian Fish Curry

3 pounds halibut fillets
½ cup vegetable oil
4 onions, chopped
2 to 3 tablespoons curry powder
1 teaspoon paprika

1½ teaspoons salt
1 teaspoon freshly ground pepper
¾ cup tomato purée
3½ cups hot water
½ cup shelled peanuts

Wash fish, pat dry, and cut into bite-size pieces. In a heavy skillet, heat oil; add onions, curry, paprika, salt, and pepper and sauté until lightly browned. Add tomato purée and reduce liquid until almost dry, stirring constantly to prevent burning. Add water, reduce heat, and simmer 20 minutes. Add fish and cook slowly for 15 minutes; do not stir after adding fish. Sprinkle with peanuts and serve.

SERVES 6 TO 8

Halibut Steaks au Poivre

6 1-inch-thick halibut steaks
½ teaspoon salt
1 teaspoon peppercorns
1 tablespoon flour
1 tablespoon vegetable oil

½ cup unsalted butter
¼ cup brandy
¼ cup tawny port
½ cup beef stock
½ cup heavy cream

Salt the fish. Crush peppercorns, preferably with a mortar and pestle, and mix with flour, coating fish with the mixture.

Brown the fish lightly in oil combined with ¼ cup butter. Lower heat and cook until fish is almost done. Add brandy and ignite. Stir in port, add stock, and heat to simmer. Remove fish to serving dish. Reduce pan juices slightly. Stir in cream and continue to simmer until sauce thickens. Correct seasonings, stir in remaining butter, and pour over fish.

SERVES 6

Poached Halibut with Green Butter

3 pounds halibut
Court Bouillon to cover (approximately
   1 quart), strained (page 190)
parsley for garnish
1 lemon, sliced, for garnish

Green Butter

1 cup butter, softened
2 hard-cooked eggs, chopped
2 tablespoons olive oil

1 large clove garlic, minced
6 sprigs watercress
8 spinach leaves
6 sprigs parsley
4 green onions, chopped
2 tablespoons capers
1 teaspoon Dijon-style mustard
juice of 2 lemons
salt and freshly ground pepper to taste

Preheat oven to 400 degrees. Grease a 9-x-13-inch baking dish.

Rinse fish and pat dry. Place in prepared baking dish and add Court Bouillon to cover. Poach gently for 25 minutes, or until fish flakes easily with fork. When done, drain well, place on heated serving dish, and garnish with parsley and lemon. Serve with Green Butter.

To prepare Green Butter: Place butter, eggs, oil, and garlic in food processor and process until creamy. Blanch watercress, spinach, parsley, and green onions. Squeeze water from vegetables, chop, and add to butter mixture with capers and mustard. Blend. Add lemon juice, salt, and pepper. Serve at room temperature in a sauceboat or small bowl.

SERVES 6

Baked Halibut Chablis

6 ¾-inch-thick halibut fillets, about 6
   ounces each
1 cup Chablis
1 teaspoon salt
1 cup fine dry bread crumbs

1 cup mayonnaise
½ cup sour cream
½ cup chopped onion
½ teaspoon paprika
parsley sprigs for garnish

Preheat oven to 500 degrees. Grease a 9-x-13 inch baking dish. (Use a metal baking dish or a dish that can withstand very high heat.)

Marinate fish in mixture of wine and salt for 4 or more hours, turning occasionally. Drain, coat with bread crumbs, and place in prepared baking dish.

Combine mayonnaise, sour cream, and onions. Divide evenly among fillets, covering each with the mixture. Sprinkle with paprika and bake for 20 minutes. Arrange on hot platter; garnish with parsley sprigs.

SERVES 6

Bass Piccata

Across Lake Washington from Seattle, football fans can watch the Seattle Seahawks during workouts in Kirkland and then drive on to nearby Juanita to dine at Peter Dow's tiny, popular Café Juanita, which specializes in northern Italian food and provided this recipe.

½ cup flour	*8 bass fillets (totaling about 1 pound)*
salt and pepper to taste	*or Petrale sole*
¼ teaspoon thyme	*6 tablespoons butter*
¼ teaspoon dill	*1 clove garlic, minced*
½ teaspoon basil	*juice of 2 lemons*
	1 tablespoon capers

Combine flour, thyme, dill, and basil. Lightly dust fillets with seasoned flour. Melt butter in skillet and add garlic. Place fillets in pan, cover, and cook over medium heat until fish is white on the edges. Turn and add lemon juice and capers. Cover and cook until bass flakes. *Do not overcook.*

SERVES 4

Sole Lindsay

2 pounds sole fillets	*½ pound Jarlsberg cheese, sliced thin*
½ cup butter, chilled and sliced thin	*½ pound cream cheese, cut into*
¼ teaspoon salt	*¼-inch sticks*
¼ teaspoon dill	*1½ pounds tiny shrimp*
freshly ground pepper to taste	*¼ cup soy sauce*
½ cup minced green onions	*parsley for garnish*

Preheat oven to 400 degrees.

Wash sole and pat dry. Place butter slices on sole and sprinkle with salt, dill, pepper, and onions. Layer Jarlsberg, cream cheese, and three-quarters of the shrimp over fillets. Roll fillets and place seam side down in baking dish. Top with remaining shrimp, and sprinkle lightly with soy sauce. Bake for 12 to 15 minutes. Garnish with parsley and serve.

SERVES 6

Ginger Scallops

1½ pounds bay scallops
6 tablespoons butter
2 tablespoons grated fresh ginger

salt and freshly ground pepper to taste
2 tablespoons minced parsley

Pat scallops dry with paper towels. Heat butter until sizzling, and sauté ginger briefly. Add scallops and continue to sauté until scallops are heated through. Season with salt and pepper and sprinkle with parsley.

SERVES 6

Herbed Scallops Sauté

1 pound scallops, cut into ½-inch
    pieces
juice of 1 lemon
salt and freshly ground pepper to taste
½ cup flour

2 tablespoons olive oil
2 tablespoons minced green onions
1 clove garlic, minced
2 tablespoons butter
2 tablespoons minced parsley

Pat scallops dry with paper towels. Sprinkle with lemon juice, salt, and pepper, and dredge with flour. Heat oil in wok or skillet until hot; add scallops and toss for 4 to 5 minutes. Add green onions, garlic, butter, and parsley, and toss quickly. *Do not overcook.* Serve immediately.

SERVES 4

Scallops Amandine

1 pound scallops
salt, freshly ground pepper, and
    paprika to taste
6 tablespoons butter
½ cup milk
½ cup flour

¼ cup toasted sliced almonds
juice of ½ lemon
1 teaspoon minced parsley
6 tablespoons butter, melted to golden
    brown

Pat scallops dry with paper towels. Season lightly with salt, pepper, and paprika. Melt butter in a large skillet. Dip scallops in milk, then in flour, and place in skillet. Sauté over medium-high heat so that scallops will brown quickly, approximately 3 minutes on each side. Arrange scallops on a hot serving platter and sprinkle with almonds. Pour on lemon juice, sprinkle with parsley, and drizzle with melted butter.

SERVES 4

Prawn and Scallop Sauté

1 pound prawns
¼ cup butter
juice of 1 lemon
3 cloves garlic, minced
1 pound scallops
1 tablespoon cognac
1 tablespoon cornstarch
2 tablespoons fish stock or chicken broth

½ cup Crème Fraîche
4 sprigs fresh basil or watercress for garnish

Crème Fraîche

1 cup heavy cream
2 tablespoons sour cream

To prepare Crème Fraîche: Combine ingredients thoroughly and let stand at room temperature for 12 to 24 hours.

Remove shells from prawns, leaving tails on, and devein. Pat scallops dry with paper towels. Melt butter in a large skillet; add lemon juice and garlic. Place prawns and scallops in butter and sauté until scallops are opaque—about 3 to 4 minutes per side. Remove to a warm platter.

Add cognac to pan juices and ignite. Dissolve cornstarch in fish stock and add, along with Crème Fraîche, and simmer until thickened. Pour sauce over shellfish and garnish with fresh basil.

SERVES 4

Asparagus–Shrimp Medley

1 pound asparagus, sliced diagonally in ¼-inch strips
3 green onions, sliced diagonally in ¼-inch strips
1 8-ounce can water chestnuts, sliced
1 clove garlic, minced

2 teaspoons grated fresh ginger
3 tablespoons vegetable oil
1 pound medium shrimp

Thickening Sauce
3 tablespoons oyster sauce
¼ cup chicken stock

1 teaspoon sugar
1 tablespoon cornstarch
1 tablespoon water

To prepare Thickening Sauce: Combine ingredients and set aside.

Stir-fry asparagus, green onions, water chestnuts, garlic, and ginger for 1 to 2 minutes in oil in skillet or wok. Add shrimp and heat thoroughly. Add Thickening Sauce and cook until thickened.

SERVES 4

Variations: Broccoli may be substituted for asparagus or the following sauce may be substituted.

2 tablespoons cornstarch
2 tablespoons water

2 tablespoons white wine
1 tablespoon soy sauce

Blend ingredients and use as above.

Herbed Shrimp Flambé

½ cup butter
½ pound fresh mushrooms, sliced
12 cherry tomatoes
1 cup celery, sliced
2 teaspoons minced fresh ginger
1 clove garlic, minced
2 pounds large shrimp, washed,
    shelled, and deveined
minced parsley

2 teaspoons minced chives
½ teaspoon tarragon
1 teaspoon dry mustard
1 teaspoon salt
¼ teaspoon freshly ground pepper
3 tablespoons fresh lemon juice
¼ cup brandy, heated
2 to 3 cups cooked rice

Melt butter in a large skillet; sauté mushrooms, tomatoes, celery, ginger, and garlic for 3 minutes. Remove from skillet. Add shrimp, sprinkle with remaining seasoning, and sauté 2 minutes, stirring constantly. Add lemon juice and return vegetables to skillet. Cover, simmer 5 minutes, then transfer to a chafing dish. Just before serving, add heated brandy and ignite. Serve over rice.

SERVES 4 TO 6

Sherried Shrimp

4 quarts salted water
2½ to 3 pounds large shrimp, washed,
    shelled, and deveined
1 pound fresh mushrooms, sliced
1 clove garlic, minced
1 cup butter, melted
2 tablespoons flour
2 cups heavy cream

½ cup sherry or white wine
dash Tabasco sauce
dash Worcestershire sauce
dash curry powder
¼ cup freshly grated Parmesan cheese
parsley for garnish
2 cups cooked rice

Preheat oven to 350 degrees. Butter a 9-inch-square baking dish.

Bring salted water to a rapid boil, add shrimp, and remove from heat. Allow shrimp to remain in the hot water for 5 minutes, then drain and set aside. Sauté mushrooms and garlic in 2 tablespoons of melted butter and set these aside also.

Heat remaining butter in skillet until foamy; add flour, stirring constantly. Slowly add the cream and sherry. When sauce has thickened, stir in Tabasco, Worcestershire, and curry powder. Add shrimp and mushrooms to sauce, and pour into prepared baking dish. Cover with grated Parmesan and bake 15 minutes. Remove from oven, garnish with parsley, and serve at once with rice.

SERVES 4

Note: Do not reheat this dish because the sauce may separate.

Shrimp Dijon

5 tablespoons butter
4 tablespoons flour
2 cups milk
salt and freshly ground pepper to taste
⅛ teaspoon cayenne
3 tablespoons minced shallots
½ cup white wine

¼ cup minced parsley
1 egg yolk
3 tablespoons Dijon-style mustard
1½ pounds large shrimp, washed,
    shelled, and deveined
½ cup freshly grated Parmesan

Preheat oven to 450 degrees.

Melt 3 tablespoons butter in a saucepan, stir in flour and cook, stirring over low heat for 5 minutes. Add milk slowly, using a wire whisk. Season with salt, pepper, and cayenne. Simmer 15 minutes, stirring occasionally. Add shallots, wine, and parsley and simmer 10 minutes more, stirring occasionally. Beat egg yolk, add 2 tablespoons of sauce to the yolk, and add to sauce, beating constantly. Remove from heat and add mustard.

Sauté shrimp in remaining butter for 4 to 5 minutes or until done. Add a third of the mustard sauce to shrimp and spoon into seafood shells or ramekins. Cover shrimp with remaining sauce, sprinkle with Parmesan, and bake for 10 to 15 minutes.

SERVES 6 AS A MAIN COURSE
OR 8 TO 10 AS A FIRST COURSE

Shrimp-stuffed Zucchini

4 6- to 8-inch zucchini
½ cup dry vermouth
2 cups chicken broth
salt and freshly ground pepper to taste
½ teaspoon thyme
1 bay leaf
1 cup mayonnaise
2 tablespoons olive oil
2 tablespoons minced parsley
2 tablespoons minced chives
2 tablespoons capers

1 tablespoon minced green onions
1 teaspoon anchovy paste
1 pound tiny shrimp
6 cooked artichoke bottoms, diced

Garnishes
4 sprigs fresh basil, chopped
16 capers
1 hard-cooked egg yolk
2 pimientos, sliced into strips

Peel zucchini; cut in half lengthwise and scoop out seeds to make boats. Place zucchini close together in skillet. Pour vermouth and broth over zucchini and add salt, pepper, thyme, and bay leaf; bring to a boil and remove from heat. Chill zucchini in broth. When ready to serve, remove zucchini from broth and drain well.

Combine mayonnaise, olive oil, parsley, chives, capers, green onions, and anchovy paste. Add shrimp and artichokes, and stir gently. Spoon into zucchini boats. Serve on individual plates and garnish.

SERVES 8

Chinese Squid

2 pounds squid
¼ cup vegetable oil
2 tablespoons minced fresh ginger
4 cloves garlic, minced
2 onions, sliced
½ pound mushrooms, sliced
1 cup celery, sliced diagonally

2 green bell peppers, sliced thin
Sauce
1½ tablespoons cornstarch
2 tablespoons soy sauce
1 tablespoon sugar
1 teaspoon white wine vinegar
½ cup beef broth

Clean squid according to following directions. Slit hoods in half lengthwise, then cut crosswise into 1-inch-wide strips. Cut each tentacle into 2 pieces. Set aside.

To prepare sauce: Combine ingredients and set aside.

Heat 2 tablespoons oil over high heat in a wok or skillet. Add ginger, garlic, and onions, and stir-fry for 1 minute. Add mushrooms, celery, and green peppers and fry for 2 minutes more. Remove vegetables from pan and set aside. Heat remaining oil in wok or skillet. Add squid and cook 1 to 2 minutes—until pieces curl. Return vegetables to pan; add sauce and cook until thickened. *Do not overcook*—overcooked squid is tough.

SERVES 6 TO 8

INSTRUCTIONS FOR CLEANING SQUID

Cleaning squid may seem intimidating, but it is really very easy. Hold the squid in one hand, grasp the head and tentacles with the other, and pull gently. The head and contents of the body should pull away together. (If the head separates, grasp the body at the pointed end and squeeze out all the contents with your thumb and fingers.) Discard the contents, and set the head and tentacles aside.

Pull out the quill-like transparent backbone and discard. Under cold running water, pull off the two flaplike fins; the spotted outer skin will peel off easily, leaving a pinkish-white cone of flesh. Rinse thoroughly again, inside and out.

Cut the tentacles from the head, just behind the eyes, and rinse thoroughly; discard the head. Keep the tentacles and the flesh in cold water until ready to use; then drain and pat dry with a paper towel (the tentacles will spatter if not dry).

Italian Squid

1 pound squid
½ cup freshly grated Parmesan cheese
½ pound ricotta cheese
½ cup minced parsley
2 cloves garlic, minced
¼ cup dry bread crumbs
1 tablespoon butter

4 green onions, chopped
2 14½-ounce cans pear-shaped
  tomatoes and liquid
1 teaspoon beef stock base
⅛ teaspoon freshly ground pepper
parsley and lemon wedges for garnish

Preheat oven to 300 degrees.

Clean squid according to preceding directions. Set bodies aside and chop tentacles. Mix Parmesan, ricotta, parsley, garlic, and bread crumbs with chopped squid and set aside. Melt butter in a medium-size skillet; add green onions and cook until soft. Add tomatoes and their liquid, stock base, and pepper. Simmer, uncovered, for 30 minutes.

Stuff squid bodies with cheese mixture, arrange in a low 1½-quart baking dish, and cover with tomato sauce. Bake, uncovered, for 20 minutes. Garnish with parsley and lemon.

SERVES 4

Crab Saint Joan

2 tablespoons butter	2 hard-cooked eggs, chopped
1 small onion, finely chopped	salt and finely ground pepper to taste
2 tablespoons flour	3 large avocados, peeled
1 cup light cream	lemon juice
¼ teaspoon nutmeg	watercress or red-leaf lettuce for
2 tablespoons minced parsley	garnish
2 cups crabmeat	

Preheat oven to 300 degrees.

Melt butter in medium skillet; add onion and sauté until transparent. Blend in flour and cook, stirring, about 5 minutes. Add cream, nutmeg, and parsley. Cook and stir sauce until smooth and thick. Add crabmeat, eggs, salt, and pepper, heat thoroughly, and keep warm over low heat.

Halve avocados, remove pits, and sprinkle with lemon juice. Place in a shallow baking dish, pour in ¼-inch warm water, and bake avocados for 10 to 15 minutes. Remove avocados from pan and fill them with hot crab mixture. Garnish with watercress or lettuce leaves and serve immediately.

SERVES 6

Crab Vermouth

½ cup butter	1½ cups chicken broth
2 tablespoons cornstarch	2 tablespoons chopped parsley
1¼ cups dry vermouth	1 tablespoon minced garlic

1 tablespoon soy sauce
1 tablespoon lemon juice

1 teaspoon sugar
2 large crabs, cracked and cleaned

Melt butter in a large kettle and add cornstarch, stirring constantly. Slowly add chicken broth and 1 cup vermouth; then add parsley, garlic, soy sauce, lemon juice, and sugar and simmer for 10 minutes. Add cracked crab (in the shells) and continue simmering until warm. Just before serving, stir in remaining vermouth.

SERVES 6

Note: Very rich and messy!

Moules Marinière

30 to 40 mussels, in shells
1 medium white or Walla Walla sweet
   onion, chopped
1 clove garlic, minced
½ cup butter

1 cup dry white wine
¼ cup parsley, chopped
salt and freshly ground pepper to taste
crusty French bread

Clean mussels thoroughly and debeard. Sauté onion and garlic in ¼ cup butter until soft. Add the wine, mussels, and parsley. Place over high heat and cook until mussels open, about 3 to 5 minutes. Remove and discard any unopened mussels. Transfer unstrained liquid to a smaller pan and reduce to half its original amount. Remove pan from heat and add remaining butter to reduced liquid. Pour this sauce over the mussels and serve immediately with French bread.

SERVES 8

Mussels Provençale

4 dozen mussels, in shells
2 cups red wine
2 cups tomato purée
1 medium onion, finely chopped
4 cloves garlic, minced
2 tablespoons basil
3 parsley sprigs

1 tablespoon lemon juice
1 teaspoon coarse salt
1 teaspoon freshly ground pepper
¼ cup butter
4 teaspoons minced parsley
½ cup freshly grated Parmesan cheese
crusty French bread

Clean mussels thoroughly, debeard, and place in a large kettle with all ingredients except butter, parsley, cheese, and bread. Bring to a boil; cover and simmer until mussels open. Remove mussels with a slotted spoon, discarding any unopened ones. Reduce the liquid to half its original amount; add butter. Arrange mussels in warm soup plates and pour liquid over them. Garnish with parsley and cheese and serve with French bread.

SERVES 8

Oysters Rockefeller

6 slices bacon
1 10-ounce package frozen chopped
*   spinach*
4 green onions, green part only,
*   minced*
½ cup minced parsley
¼ cup minced celery leaves
½ cup butter, softened

1 to 2 teaspoons lemon juice to taste
salt and freshly ground black pepper
*   to taste*
¼ teaspoon Tabasco sauce
rock salt
2 dozen oysters and 2 dozen shells
¼ cup bread crumbs
¼ cup Parmesan cheese

Preheat oven to 450 degrees.

Fry bacon; drain and crumble. Cook spinach according to package instructions, drain, and squeeze dry. Combine onions, parsley, and celery leaves with bacon; add to softened butter. Add lemon juice, salt, pepper, and Tabasco and mix well. Fill broiler trays with rock salt and bake until hot. Place oyster shells on salt, add oysters, and cover with spinach sauce. Sprinkle with bread crumbs and Parmesan, place in oven, and cook until oysters curl at the edges.

SERVES 4 TO 6

Portuguese Clams

3 tablespoons olive oil
½ cup chopped onions
2 large cloves garlic, minced
3 tablespoons bread crumbs
1 to 1½ cups peeled, finely chopped
*   tomatoes*

3 hard-cooked eggs, whites and yolks
*   chopped separately*
3 to 4 dozen small clams, in shells
2 cups white wine
salt to taste
chopped parsley for garnish

Heat oil in a large skillet; add onions and garlic. Sauté, stirring, for 5 minutes. Add crumbs, tomatoes, and egg yolks. Cook about 20 minutes, or until thick. Set aside.

Wash and scrub clams; steam in white wine until the shells open. Place clams, still in their shells, in a heated shallow bowl, discarding any clams that have not opened. Add 1 cup of the clam–wine nectar to the tomato mixture and bring to a boil. Salt to taste and pour over clams. Garnish with the chopped egg whites and parsley.

SERVES 6

Italian Clam Stew

3 dozen small clams, in shells
¼ cup olive oil
3 cloves garlic
4 anchovy fillets, chopped
2 tablespoons minced parsley
1 cup dry red wine

¼ cup tomato paste
3 cups water
½ teaspoon salt
½ teaspoon freshly ground pepper
1 teaspoon oregano
4 1-inch slices from baguette of French bread, fried in additional olive oil

Wash and scrub clams. Heat oil in a large saucepan, add garlic, and brown. Discard garlic, add anchovies, parsley, and wine, and simmer 5 minutes. Add tomato paste, water, salt, and pepper, and cook 5 minutes more. Add clams, cover, and cook until shells open. Add oregano and cook 2 minutes longer.

Place a slice of French bread in each dish and pour stew over bread.

SERVES 4

Cioppino

2 onions, chopped into medium-size pieces
4 cloves garlic, finely minced
¼ cup minced parsley
½ cup diced celery
2 green bell peppers, seeded and cut into rings
¼ cup olive oil
1 cup butter
2 tablespoons sugar
1 8-ounce can tomato sauce
2 6-ounce cans tomato paste
2 28-ounce cans tomatoes and liquid, puréed in blender or food processor
¼ teaspoon allspice

¼ teaspoon rosemary
¼ teaspoon oregano
¼ teaspoon thyme
¼ teaspoon basil
6 peppercorns
pinch cayenne
1 bay leaf
1 cup red wine
1 lemon, sliced thin
1 cup clam broth
2 pounds cracked crab
2 pounds prawns, washed, shelled, and deveined
2 pounds clams, in shells
1 to 2 pounds white fleshy fish such as halibut or cod

In a large soup kettle, sauté onions, garlic, parsley, celery, and green bell peppers in oil and butter until golden brown. Add sugar, tomato sauce, tomato paste, tomatoes, spices, and herbs. Bring to a boil, reduce heat, and simmer 15 minutes. Add wine and cook slowly for 1 hour. The dish may be prepared ahead to this point and set aside.

Bring sauce to a boil; add lemon, clam broth, and seafood. Simmer for 20 minutes or until clams open. Serve in large bowls.

SERVES 12

Variation: Scallops and mussels may be substituted for part of the seafood above. *Do not omit the white fish.*

Paella

2 dozen small clams	1 green bell pepper, seeded and
1 quart mussels, debearded	chopped
1 teaspoon oregano	½ teaspoon ground coriander
2 peppercorns, crushed	1 teaspoon capers, chopped
1 clove garlic, minced	3 tablespoons tomato sauce
1½ teaspoons salt	2¼ cups rice, washed and drained
6 tablespoons olive oil	4½ cups clam liquid and water, boiling
1 teaspoon vinegar	1 teaspoon saffron
1½ pounds chicken parts	1 pound prawns, washed, shelled, and
2 ounces ham, cut in strips	deveined
1 chorizo, sliced	1 10-ounce package frozen peas
1 ounce salt pork, finely chopped	1 10-ounce package frozen artichoke
1 onion, chopped	hearts
	1 2½-ounce can pimientos

Scrub clams and mussels, and steam in ½ inch of water, discarding any that do not open. Set clams and mussels, still in their shells, aside in their liquid. Combine oregano, peppercorns, garlic, salt, 2 tablespoons of olive oil, and vinegar and rub chicken parts with the mixture.

Heat remaining olive oil over medium-high heat in a deep, heavy skillet and brown chicken. Reduce heat to medium and add ham, chorizo, salt pork, onion, green pepper, coriander, and capers. Cook 10 minutes more. Add tomato sauce, rice, boiling liquid, saffron, and prawns. Mix well, cover, and cook rapidly until liquid is absorbed— about 45 minutes.

Add peas, artichokes, and pimientos. Arrange clams and mussels on top; cover and cook 5 minutes more before serving.

SERVES 12

Seafood Ramekins

1 cup bread crumbs
1 cup crabmeat
1 cup tiny shrimp
3 or 4 green onions, chopped

1 cup chopped celery
1 cup mayonnaise
1 tablespoon Worcestershire sauce
½ cup chopped parsley.

Preheat oven to 350 degrees.

Reserve ¼ cup crumbs for topping; lightly toss together remaining ingredients. Spoon into seafood shells or ramekins and sprinkle reserved crumbs on top. Bake for 30 minutes.

SERVES 6

Seafood Strudel

2 tablespoons unsalted butter
2 tablespoons flour
½ teaspoon Dijon-style mustard
¼ teaspoon salt
dash cayenne
¾ cup milk, at room temperature
2 tablespoons heavy cream
½ pound phyllo sheets
¾ cup unsalted butter, melted
6 tablespoons freshly grated Parmesan
    cheese
¼ teaspoon dry mustard

1 pound cooked crabmeat, shrimp,
    lobster, halibut or a combination
    of all, in bite-size chunks
½ cup grated Swiss cheese
2 hard-cooked eggs, chopped
¾ cup sour cream
¼ cup chopped shallots
2 tablespoons minced chives
1 large clove garlic, minced
6 tablespoons minced parsley
minced parsley for garnish
crab claws for garnish (optional)

Melt 2 tablespoons butter in a small saucepan over medium heat. Stir in flour and cook, stirring constantly, until mixture begins to bubble. Add mustard, salt, cayenne, and milk; cook, stirring continually, until mixture bubbles and thickens. Add cream and adjust seasonings if necessary. Cover, and chill until very thick and firm—about 2 hours.

Brush each phyllo sheet with melted butter (keep sheets you are not working with soft by placing them under waxed paper covered by a damp dishtowel). Stack 1 on top of the other, until ready to roll up.

Preheat oven to 375 degrees and butter a baking sheet.

Combine ¼ cup Parmesan and dry mustard in a small bowl, then sprinkle mixture on prepared phyllo. Spread seafood evenly on phyllo and sprinkle with Swiss cheese and chopped eggs; dot with sour cream. Sprinkle with shallots, chives, garlic, and ¼ cup parsley; dot with chilled sauce. Roll up sheets lengthwise, place on prepared baking sheet, and brush with some of the melted butter. Slice diagonally with serrated knife into 1½-inch pieces and push slices together to re-shape roll. Add remaining parsley to remaining butter and brush strudel again. Brush 3 more times during baking, reserving a little butter to brush on just before serving. Bake 35 to 40 minutes, until crisp and golden brown. Garnish with crab claws and serve.

SERVES 8

Court Bouillon

This is a flavored liquid in which fish or shellfish can be completely immersed and poached.

¾ cup diced celery
½ cup diced carrots
½ cup chopped onion
1 cup white wine
½ cup minced parsley
1 tablespoon chopped fresh thyme or
    1 teaspoon dried thyme

1 bay leaf
1 tablespoon salt
3 pounds fish trimmings (head, bones,
    tails, and fins), tied in a cheese-
    cloth bag
8 whole peppercorns
3 quarts cold water

Combine all ingredients in stock pot; cover and bring to a boil. Reduce heat and simmer for 30 minutes. Skim and cool. Remove fish trimmings and strain the bouillon through a double thickness of cheese-cloth.

YIELD: APPROXIMATELY 3 QUARTS

Fumet de Poisson

3 tablespoons oil
⅓ cup chopped onions
⅓ cup sliced carrots
⅓ cup sliced celery
4 cups white wine
4 cups water
2 pounds fish trimmings (heads,
    bones, tails, and fins)

dash of fennel
4 parsley sprigs, stems removed
1 bay leaf
1 teaspoon salt
½ teaspoon freshly ground pepper
lemon juice

Heat oil in a large stockpot and sauté vegetables until barely brown. Add wine, water, and fish trimmings. Bring to a boil, add remaining ingredients, and simmer uncovered for 2 hours. Skim, then strain through double thickness of cheesecloth.

YIELD: 2 QUARTS

Note: Broth may be refrigerated or frozen. If refrigerated, boil every 2 days to keep from spoiling. This concentrated, gelatinous *fumet* can be used as the basic liquid in making sauces to be served with fish.

Hot Caper Sauce

This goes well with salmon or other highly flavored fish.

4 egg yolks
juice of 1 lemon
2 cups butter, melted
salt and white pepper to taste

2 tablespoons chopped capers
¼ cup minced parsley
1 tablespoon white wine vinegar

In a heavy pan, beat together egg yolks and juice over low heat; cook slowly for 2 minutes. Add melted butter to egg yolks, stirring constantly with a whisk, and continue to cook another 1 to 2 minutes. Add remaining ingredients and serve.

YIELD: 2½ CUPS

Brown Butter Sauce

This sauce is especially good with salmon.

½ cup butter
2 tablespoons minced parsley

1 tablespoon chopped capers
1 teaspoon vinegar

Over high heat, melt butter in a saucepan and cook until it begins to brown. Add parsley, capers, and vinegar and continue cooking until sauce turns dark brown. Serve immediately.

YIELD: ½ CUP

Watercress-Dill Sauce

Serve with salmon or white fish.

½ cup watercress leaves
¼ cup chopped fresh dill or
   1 tablespoon dried dill
¼ cup chopped green onions
2 cloves garlic, minced
4 anchovy fillets

1 cup mayonnaise
1 tablespoon brandy
juice of ½ lemon
½ cup sour cream
salt and freshly ground pepper to taste

In blender or food processor combine all ingredients and process until smooth. Chill.

YIELD: 2½ CUPS

Green Sauce

Serve with salmon.

¾ cup fresh spinach
2 tablespoons fresh chives
¼ cup minced parsley

1 cup mayonnaise
2 tablespoons tarragon wine vinegar

In blender or food processor, combine all ingredients and process until smooth. Chill.

YIELD: 2 CUPS

Avocado Mayonnaise

Serve with salmon or other barbecued fish.

½ cup mashed avocado
¼ cup lemon juice
2 tablespoons minced parsley

1 teaspoon Worcestershire sauce
1 small clove garlic, minced
1 cup mayonnaise

Combine avocado, lemon juice, parsley, Worcestershire, and garlic. Gently fold in mayonnaise. Chill.

YIELD: 1½ CUPS

White Butter

Serve with salmon or white fish.

¼ cup white wine vinegar	6 finely minced shallots
¼ cup dry white wine	salt and white pepper to taste
2 tablespoons minced parsley	1 cup unsalted butter, softened

In a saucepan, combine all ingredients except butter and simmer until liquid is reduced almost completely. Over low heat, beat in butter, about 2 tablespoons at a time, whisking constantly; never allow the butter to melt. The mixture will be fluffy and almost white when ready.

YIELD: 1½ CUPS

The Skykomish, a great white-water river, flows near the town of Index in the Cascade foothills northeast of Seattle. Snow still remains on the peaks of Mount Index in early summer.

Poultry

:==:

Roast Cornish Game Hens

6 Cornish game hens, about
   1½ pounds each
1½ teaspoons salt
¾ teaspoon pepper
7 tablespoons tarragon

6 cloves garlic
garlic salt
¾ cup butter
¾ cup dry white wine
2 tablespoons flour
1 cup cold water

Preheat oven to 450 degrees.

Wash hens under cold running water; drain and pat dry. Sprinkle ¼ teaspoon salt, ⅛ teaspoon pepper, and 1 tablespoon tarragon inside of each hen. Place 1 clove of garlic inside each and liberally sprinkle outside of each with garlic salt. Truss if desired and set aside.

Make a basting sauce by melting butter in saucepan and stirring in wine and remaining tablespoon tarragon. Place hens in a shallow roasting pan without a rack. Roast 1 hour, or until hens are brown and tender, basting often with basting sauce. Place hens on platter and keep warm. Reserve pan drippings.

For gravy, whisk together flour and water and stir into drippings in pan. Bring to a boil, stirring until thickened. Pass separately.

SERVES 6

Variation: Chicken breasts also may be prepared in this manner.

Game Hen Dijon

2 tablespoons butter
1 tablespoon Dijon-style mustard
½ teaspoon salt
½ teaspoon pepper
2 Cornish game hens, about
    1½ pounds each
zest of ½ lemon

1 teaspoon Dijon-style mustard
½ cup Béchamel Sauce (page 135)
¼ teaspoon salt
1 cup light cream
1 teaspoon butter
4 bread rounds, 3 inches in diameter
1 tablespoon butter

Preheat oven to 450 degrees. Grease a roasting pan.

Combine first 4 ingredients and mix to a smooth paste. Spread paste over breasts, legs, and wings of hens. Put hens in prepared pan and roast 1 hour, basting occasionally with pan juices. When hens are cooked, cut in half, arrange in a shallow pan, and keep warm. Save pan drippings.

Mince lemon zest. Cover with water, bring to a boil, and simmer for 10 minutes and drain.

To drippings in roasting pan, add 1 teaspoon mustard and cook over low heat, stirring thoroughly. Add Béchamel Sauce and ¼ teaspoon salt. Stir in cream, bring sauce just to a boil, and correct seasonings. Add the blanched lemon zest and 1 teaspoon butter.

Sauté both sides of bread rounds in 1 tablespoon butter until golden brown, drain on crumpled paper towels, and arrange on serving platter. Place game hens in sauce, turning to coat and heat through, then transfer to rounds and spoon on additional sauce.

SERVES 2 TO 4

Coq au Vin

3 chickens, about 3 pounds each, cut
    into parts
½ cup butter
¼ cup brandy
3¼ cups dry red wine
1 tablespoon salt
¼ teaspoon nutmeg
½ teaspoon rosemary
1 bay leaf
1 tablespoon powdered chicken stock
    base (powdered seasoning for
    dissolving in water)

3 cloves garlic, minced
1¼ pounds fresh button mushrooms
1½ tablespoons lemon juice
4 slices extra-thick bacon
1 pound small onions, simmered until
    tender and thoroughly drained
2 teaspoons sugar
⅓ cup cornstarch
⅓ cup water
1 7-ounce jar green pimiento-stuffed
    olives, drained

Brown chicken pieces, a few at a time, in ¼ cup butter, turning to brown on all sides. Warm brandy slightly; ignite 1 tablespoon and pour, flaming, over the chicken. Pour on remaining brandy and let flame on chicken. Pour in wine and loosen the browned drippings. Transfer chicken and liquid to a large casserole with a lid and add salt, nutmeg, rosemary, bay leaf, stock base, and garlic. Cover and simmer gently for 45 minutes or until chicken is barely tender. Remove from heat.

Break off mushroom stems, slice, and sauté with caps in remaining butter and lemon juice for a few minutes. Transfer mushrooms and juices to the chicken.

Preheat oven to 350 degrees.

Chop the bacon fine, sauté until crisp, remove from pan, and drain. Pour off all but 2 tablespoons of bacon drippings, add onions to the pan, and sprinkle with sugar. Heat onions, stirring gently until lightly browned, and add to the chicken.

Blend cornstarch with water to make a paste. Drain the wine and juice from the chicken into a saucepan and heat to boiling; stir in cornstarch paste and cook until thickened, stirring constantly. Pour over the chicken, add olives, and sprinkle with crumbled bacon. (At this point, chicken may be cooled and refrigerated for finishing later.) Cover and bake for 30 minutes, or, if chicken was refrigerated, bake 1 hour and 15 minutes.

SERVES 8 TO 10

Stuffed Chicken Legs with Tomato-Zucchini Sauce

Tomato–Zucchini Sauce

¼ pound zucchini (1 small zucchini)
pinch of salt
2 tablespoons unsalted butter
¼ cup minced fresh basil
1 small clove garlic, minced
1½ tablespoons minced shallot
juice of 1 large lemon
⅓ cup olive oil
2 large tomatoes (⅔ pound), peeled,
    seeded, and coarsely chopped
salt and freshly ground pepper to taste

Basil Stuffing

3 tablespoons olive oil
1½ tablespoons minced shallot
3 tablespoons fine bread crumbs
½ cup whole-milk ricotta cheese
½ cup freshly grated imported Bel
    Paese cheese (about 2 ounces)
¼ cup plus 2 tablespoons freshly
    grated Parmesan cheese
1 egg yolk
1 small clove garlic, minced
2½ tablespoons minced fresh basil

1½ tablespoons unsalted butter at
    room temperature
salt and freshly ground pepper to taste

Chicken

*4 large chicken legs (drumsticks with
    thighs attached), skin intact*
white paper frills for garnish (optional)
4 sprigs basil for garnish

To prepare sauce: Grate zucchini, sprinkle lightly with salt and let drain in colander 30 minutes. Rinse and squeeze dry. Melt butter in a small heavy skillet over medium-high heat. Add zucchini and stir until cooked, about 3 minutes. Transfer to bowl and stir in basil, garlic, shallot, and lemon juice. Whisk in olive oil, a drop at a time, mix in tomatoes, and add salt and pepper to taste. Set aside.

To prepare stuffing: Heat olive oil in a small skillet over medium heat. Add shallots and stir until translucent, about 3 minutes. Mix in bread crumbs, remove from heat, and cool to room temperature. Using fork, mix in ricotta, Bel Paese, Parmesan, egg yolk, garlic, basil, butter, salt, and pepper. Set aside.

To prepare chicken: Preheat oven to 325 degrees. Generously butter large gratin or other shallow baking pan.

Pat chicken legs dry. Gently loosen skin from legs with fingers (being careful not to pierce skin) as far down legs as possible. Spread a layer of stuffing under loosened skin. Transfer chicken to prepared pan. Bake, basting occasionally, until juices run yellow when chicken is pierced with a fork—about 40 to 45 minutes. Transfer to serving platter and keep warm.

After discarding all fat from pan, pour in sauce, place over medium heat, and bring to a boil. Boil 2 minutes, scraping up any browned bits clinging to bottom of pan, and pour sauce over chicken. Arrange white paper frills on legs, if desired, garnish chicken with basil, and serve.

SERVES 2 TO 4

Variation: Basil stuffing may also be used with roast chicken. To prepare, sauté minced liver with shallot and after adding basil, stir in 1 small tomato, peeled, seeded, and chopped.

Crab-Stuffed Chicken Breasts

3 large whole chicken breasts, halved,
    boned, and skinned
salt and pepper to taste
½ cup chopped onion
½ cup chopped celery
3 tablespoons butter
5 tablespoons white wine

1 cup flaked crabmeat
½ cup cubed herb-seasoned stuffing
2 tablespoons flour
½ teaspoon paprika
6 tablespoons butter, melted
¾ cup Hollandaise Sauce (page 128)

Preheat oven to 375 degrees.

Pound chicken breasts to flatten; sprinkle with salt and pepper. Sauté onion and celery in 3 tablespoons butter until tender. Remove from heat and add 3 tablespoons wine, crabmeat, and stuffing. Toss to blend. Divide mixture among chicken breasts (about 2 tablespoons each); roll up and secure with toothpicks.

Combine flour and paprika and coat chicken. Place chicken in a baking dish, drizzle with melted butter, and bake uncovered for 45 minutes. Transfer to a platter and keep warm. Add remaining wine to Hollandaise Sauce and spoon over chicken. Serve at once.

SERVES 6

Kalaloch Crab Chicken

Chicken
3 large whole chicken breasts, halved,
    boned, and skinned
6 tablespoons butter
6 large Dungeness crab legs, shelled
salt and pepper to taste
garlic powder to taste
vegetable oil for deep-frying
1 cup Allemande Sauce

Allemande Sauce
3 tablespoons butter
2 tablespoons flour
2¼ cups chicken broth
pinch of nutmeg
salt and pepper to taste
1 egg yolk
2 tablespoons heavy cream
1 tablespoon lemon juice

To prepare chicken: Pound the chicken breasts to flatten. In the center of each breast place 1 tablespoon butter, meat from 1 crab leg, salt, pepper, and garlic powder. Roll up breasts and secure with toothpicks.

Preheat oil in a wok, deep skillet, or deep fryer to medium-high and deep-fry the rolled breasts 7 to 10 minutes, or until brown and firm. Serve with Allemande Sauce.

SERVES 4 TO 6

To prepare sauce: Melt 2 tablespoons butter in saucepan. Stir in flour to make a smooth paste and cook slowly 2 to 3 minutes. Gradually add 1½ cups broth and stir over low heat until thickened. Add nutmeg, salt, and pepper, stir in remaining broth, blending well, and cook over medium heat until reduced to 1¾ cups. Remove from heat.

Beat egg yolk with cream and add 2 tablespoons sauce. Add egg mixture to remaining sauce, return to low heat, and stir until slightly thickened. Just before serving, stir in juice and remaining butter.

YIELD: 2½ CUPS

Sesame Chicken

Chicken

6 tablespoons flour
½ teaspoon salt
¼ teaspoon freshly ground pepper
2 large whole chicken breasts, halved
    and boned
2 eggs
¼ cup milk
3 tablespoons sesame seeds
vegetable oil for deep-frying

1 cup Caledonia Sauce

Caledonia Sauce
3 tablespoons butter
2 tablespoons flour
2½ cups strained chicken broth
pinch of nutmeg
salt and pepper to taste
½ cup heavy cream

To prepare chicken: Combine 2 tablespoons flour, salt, and pepper in a clean paper or plastic bag. Add chicken and shake bag so chicken will be coated. Beat eggs with milk and mix remaining flour with sesame seeds. Dip each chicken piece into egg mixture, then roll in sesame-seed mixture.

In a deep skillet, heat oil to medium high.

Deep-fry chicken for 15 minutes, or until golden and tender. Drain on crumpled paper towels and serve with Caledonia Sauce.

SERVES 4

To prepare sauce: Melt 2 tablespoons butter in saucepan. Stir in flour to make a smooth paste and cook slowly 2 to 3 minutes. Gradually add 1½ cups chicken broth, stirring over low heat until thickened. Add nutmeg, salt, and pepper. Add remaining cup of broth, bring to a boil, reduce heat, and simmer, stirring frequently, until sauce is reduced to 1½ cups. Stir in remaining cream and butter.

YIELD: 2 CUPS

Note: Be sure to strain the chicken broth, as this sauce should be very white and delicate.

Chicken in Phyllo

Chicken
¼ cup butter
3 large whole chicken breasts, halved,
    boned, and skinned
salt and pepper to taste
6 sheets phyllo
½ cup butter, melted
¼ cup fine bread crumbs
18 large spinach leaves

3 medium carrots, cut in julienne
    strips
1 cup Mustard Sauce
parsley or spinach leaves for garnish
carrot curls for garnish

Mustard Sauce
¼ cup Dijon-style mustard
1 cup light cream

Preheat oven to 400 degrees. Oil a baking sheet.

To prepare chicken: Melt butter in skillet and sauté chicken breasts quickly (about 3 minutes on each side) until just firm. Sprinkle with salt and pepper and set aside, leaving pan juices in the skillet.

Steam carrot strips briefly, until tender but still crisp. Cool. Brush a sheet of phyllo with melted butter, fold in half, brush again, and sprinkle with bread crumbs. Lay 3 spinach leaves at one end. Place a piece of chicken on spinach and top with a few carrot strips. Fold phyllo sides inward, roll up phyllo, and place seam side down on prepared baking sheet. Brush with butter. Repeat procedure for remaining phyllo and bake about 15 minutes or until lightly browned.

To prepare sauce: Stir mustard into skillet with pan juices. Whisk in cream, blending thoroughly. Simmer until sauce is slightly thickened and reduce to 1 cup.

Arrange chicken on serving platter and garnish with parsley or spinach leaves and carrot curls. Pass sauce separately.

SERVES 6

Chicken Breasts Florentine

2 large whole chicken breasts, halved,
    boned, and skinned
salt and pepper
pinch of nutmeg
½ pound spinach, chopped, lightly
    steamed, and drained
4 thin slices boiled ham
4 thin slices Swiss cheese
2 eggs

1½ tablespoons heavy cream
1 tablespoon chopped parsley
⅓ cup freshly grated Parmesan cheese
⅓ cup flour
½ cup vegetable oil
½ cup butter
½ cup dry vermouth or white wine
½ cup chicken broth
juice of ½ lemon

Pound chicken breasts very thin with a wooden mallet and sprinkle with salt, pepper, and nutmeg. Divide spinach into 4 equal portions, and place a portion on the center of each chicken breast. Place a slice of ham and cheese on top of the spinach; fold sides of breast inward, completely covering the ingredients, sealing edges with a meat mallet.

Beat eggs in a mixing bowl; add cream, parsley, and Parmesan. Dust each breast with flour and dip in egg mixture, coating well.

Heat oil in a heavy skillet until very hot and sauté breasts, 1 at a time, until crisp and golden. Transfer to a warm platter.

Melt butter in the skillet and add wine, cooking until it evaporates—5 or 6 minutes. Add broth and cook 5 more minutes. Add lemon juice, cook 3 minutes, pour over the breasts, and serve.

SERVES 4

Soyu Chicken

¾ cup soy sauce
½ cup water
½ cup sugar
4 pieces star anise

2 tablespoons sesame oil
6 green onions
3 to 4 pounds chicken thighs or breasts

Combine all ingredients except chicken in a large pot and bring to a boil. Wash chicken and place in the sauce. Cover pot and return to boiling; lower heat and simmer 20 to 30 minutes or until chicken pieces are tender.

SERVES 6

Note: To use leftovers, store the sauce and chicken separately. When reheating, heat sauce first; then put chicken in.

Chinese Smoked Chicken

1 3- to 4-pound whole chicken or chicken parts, washed and patted dry

Marinade

1 green onion, chopped
6 tablespoons soy sauce

2 tablespoons hoisin sauce
2 tablespoons dry white wine
1 teaspoon brown sugar
1 teaspoon minced ginger
1 teaspoon salt
1 teaspoon liquid smoke

To prepare marinade: Combine ingredients and mix well. Add chicken and marinate several hours or overnight.

Preheat oven to 400 degrees.

Roast chicken on a rack for about 1 hour, basting often. Cover with foil for the last 15 minutes to prevent skin from turning dark. Cool slightly and serve.

SERVES 4

Chicken and Artichoke Hearts

Chicken

1½ cups chicken broth
4 large whole chicken breasts
1 8½-ounce can artichoke hearts
   (not marinated) drained
2 tablespoons butter
1 pound mushrooms, sliced

Sauce

¼ cup butter
¼ cup flour
¼ teaspoon salt

dash white pepper
¾ cup light cream
2 tablespoons sherry
½ cup freshly grated Parmesan cheese

Topping

½ cup bread crumbs
1 tablespoon butter
2 teaspoons minced parsley
2 tablespoons minced green onion tops
½ teaspoon chervil

To prepare chicken: In a frying pan, bring chicken broth to a simmer and add chicken breasts in single layer. Cover and poach until tender—about 20 minutes. Lift from broth and cool, reserving ¾ cup broth for sauce. Carefully remove skin and bones and place chicken in shallow baking dish. Cut artichoke hearts in half and arrange over breasts in a frying pan.

Over medium heat, melt butter in a frying pan and sauté mushrooms lightly. Drain and spoon over chicken. (At this point the dish may be covered and refrigerated.)

To prepare sauce: Melt butter and add flour, salt, and pepper, stirring for about 3 minutes or until smoothly blended. Gradually add reserved chicken broth and cream, stirring until thickened. Stir in sherry and Parmesan until cheese is melted and mixture blended. (Cover and refrigerate if preparing to use later.)

Preheat oven to 325 degrees.

To prepare topping: Sauté bread crumbs lightly in butter. Stir in parsley, green onion tops, and chervil.

If necessary, warm sauce over low heat until it liquifies. Pour over chicken and sprinkle topping on. Bake chicken uncovered for 30 minutes. Do not overcook or sauce will separate.

SERVES 6 TO 8

Java Chicken Curry

5 medium onions
5 small dried hot red chili peppers,
 seeds removed
1 tablespoon chopped ginger
10 cloves garlic
1½ teaspoons salt
½ teaspoon turmeric
1 3- to 4-pound chicken or chicken
 parts

¼ cup vegetable oil
1 16-ounce can whole tomatoes and
 liquid
⅓ cup water
1 tablespoon soy sauce
1 teaspoon grated lemon zest
1 tablespoon curry powder
1 to 2 tablespoons brown sugar

Slice 3 onions and set aside. Cut remaining 2 onions in chunks. In a food processor, using metal blade, process the 2 onions, chili peppers, ginger, and garlic until puréed.

Mix together salt and turmeric and rub into chicken. Heat oil in a large frying pan over medium-high heat, add chicken, and cook, turning once, until browned (about 10 minutes). Remove chicken and add sliced onion and puréed onion mixture to pan. Cook, stirring occasionally, until sliced onion is very limp.

Process tomatoes and their liquid until smooth; add to onions along with water, soy sauce, lemon zest, curry powder, and brown sugar. Return chicken to pan, cover, and simmer for 45 minutes.

With slotted spoon, remove chicken pieces to serving platter and keep warm. Boil sauce, uncovered, stirring constantly, until reduced to about 3 cups. Skim off fat and spoon sauce over chicken.

SERVES 4 TO 6

Chicken T

3 whole chicken breasts
1 teaspoon salt
1 onion
7 cloves
5 peppercorns
5 stalks celery
3 sprigs parsley
6 medium tamales
1 4-ounce can green chilis, seeded and
 cut into strips

1 cup tomato sauce
1 cup ripe olives, pitted and sliced
½ cup seedless raisins
2 teaspoons chili powder
1 cup beef broth
3 ounces dry sherry
1 cup grated sharp Cheddar cheese
½ cup freshly grated Parmesan cheese

Preheat oven to 350 degrees. Butter a 9-x-13-inch glass pan.

Combine chicken, salt, onion, cloves, peppercorns, celery, and parsley in pan. Cover with cold water and bring to a boil. Allow to simmer about 1 hour or until tender. Cool in broth, then bone the chicken.

Cut tamales into ¾-inch-thick slices and line prepared pan with half of them. Cover with thick slices of boned chicken and add chili strips and remaining tamales.

Combine tomato sauce, olives, raisins, chili powder, broth, and sherry and pour over contents of pan. Sprinkle with Cheddar and Parmesan, and bake uncovered for 1 hour.

SERVES 6

Chicken Cacciatore

¼ cup olive oil
2 ounces salt pork
¼ cup butter
½ pound onions, peeled and diced
2 whole chickens (2¼ pounds each), quartered
2 chicken livers, finely chopped
2 chicken gizzards, finely chopped
2 cloves garlic, minced

1½ teaspoons rosemary, crushed
¼ cup chopped parsley
½ teaspoon salt
¼ teaspoon freshly ground pepper
2 cups canned tomatoes
1 6-ounce can tomato paste
1 cup sherry
¼ pound mushrooms, sliced

In a large pot heat oil, salt pork, and butter. Add onions and brown slowly. Add chicken, livers, and gizzards and sauté until browned— about 10 minutes. Add garlic, rosemary, parsley, salt, and pepper; stir well and cook 5 minutes. Add tomatoes, tomato paste, sherry, and mushrooms, cover, and cook slowly for 45 minutes. Correct seasoning and skim if necessary.

SERVES 8

Country Captain Chicken

⅓ cup flour
1 teaspoon salt
¼ teaspoon pepper
3 to 4 pounds chicken pieces
¼ cup butter
½ cup chopped onion
½ cup chopped green bell pepper

2 cloves garlic, minced
2 teaspoons curry powder
1 teaspoon thyme
1 28-ounce can stewed tomatoes
½ cup raisins
½ cup toasted sliced almonds (optional)

Combine flour, salt, and pepper in a bag; add chicken and shake well to coat chicken. Melt butter in a large skillet; brown chicken and remove from skillet. Add onion, green pepper, garlic, curry, and thyme and sauté until tender. Add tomatoes, breaking them up with a fork. Simmer uncovered for 10 minutes.

Return chicken to skillet and simmer, covered, over medium-low heat for 40 minutes or until chicken is tender. Add raisins and cook 5 minutes longer. Garnish with almonds.

SERVES 4

Note: Flavor improves if chicken is cooked a day ahead. Reserve raisins and almonds, reheat chicken, and add almonds and raisins for the final 5 minutes of reheating.

Chutney Chicken

8 chicken breasts
salt and pepper to taste
1½ cups orange juice
½ cup raisins
½ cup chutney
½ teaspoon thyme
2 teaspoons cinnamon
½ teaspoon curry powder
½ cup toasted slivered almonds

Preheat oven to 350 degrees.

Arrange chicken in 9-x-13-inch baking dish and sprinkle with salt and pepper. Combine orange juice, raisins, chutney, thyme, cinnamon, and curry, pour over chicken, and bake for 1 hour, basting occasionally. Add toasted almonds and serve with rice.

SERVES 6 TO 8

Orange Chicken

½ cup butter
2 2- to 3-pound chickens or chicken parts
2 teaspoons salt
½ teaspoon pepper
2 teaspoons paprika
3 large onions, sliced
1 12-ounce can frozen orange juice concentrate
½ cup honey
¼ cup lemon juice
2 teaspoons ground ginger
1 teaspoon nutmeg
1 cup whole olives, pitted
1 large can mandarin oranges or 1 cup seedless orange sections

Preheat oven to 350 degrees.

Melt butter in heavy skillet, add chicken, and brown on all sides. Sprinkle with salt, pepper, and paprika. Transfer chicken to a heavy casserole and keep warm. Separate onions into rings and sauté in same skillet until tender. Arrange over chicken.

Combine orange juice concentrate, honey, lemon juice, ginger, and nutmeg. Pour into skillet and bring to a boil, stirring constantly. Stir in olives and pour over chicken. Bake, covered, for 1 hour. Garnish with orange sections and serve immediately.

SERVES 8

Liz's Chicken

½ cup butter, melted
½ cup honey
¼ cup prepared mustard

1 teaspoon curry powder
salt and pepper to taste
3½ pounds chicken parts

Preheat oven to 350 degrees. Grease a 9-x-13-inch baking dish.

Combine butter, honey, mustard, curry powder, salt, and pepper. Place chicken in baking dish, pour honey mixture over chicken, and bake uncovered for 40 minutes.

SERVES 6

Parmesan Chicken

1 cup very dry bread crumbs
⅔ cup dry grated Parmesan cheese
  (this is a case where freshly grated
  cheese won't work)
1 teaspoon salt
¼ teaspoon pepper

¼ teaspoon minced parsley
⅛ teaspoon garlic powder
⅛ teaspoon paprika
4 whole chicken breasts, halved
½ cup butter, melted
juice of ½ lemon

Combine bread crumbs, Parmesan, salt, pepper, parsley, garlic powder, and paprika. Dip chicken in melted butter, then in crumb mixture. Sprinkle with lemon juice and refrigerate for ½ hour.

Preheat oven to 350 degrees.

Bake chicken in a shallow pan or on a rimmed cookie sheet for 45 minutes to 1 hour.

SERVES 6 TO 8

Tandoori Chicken

2 cups plain yogurt
1 onion, chopped
2 cloves garlic, minced
2 teaspoons grated fresh ginger
1 tablespoon coriander
1 teaspoon cumin seed
1 teaspoon turmeric
¼ teaspoon cinnamon

¼ teaspoon ground cloves
¼ teaspoon nutmeg
¼ teaspoon mace
¼ teaspoon cardamom
3 tablespoons lemon juice
salt to taste
cayenne to taste
2 2- to 3-pound chickens, halved

Thoroughly combine everything but the chicken. Pour sauce over chickens and marinate uncovered at least 3 hours at room temperature or covered all day in the refrigerator. Cook over a medium-hot charcoal fire for 45 minutes or until done. Baste and turn often.

SERVES 4

Italian Stir-fried Chicken

3 tablespoons olive oil
1 clove garlic, minced
2 large whole chicken breasts,
    skinned, boned, and cubed
1 cup green beans (preferably Italian
    green beans), cut into 1-inch
    diagonal pieces
½ cup chopped green bell peppers

¼ cup chopped green onions, white
    part only
½ teaspoon salt
4 medium tomatoes, quartered
4 anchovies, mashed
2 tablespoons pimiento, diced
1 tablespoon capers
2 tablespoons lemon juice
½ teaspoon cayenne

Place wok or skillet over high heat until very hot. Add oil and garlic; stir-fry about 30 seconds. Add chicken, beans, green pepper, onions, and salt and continue stirring until chicken is cooked through—about 3 minutes. Add tomatoes, anchovies, pimiento, capers, and lemon juice and stir-fry 1 minute more. Turn onto a warm platter, sprinkle with cayenne and serve.

SERVES 4

Sesame-Seed Chicken

2 cups firmly packed brown sugar
1 cup soy sauce
2 cloves garlic, minced
2 teaspoons sesame oil

1 3- to 4-pound chicken or chicken
    parts
¼ cup toasted sesame seeds
1 pound snow peas, blanched

Combine brown sugar, soy sauce, garlic, and oil in saucepan. Cook over medium heat until syrupy. Pour over chicken and marinate several hours or overnight.

Preheat oven to 375 degrees.

Pour off marinade and reserve. Bake chicken on a rack for 45 minutes, basting chicken with marinade every 15 minutes. Sprinkle each piece of chicken with toasted sesame seeds for the last 5 minutes of cooking. Serve on a bed of sugar peas.

SERVES 4

Chicken Francis

Bothell, a dairy-farming community north of Seattle, is the site of one of the area's finest French restaurants, Gerard's Relais de Lyon. The restaurant, in what looks to be a former farmhouse, is owned by Gerard Parrat, who contributed this recipe.

⅓ cup finely chopped pimiento
¼ cup capers
1 clove garlic
2 teaspoons salt
½ teaspoon black pepper
½ teaspoon dill

½ teaspoon tarragon
1⅓ cups olive oil
¾ cup red wine vinegar
2 chickens, about 2½ pounds each,
*   quartered*

Combine all ingredients except chicken to make a marinade. Add chicken and marinate 24 hours.

Preheat oven to 425 degrees.

Remove chicken from marinade and bake for 20 to 30 minutes. Before serving place under broiler until lightly browned.

SERVES 4

Chicken Livers Français

½ pound mushrooms, sliced
6 tablespoons butter
¾ pound chicken livers
1 small clove garlic, minced
4 tablespoons flour
1 teaspoon salt
¼ teaspoon pepper

1 cup milk
2 cups broccoli flowerets
1 tablespoon lemon juice
1 cup sour cream
2 tablespoons freshly grated Parmesan
*   cheese*

Preheat oven to 350 degrees. Butter a 2-quart baking dish.

Sauté mushrooms in 2 tablespoons butter. Remove with slotted spoon and set aside. Melt remaining butter and add chicken livers and garlic. Sauté until brown and tender, remove with a slotted spoon, and set aside. To pan juices add 3 tablespoons flour, salt, and pepper, stirring until smooth. Add milk and heat, stirring constantly, until thickened. Stir in livers and mushrooms and remove from heat.

Steam broccoli until tender but still crisp and arrange in prepared baking dish. Sprinkle with lemon juice and top with liver mixture. Combine sour cream and remaining tablespoon of flour and spread over liver mixture. Top with Parmesan and bake uncovered for 30 minutes.

SERVES 4

Chicken Livers in Port

2 green onions, chopped
¼ cup butter, melted
½ pound chicken livers, cut into small
    pieces
¼ teaspoon sage

¼ teaspoon salt
1 tablespoon lemon juice
⅓ cup port
⅛ teaspoon freshly ground pepper

Sauté green onions in melted butter. Add livers and sauté 3 to 5 minutes. Add sage, salt, lemon juice, port, and pepper. Cook slowly for 8 minutes, stirring occasionally. Serve on toast points, scrambled eggs, or baked potatoes.

SERVES 2 TO 3

Duck with Plum Sauce

1 quartered Long Island duckling with
    giblets, neck, and wing tips
2 tablespoons vegetable oil
2 cups beef broth
1¼ cups tawny port
1 16-ounce can purple plums, drained
1 tablespoon lemon juice

¼ cup cognac
3 tablespoons sugar
3 tablespoons red wine vinegar
2 tablespoons arrowroot
chopped parsley and additional plums
    for garnish

Cut giblets, neck, and wing tips into small pieces; brown in vegetable oil. Remove fat, add beef broth and 1 cup port, and simmer slowly for 2 hours. Strain and set aside.

Meanwhile, soak plums in lemon juice and cognac for 1 hour. Preheat oven to 450 degrees.

In a separate pan, simmer sugar and wine vinegar until mixture is a caramel color. Pour into strained broth and simmer 10 minutes more. Mix arrowroot with remaining port, add to broth, and stir until thickened. Add plum mixture to sauce and simmer for 10 minutes or until slightly thickened. Set aside.

Roast duckling at 450 degrees for 20 minutes. Reduce heat to 350 degrees and roast 1 hour more. Duckling should be pink. Spoon some sauce over duckling and serve remaining sauce separately. Garnish with chopped parsley and additional plums.

SERVES 4

Stir-fried Wild Duck

3 tablespoons vegetable oil	2 tablespoons oriental plum sauce
4 green onions, chopped, white and green parts separate	1 1-inch piece of ginger, peeled and minced
2 whole wild duck breasts, cut in bite-size pieces	1 teaspoon sugar
	1 teaspoon soy sauce

Heat oil in a wok over medium-high heat until melted and hot. Add white parts of green onions and sauté briefly—about 45 seconds. Remove with slotted spoon and drain.

Place duck in wok and stir-fry until just past the pink stage. (Do not overcook or meat will toughen.) Remove duck with slotted spoon and drain. Add plum sauce, ginger, sugar, and soy sauce to wok and stir until thoroughly mixed. Reduce heat and simmer, stirring constantly, until sauce begins to glisten—about 1 to 2 minutes. Add duck and onions and mix thoroughly with sauce. Transfer to a heated serving platter and garnish with green onion tops.

SERVES 2

Wild Duck with Apricot Sauce

2 wild ducks	Sauce
salt and freshly ground pepper to taste	⅓ cup beer
2 tablespoons butter, softened	⅓ cup apricot preserves
1 lemon, halved	1 tablespoon Worcestershire sauce
1 strip bacon, halved	1 tablespoon dry mustard
	1 teaspoon finely minced orange zest

Preheat oven to 450 degrees.

To prepare sauce: Combine ingredients in pan and bring to a boil, stirring constantly. Remove from heat.

Sprinkle ducks inside and out with salt and pepper and rub skin with softened butter. Place a lemon half in each cavity. Put each duck, breast side up, on roasting rack with half a strip of bacon over breast. Brown for 25 minutes, then reduce oven temperature to 425. Spoon some sauce over the ducks and cook 30 to 40 minutes more, basting frequently and using up remaining sauce.

SERVES 4

Barbecued Turkey Roll

1 rolled boneless turkey	Marinade
hickory chips that have been soaked in	2 cups white wine
water	1 package Italian salad dressing mix
	¾ cup vegetable oil
	½ cup soy sauce

To prepare marinade: Combine ingredients and pour over turkey. Marinate turkey 24 hours, turning occasionally.

Prepare a low fire (grey coals) in a covered barbecue. Add a handful of wet hickory chips to coals when you begin cooking. Cook turkey about 8 inches above coals for 30 to 40 minutes on each side. Serve turkey hot or cold, thinly sliced, on a large platter.

SERVES 8

Note: Rolled boneless turkeys are readily available frozen. Thaw in refrigerator.

Honey-Orange Marinade

¼ cup butter, melted	¼ cup coarsely chopped parsley
1 cup orange juice	1 tablespoon dry mustard
3 tablespoons lemon juice	2 medium cloves garlic, minced
¼ cup honey	

Combine all ingredients and mix well. Use to marinate chicken for at least 4 hours. This is enough for 1 chicken, which should be broiled or barbecued. Do not baste the chicken while cooking.

YIELD: APPROXIMATELY 2 CUPS

Northwest Game Sauce

1 small onion, chopped
¼ cup butter
1 pound pitted plums, puréed
1 teaspoon grated fresh ginger
2 tablespoons chili sauce

¼ cup lemon juice
2 tablespoons soy sauce
¼ cup firmly packed brown sugar
¼ cup sour cream (optional)

Sauté onion in butter. Add remaining ingredients except sour cream and simmer for 15 minutes. Stir in sour cream just before serving. Serve with roasted duck or pheasant and wild rice.

YIELD: 3 CUPS

Autumn leaves in the Methow Valley, a resort and cattle area near Lake Chelan in eastern Washington.

Meats

━━━

Roquefort Sauce for Steak

¾ cup dry white wine
1 cup heavy cream
¼ pound Roquefort cheese, softened

½ cup butter, softened
white pepper to taste

In a saucepan, reduce wine over high heat to 1 tablespoon. Add heavy cream, and reduce liquid by half over moderate heat. In a bowl, combine Roquefort cheese and butter with a fork until smooth. Gradually whisk cheese mixture into cream mixture, a little at a time, and simmer sauce for 3 minutes. Strain through a fine sieve into a bowl and add white pepper to taste.

YIELD: ABOUT 1½ CUPS

Dog's Breath Chili

Winner of the first Seattle Times *Gasworks Park Washington State Chili Cook-off and Lake Union Duck Stampede.*

Chili
1½ medium onions, chopped
1 green bell pepper, including seeds,
    chopped

2 celery stalks, chopped
vegetable oil to cover bottom of kettle
3 pounds lean ground beef
1 pound top sirloin, cut into small
    cubes

1 6-ounce can tomato paste
1 15-ounce can tomato sauce
1 16-ounce can stewed tomatoes
3 small cloves garlic, chopped
3 ounces (yes, 3 ounces!) chili powder
    (¾ cup)
1 to 2 teaspoons pepper
1 to 2 teaspoons oregano
1 3-inch piece hot green chili pepper,
    chopped
1 8-ounce can chili salsa
salt and garlic salt to taste
1 cup beer

pinch of Red Man Chewing Tobacco
    (optional)
4 cups small red kidney beans
    (optional)

Accompaniments (optional)
2 cups grated Cheddar cheese
2 red onions or Walla Walla sweet
    onions, chopped
2 cups sour cream
2 avocados, chopped
2 large tomatoes, chopped

Sauté onion, bell pepper, and celery in oil until onion is transparent. Add meats and stir until brown—15 to 20 minutes. Add remaining ingredients and simmer 2½ hours, stirring occasionally. Cook beans separately and add at serving time. Serve with any or all of the garnishes.

Serves 6 to 8 with hearty appetites. (This yields 1 gallon or, with beans, 1½ gallons.)

Curried Flank Steak

1 2-pound flank steak
3 tablespoons butter, softened
2 tablespoons Dijon-style mustard
1 teaspoon curry powder
1 teaspoon Worcestershire sauce
½ teaspoon salt
¼ teaspoon pepper
½ cup dry sherry

1 cup sour cream
3 tablespoons brandy
1 pound mushrooms, sliced
2 tablespoons butter
2 tablespoons chopped parsley for
    garnish
1 cup fluted mushroom caps for
    garnish

Place steak in a shallow dish. Make a paste of softened butter, mustard, curry powder, Worcestershire, salt, and pepper. Spread mixture over steak, cover with sherry, and turn meat so that marinade coats both sides. Refrigerate for 4 hours or more, removing from the refrigerator 1 hour before broiling.

Preheat oven to broil. Place meat in a preheated broiler pan and quickly brown—about 2 to 3 minutes per side. Place meat on a heat-proof platter and keep warm. Deglaze broiler pan with brandy, then add sour cream to pan juices and stir.

In a small skillet, sauté sliced mushrooms in 2 tablespoons butter over moderate heat. Add a dash of sherry to mushrooms, then add mushrooms to cream sauce in broiler pan. Cut meat into diagonal slices, pour on sauce, and place platter under broiler for 1 minute. Garnish with fluted mushrooms and parsley.

SERVES 4

Lobster-Stuffed Tenderloin of Beef

3 to 4 pounds whole beef tenderloin
1 4-ounce frozen lobster tail
1 tablespoon butter, melted
1½ teaspoons lemon juice
6 slices bacon, partially cooked
½ cup chopped green onion

½ cup butter
½ cup dry white wine
⅛ teaspoon garlic salt
fluted whole mushrooms and
  watercress for garnish

Preheat oven to 425 degrees.

Cut beef tenderloin lengthwise to within ½ inch of end and spread flat to butterfly, in effect doubling length of tenderloin. Place frozen lobster tail in boiling water to cover. Return water to boiling, reduce heat, and simmer 5 to 6 minutes. Carefully remove lobster from shell. Cut lobster meat in half lengthwise and place halves end to end on beef. Combine the melted butter and lemon juice and drizzle on lobster. Close meat around lobster and tie roast together securely with string at 1-inch intervals. Place on rack in shallow roasting pan, and roast approximately 40 minutes, until meat thermometer registers 140 degrees for rare, then lay bacon slices on top of roast and roast 5 minutes more. (If medium-rare meat is preferred, internal temperature should be 160 degrees; well-done, 170.)

Meanwhile, in saucepan, cook green onion in the remaining butter over very low heat until tender, stirring frequently. Stir in wine and garlic salt and heat through. To serve, slice roast and spoon wine sauce over it, garnishing platter, if desired, with fluted mushrooms and watercress.

SERVES 8

Variation: Four ounces of fresh crabmeat may be substituted for lobster.

Kaldolma with Beef

8 large cabbage leaves
⅓ cup Parmesan cheese

Sauce

2 6-ounce cans tomato sauce
½ cup firmly packed brown sugar
¼ cup wine vinegar
2 tablespoons Worcestershire sauce
2½ teaspoons salt
2 teaspoons chili powder
2 teaspoons dry mustard

Stuffing

1 egg
1 pound lean ground beef
¾ cup cooked rice, well drained
½ cup finely chopped onion
1 teaspoon salt
1 teaspoon Worcestershire sauce
¼ teaspoon pepper
¼ cup freshly grated Parmesan cheese

Preheat oven to 350 degrees. Grease a shallow 2-quart baking dish.

Steam cabbage leaves until just tender—about 10 minutes. Combine sauce ingredients in a small bowl and set aside.

Combine stuffing ingredients. Place approximately ⅓ cup of stuffing in center of each cabbage leaf, then fold leaf over stuffing and secure with toothpicks. Pour 1 cup of sauce into prepared baking dish. Place cabbage rolls in dish and pour remaining sauce over them. Bake for 45 minutes, sprinkle with ⅓ cup Parmesan, and bake 5 minutes more.

SERVES 4

Imperial Beef Paprika

8 pounds beef chuck, cut into 1-inch
  cubes
1½ cups flour
1 tablespoon plus 1 teaspoon salt
2 teaspoons freshly ground pepper
1 teaspoon savory
⅔ cup butter
1 to 2 tablespoons vegetable oil
2 pounds yellow onions, peeled and
  sliced

2 pounds mushrooms, sliced
2 cloves garlic, minced
¼ teaspoon oregano
4 teaspoons paprika or 2 to 3 teaspoons Hungarian paprika
2 cups Burgundy wine
1 6-ounce can tomato paste
1 cup sour cream
chopped parsley for garnish
8 cups cooked noodles

Shake meat cubes in a bag with flour, 1 tablespoon salt, 1 teaspoon pepper, and ½ teaspoon savory. Brown meat in small batches in butter and oil over medium-high heat in a Dutch oven. Remove meat. Sauté onions, mushrooms, and garlic in the Dutch oven until tender but not brown.

Return meat to Dutch oven. Season with oregano and remaining salt, pepper, and savory. Sprinkle paprika over surface of meat until it is red, stir, then redden surface again. Add 1 cup Burgundy and the tomato paste. Cover Dutch oven and simmer meat slowly, stirring occasionally, for about 3 hours, or until fork-tender. Add more wine as needed to keep mixture from thickening too rapidly.

Just before serving, stir in sour cream and garnish with chopped parsley. Serve over noodles.

SERVES 12 TO 16

Note: This dish improves if allowed to stand and is best if made the day before. Reheat and add sour cream at the last minute.

Steak in a Bag

1 cup bread crumbs (3 or 4 slices) from egg bread
2 cups grated sharp Cheddar cheese
¼ cup butter, softened
¼ cup vegetable oil

1 teaspoon minced garlic
2 teaspoons seasoned salt
2½ teaspoons lemon pepper
2 to 3 pounds 2½-inch thick sirloin steak

Preheat oven to 375 degrees.

Mix bread crumbs with 1 cup cheese. In a separate bowl, mix butter, oil, garlic, salt, and pepper. Spread this mixture evenly on both sides of steak, then pat top of steak with bread–cheese mixture, coating well.

Place steak in a brown paper bag, fold the end closed, and secure with paper clips. Sprinkle bag lightly with water to prevent burning and place on rimmed baking sheet. Bake meat in bag for 30 minutes for rare steak. For medium-rare, bake at 425 degrees for an additional 15 minutes. For medium-well-done steak reduce heat to 375 degrees at this point and bake for an additional 5 minutes.

SERVES 4 TO 6

Popover Pizza — Just for Kids

½ pound bulk pork sausage
½ pound lean ground beef
1 15-ounce can tomato sauce

1 cup plus 2 tablespoons flour
1 teaspoon oregano
¼ teaspoon salt

12 ounces mozzarella cheese, sliced
2 eggs
1 tablespoon corn oil

1 cup milk
¼ teaspoon salt
¼ cup grated Parmesan cheese

Preheat oven to 425 degrees.

In a medium skillet, cook and stir meat until crumbly. Drain off fat and add tomato sauce, 2 tablespoons flour, oregano, and salt. Heat to boiling, and cook, stirring, for 1 minute. Pour into a 9-x-13-inch un-greased baking pan and cover with mozzarella slices.

Beat together eggs, oil, milk, salt, and remaining flour and pour over cheese and meat. Sprinkle with Parmesan and bake until pizza is puffy and cheese has melted—about 25 to 30 minutes. Serve immediately.

SERVES 4 TO 6

Note: May also be cut into small squares and served as an appetizer.

Beef Vinaigrette

1½ to 2 pounds top round, cut paper
    thin
salt, pepper, and minced garlic to taste

Vinaigrette Marinade
¾ cup olive oil
5⅓ tablespoons wine vinegar
3 cloves garlic, finely minced
juice of 1 lemon
2 teaspoons dry mustard

1 tablespoon minced red onion
1½ tablespoons oregano
1 tablespoon minced parsley
2 teaspoons seasoning salt
½ teaspoon coarsely ground black
    pepper
1 teaspoon salt
1 red onion, sliced thin
parsley for garnish

Season strips of top round with salt, pepper, and garlic, and broil quickly. When meat reaches desired doneness, set aside. Thoroughly combine marinade ingredients and set aside also.

Separate onion slices into rings. In a large shallow pan, place a layer of beef, then a layer of onion rings. Cover well with vinaigrette. Repeat until beef, onion, and vinaigrette are used up. Cover and refrigerate, occasionally spooning vinaigrette over beef and onions.

Marinate in refrigerator for several hours or up to 4 days. Allow to stand at room temperature 15 to 20 minutes before serving. To serve, garnish with fresh parsley and serve with beef and onions swimming in marinade. Serve with crusty French bread.

SERVES 6 TO 8

Beef Stroganoff

1 cup butter
1½ cups minced onion
1½ pounds mushrooms, sliced
3½ pounds beef top round, cut in
    ¼-x-¼-x-2-inch strips
6 tablespoons flour

3 cups beef bouillon
1 teaspoon salt
6 tablespoons tomato paste
2 teaspoons Worcestershire sauce
1 cup sour cream

Melt ⅓ cup butter in a large saucepan or Dutch oven. Sauté onions and remove to a warm dish. Melt another ⅓ cup butter, sauté mushrooms and add to onions. Roll beef strips in flour. Melt remaining butter and brown beef lightly. Add onions and mushrooms to the saucepan. Add bouillon and salt and cover. Simmer gently until beef is fork–tender—about 1½ hours.

Add tomato paste, Worcestershire, and sour cream, stirring to combine ingredients. Heat thoroughly and serve over rice or buttered noodles.

SERVES 10 TO 12

African Ground-Nut Stew

2 pounds lean ground beef
1 onion, chopped
¼ teaspoon thyme
¼ teaspoon oregano
¼ teaspoon freshly ground pepper
¼ teaspoon cayenne
2 6-ounce cans tomato paste
1 tablespoon Worcestershire sauce
½ cup catsup
2 cups beef broth
2 cups ground peanuts
2 cups uncooked white or brown rice

Condiments
4 to 6 hard-cooked eggs, diced
1 green bell pepper, diced
2 cups mandarin orange sections,
    fresh, or canned and drained
1 cucumber, diced
1 onion, diced and sautéed
½ cantaloupe, diced
fresh or canned pineapple chunks,
    drained
grated coconut
2 to 3 bananas, diced

In a large skillet, brown ground beef with onion, thyme, oregano, pepper, and cayenne. Add tomato paste, Worcestershire, catsup, and broth. Simmer, covered, over low heat for about 2 hours. Add 1 cup ground peanuts, cover, and continue to simmer for ½ hour more.

Cook rice separately according to package directions. In each serving bowl place a spoonful of rice and top with hot stew sprinkled with remaining peanuts. Serve condiments separately.

SERVES 8

Goulash Szegetti

This Hungarian casserole is one of those dishes that improves with time—it has to be prepared several days before it is to be cooked.

¼ cup butter	salt and pepper to taste
3 cups chopped onions	1 pound sauerkraut
1 pound lean pork, cut into bite-size pieces	¼ cup white wine
1 pound sirloin of beef, cut into bite-size pieces	2 cups heavy cream
	1 cup uncooked white rice

Sauté 2 cups onion in 2 tablespoons butter. Remove onion and set aside. Brown pork and beef in same pan. Season with salt and pepper, return onions to pan, and cook slowly over low heat until meat is tender—about 1 hour. In a separate pan, melt remaining butter and lightly brown remaining onion with the sauerkraut. Add wine, cover, and cook slowly for 20 minutes.

Steam rice according to package directions. Place cooked rice in bottom of a 3-quart casserole, cover with meat mixture, and top with sauerkraut mixture. Pour in cream, cover, and refrigerate for 4 to 5 days.

Preheat oven to 325 degrees. Bake goulash, uncovered, for 2 hours.

SERVES 6 TO 8

Stuffed Beef

1 7-pound beef rump roast, trimmed	½ cup Greek olives
1 tablespoon olive oil	1 cup marinated mushrooms, sliced
1 tablespoon chopped parsley	½ pound provolone cheese
1 teaspoon rosemary	¼ pound Canadian bacon
1 teaspoon tarragon	¼ pound Italian salami
2 large cloves garlic, minced	1 teaspoon pepper

Preheat oven to 400 degrees.

Butterfly beef by carefully removing the bone and spreading the meat flat, in effect doubling the width of the roast. In a small bowl, combine olive oil, herbs, and garlic. Rub this mixture over the butterflied roast. Layer the olives, mushrooms, cheese, bacon, salami, and pepper on the roast.

Roll the roast, jelly-roll fashion, and tie at 1-inch intervals with string. Set in a broiler pan on a rack and place in oven. Immediately reduce heat to 325 degrees. Roast, allowing 15 minutes per pound or until internal temperature reaches 140 degrees on a meat thermometer for rare. (If medium-rare beef is preferred, internal temperature should be 160 degrees; well-done, 170.)

Turn oven temperature to broil and broil roast 5 inches from heat for 2 to 3 minutes until brown. Transfer to carving board and let rest 10 minutes before carving.

SERVES 10 TO 12

Stroganoff Sandwiches

2 cloves garlic, minced
2/3 cup vegetable oil
3 tablespoons wine vinegar
1 tablespoon Dijon-style mustard
salt and pepper
2 pounds sirloin, round, or flank steak
1/4 cup butter
1/4 teaspoon salt
2 cups thin-sliced onions

1/2 cup butter, softened
1 teaspoon minced parsley
1/8 teaspoon thyme
1/8 teaspoon oregano
6 French rolls, split lengthwise
1 1/2 cups sour cream
2 tablespoons prepared horseradish
1/4 cup chopped parsley

Combine garlic, oil, vinegar, mustard, salt, and pepper as marinade. Score steak and marinate in a shallow glass dish for 4 to 6 hours. When ready to serve, melt butter with salt, add onions, and cook over low heat for 20 minutes. Set aside and keep warm.

Preheat oven to 350 degrees.

Mix softened butter with herbs and butter inside of rolls. Wrap rolls in aluminum foil and bake for 20 minutes. Broil or barbeque steak 3 to 5 minutes per side. Slice diagonally and keep warm. Warm sour cream with horseradish over low heat.

To make sandwiches, place sliced meat on bottom half of each roll, cover with onions, and top with horseradish sauce. Sprinkle with parsley and cover with top half of roll.

SERVES 6

Toshi Spring Rolls

1 pound lean ground beef	½ cup chopped white onion
½ cup cooked chopped spinach, well drained	¼ teaspoon pepper
	1 teaspoon salt
½ pound large shrimp, shelled, deveined, and finely chopped	1 clove garlic, minced
	1 package egg roll wrappers (25)
2 cups bean sprouts	oil for deep-frying
1½ cups grated carrots	

Sauté ground beef and drain. Add all remaining ingredients except egg roll wrappers and oil. Stir-fry in wok until barely cooked. Spoon ¼ cup of this mixture onto center of each egg roll wrapper, moisten all edges of wrapper, and roll wrapper diagonally to center. Fold in corners and continue rolling into a cylinder. Deep-fry until golden brown, drain, and serve immediately with Ginger Mayonnaise (page 27) or Sweet and Sour Plum Sauce (page 28).

SERVES 8

Steak au Poivre Vert

Served at Phillipe Gayte's Le Provençal in Kirkland, across Lake Washington. Get there by driving over a floating bridge or, better, by sailing to Kirkland's Marina Park, which offers free moorage and a chance to visit the historic boats of a nearby floating museum.

4 individual New York or Spencer steaks	½ cup white wine or ¼ cup brandy
	¾ cup heavy cream
1½ tablespoons vegetable oil	¼ pound butter
1½ tablespoons butter	2 teaspoons green peppercorns
3 shallots, chopped	salt to taste
1 teaspoon Dijon-style mustard	chopped parsley for garnish

In a large frying pan, sauté steaks over high heat in mixture of oil and butter. Remove meat to a warm platter, cover with foil, and keep warm. In the same pan, sauté shallots until lightly browned. Drain grease from the pan. Add mustard and wine and mix well with a whisk until moisture has evaporated—several minutes. Add cream and bring to a low boil, stirring constantly, over medium heat until sauce thickens—4 to 5 minutes. Reduce heat.

Add ¼ pound butter, cut into small bits, and melt. Add peppercorns and season to taste. Pour sauce over steaks and sprinkle with chopped parsley.

SERVES 4

Heavenly Beef Casserole

1 pound ground beef	½ pint sour cream
2 cloves garlic, minced	6 green onions, chopped fine
1 teaspoon sugar	12 ounces small egg noodles
1 teaspoon salt	1 pound mozzarella cheese, grated
1 15-ounce can tomato sauce	2 tablespoons minced parsley
2 ounces cream cheese, softened	

In a large frying pan, brown the meat and drain off all fat. Add garlic, sugar, salt, and tomato sauce and simmer 30 minutes. Meanwhile, place cream cheese in a medium-size bowl and add green onions and sour cream, mixing thoroughly.

Preheat oven to 350 degrees. Grease a 9-x-13-inch baking dish.

Cook and drain the noodles. In the baking dish, spread half of the noodles, cover with half of the cream cheese mixture, and top with half of the mozzarella. Cover with all the meat sauce. Put in remaining noodles, cream cheese mixture, and mozzarella. Bake uncovered for 30 minutes. Sprinkle minced parsley over top and serve.

SERVES 8 TO 10

Orange Brandied Beef

3¼ pounds chuck steak, cut into 1-inch cubes	½ cup plus 3 tablespoons brandy
	8 carrots, peeled and sliced
1½ teaspoons salt	2 cloves garlic, minced
¼ teaspoon freshly ground pepper	1½ tablespoons grated lemon zest
3 tablespoons olive oil	⅓ cup fresh orange juice
1 tablespoon grated orange zest	½ cup chopped parsley
1½ pounds small onions, peeled	1 orange, sliced thin, for garnish
2 cups condensed beef broth	

Sprinkle meat generously with salt and pepper, then sauté briefly in oil in a heavy pan. Add orange zest, onions, beef broth and ½ cup brandy. Simmer 2 hours, covered.

Add carrots, garlic, and lemon zest and simmer 25 minutes more or until carrots are tender. Stir in orange juice, parsley, and remaining brandy. Garnish with orange slices.

SERVES 6

Veal Normandy Northwest Style

3 large Golden Delicious apples, peeled
   and cored
¼ cup lemon juice
1 pound veal scallops, pounded very
   thin
flour

salt and freshly ground pepper to taste
¼ cup butter
1½ tablespoons vegetable oil
⅓ cup brandy or Calvados
1 cup heavy cream
chopped parsley for garnish

Cut apples into ½-inch cubes, cover with lemon juice, and set aside.

Dust veal with flour, salt, and pepper. Combine butter and oil in a large frying pan over medium-high heat and sauté veal until golden brown—2 to 3 minutes per side. Do not overcook. Remove veal to platter and keep warm.

Add apples, with lemon juice, and brandy to pan. Cook 2 to 3 minutes over medium heat, stirring gently with wooden spoon to loosen browned bits from the pan. Reduce heat, add cream, and continue to cook, stirring frequently, until sauce reaches a consistency to coat spoon. Taste and season if necessary. Spoon sauce over meat and sprinkle chopped parsley over the top.

SERVES 4

Variation: The sauce is also excellent with pork.

Veal Birds Allegrini

8 Italian sausage links
¼ cup chopped parsley
2 cloves garlic, minced
5 green onions, chopped
½ cup butter, softened

2 teaspoons Italian seasoning
8 veal scallops, pounded about ¼ inch
   thick
salt and pepper to taste

Preheat oven to 350 degrees. Grease a baking pan.

Remove casings and partially cook sausage, then drain and chop fine. In another pan, sauté parsley, garlic, and green onions until tender. Combine with sausage, butter, and Italian seasoning to make a paste.

Salt and pepper the veal and place 2 to 3 tablespoons of paste on each piece. Roll up in a "bird" and tie with string to secure. If there is leftover paste, spread on top of the birds. Lay the birds in prepared baking pan and bake until veal is cooked and filling is very hot— approximately 15 minutes. Remove birds to a platter, baste with pan drippings, and serve.

SERVES 4

Veal Parmigiana

1 pound veal scallops, pounded thin
salt and freshly ground pepper to taste
1 egg
2 tablespoons water
⅓ cup freshly grated Parmesan cheese
⅓ cup fine, dry bread crumbs
¼ cup olive oil or vegetable oil
3 tablespoons butter
1 medium onion, minced

1 clove garlic, minced
1 6-ounce can tomato paste
1 cup hot water
1 cup white wine
1 teaspoon salt
½ teaspoon dried marjoram
½ pound mozzarella or Monterey jack
    cheese, sliced thin

Preheat oven to 350 degrees.

Cut veal into 8 pieces and sprinkle with salt and pepper. Beat egg with water. Combine cheese and bread crumbs. Dip veal in egg, then coat with cheese mixture.

Heat oil and butter in a large skillet. Sauté veal over medium-high heat, then lay in a shallow, wide baking dish. In the same skillet, cook onion and garlic until soft, adding more oil and butter if necessary. Add the tomato paste, hot water, wine, salt, and marjoram. Simmer to reduce sauce slightly. Pour most of the sauce over the veal, top with sliced mozzarella, and pour remaining sauce over the cheese. Bake for 20 to 25 minutes.

SERVES 4

Veal Sauté

1 pound veal sirloin cut into 10 to 12
    pieces
3 tablespoons flour
salt and freshly ground pepper to taste

1 tablespoon olive oil
4 to 5 tablespoons butter
3 tablespoons dry white wine or extra
    dry vermouth

1½ teaspoons lemon juice

½ pound mushrooms, sliced

2 cups cooked white rice

Sprinkle veal with flour, salt, and pepper. Heat olive oil and 1 table-spoon butter. When pan is hot, sauté veal on both sides, but do not brown. Remove from pan and keep warm. Add wine to pan juices, heat gently, and add remaining butter and lemon juice. Sauté mush-rooms separately. Place veal slices on platter and top with mushrooms and sauce.

Serve over white rice.

SERVES 4

Stuffed Lamb with Orange Mint Sauce

1 6- to 8-pound leg of lamb

salt and freshly ground pepper to taste

⅔ cup chopped onion

⅔ cup chopped celery

3 tablespoons butter

2 tablespoons grated orange zest

10 slices cinnamon–raisin bread, cut into small cubes

1 egg, beaten

Orange Mint Sauce

1¾ cups orange juice

⅓ cup firmly packed brown sugar

¼ cup butter

1 tablespoon cornstarch

¼ cup chopped fresh mint or 1 table-spoon dried mint flakes

1 tablespoon grated orange zest

1½ teaspoons ground ginger

½ to ¾ teaspoon ground cloves

2 teaspoons salt

1 10½-ounce can mandarin oranges, drained

Preheat oven to 325 degrees.

Butterfly the leg of lamb by carefully removing the bone (being careful not to pierce the outer skin) and spreading the meat flat, in effect doubling its width. Sprinkle lamb with salt and pepper.

Sauté onion and celery in melted butter until tender. In a bowl, toss onion and celery with orange zest and bread cubes. Blend in egg. Spread stuffing over lamb, roll up, and tie with string. Roast approxi-mately 2 hours or until meat thermometer registers 160 degrees for medium rare. (Temperature should be 175 to 180 for well done.)

To prepare sauce: Mix together all ingredients except mandarin oranges and add to pan drippings from the roast. Heat until thick-ened, then add oranges. Pass separately to spoon over sliced lamb.

SERVES 6 TO 8

Note: To cook on covered barbecue, allow 1½ to 2 hours.

Barbecued Lamb

1 6- to 7-pound leg of lamb	2 teaspoons salt
1 clove garlic, minced	½ teaspoon oregano
¾ cup oil	½ teaspoon basil
¼ cup red wine vinegar	⅛ teaspoon freshly ground pepper
½ cup chopped onion	1 bay leaf, crushed
2 teaspoons Dijon-style mustard	

Butterfly the leg of lamb by carefully removing the bone (being careful not to pierce the outer skin), and spreading the meat flat, in effect doubling its width. Place lamb, fat side down, in a shallow pan. In bowl or blender, make a marinade by combining remaining ingredients and blending well. Pour marinade over lamb, cover tightly, and refrigerate overnight, turning lamb at least once.

Remove lamb from refrigerator 1 hour before cooking. Barbecue over hot coals about 40 minutes for medium rare. Turn occasionally and baste with marinade every 10 minutes. Slice diagonally when serving.

SERVES 6 TO 8

Rack of Lamb with Mustard and Parsley-Crumb Coating

2 racks of lamb
parsley or watercress for garnish

Mustard Coating

1 clove garlic
½ teaspoon salt
½ teaspoon thyme
3 tablespoons Dijon-style mustard
3 tablespoons olive or vegetable oil

Parsley–Crumb Coating

¾ cup bread crumbs
6 tablespoons butter
¼ cup minced parsley
½ teaspoon minced garlic
½ teaspoon thyme
salt and freshly ground pepper to taste

Preheat oven to 475 degrees.

Score the racks of lamb on the top. Mash the garlic and salt together in a bowl, add the thyme, and whisk in the mustard and oil. Spread the mixture over the lamb and roast for 15 minutes. In a skillet, combine ingredients for crumb coating, stirring over medium heat for 2 to 3 minutes, being careful not to let the crumbs brown. Remove from heat.

After the lamb has roasted for 15 minutes, remove from oven and pat on the crumbs. Reduce heat to 450 degrees and roast the lamb 10 to 15 minutes more or until the crumb mixture is golden and the lamb is rare (140 degrees on a meat thermometer). (If medium-rare meat is preferred, internal temperature should be 160 degrees; well-done, 170.) Garnish and serve with Spinach Rockefeller (page 250).

SERVES 6

Indian Lamb Curry

1 pound lamb shoulder, leg, or shank, cut into 1-inch cubes
¼ cup vegetable oil
1 to 2 small dried hot red chili peppers
1 26-ounce can whole peeled tomatoes
2 teaspoons unsweetened coconut or more if preferred
1 9-ounce package frozen peas or beans (optional)

Marinade
1 large onion, chopped
1 tablespoon ground coriander
1 heaping teaspoon turmeric
½ teaspoon ground cumin
½ teaspoon ground pepper
pinch of cayenne
2 cloves garlic, minced
1 inch fresh ginger, grated

Mix marinade ingredients and marinate lamb in covered container overnight.

Heat oil until hot and break the pepper or peppers into it. (The hotness of this dish is determined by the number of peppers used.) Sauté the meat mixture in the oil and remove the peppers. Add the tomatoes and coconut; salt to taste, and simmer until sauce is the consistency of spaghetti sauce. If necessary, add more coconut for thickening. Add frozen vegetable for contrasting color if desired. Serve with Rice for Indian Lamb Curry (page 159).

SERVES 4

Note: Not only can curry be prepared ahead, but the flavor improves with age.

Mediterranean Lamb Shanks

4 meaty lamb shanks, uncracked
2 tablespoons lemon juice
salt and freshly ground pepper to taste
2 tablespoons olive oil
1 clove garlic, minced
½ teaspoon oregano
1 onion, quartered

1 cup bouillon or combination of bouillon and dry white wine
1 9-ounce package frozen artichoke hearts
1 teaspoon cornstarch
¼ cup water

Preheat oven to 300 degrees.

Rub shanks with 1 tablespoon lemon juice and salt and pepper to taste. In a skillet, sauté shanks in olive oil, turning until evenly browned on all sides. Transfer shanks to casserole and sprinkle with remaining lemon juice, garlic, and oregano. Add onion and bake, covered, for 2½ hours. Add bouillon and artichoke hearts. Raise heat to 350 degrees and bake, covered, for 20 to 30 minutes more, or until artichokes are tender.

Transfer lamb and artichokes to a hot platter and keep warm. Thicken juices in casserole with cornstarch blended with water and serve sauce separately.

SERVES 4

Leg of Lamb with Rosemary Stuffing

1 6½-pound leg of lamb
½ cup sliced carrots
½ cup sliced onions
2 cloves garlic, sliced
2 cups lamb stock or beef broth

4 ounces pork fat or beef suet
1 clove garlic, minced
¼ teaspoon ground rosemary
¼ teaspoon salt
⅛ teaspoon freshly ground pepper

Stuffing
¾ cup fresh bread crumbs
2 tablespoons milk
2 tablespoons minced green onions
2 tablespoons butter
8 ounces raw lamb

Mustard Sauce Coating
½ teaspoon ground rosemary
1 clove garlic, minced
1 tablespoon soy sauce
½ cup Dijon-style mustard
¼ cup olive oil or vegetable oil

Preheat oven to 350 degrees.

Butterfly the leg of lamb by carefully removing the bone (being careful not to pierce the outer skin), and spreading the meat flat, in effect doubling its width.

To prepare stuffing: Moisten crumbs with milk to make a fine paste. Sauté green onions in butter. Grind raw lamb with fat or suet. Thoroughly mix together the crumbs, green onions, and ground meat. Stuff leg of lamb with this mixture and tie or close with skewers.

Combine coating ingredients, place lamb on roasting rack, bottom side up, and paint with coating. Turn lamb and paint upper (fat) side, reserving 3 tablespoons of coating for sauce. Arrange carrots, onions, and garlic around lamb. Insert meat thermometer in thickest part of meat, place in oven, and roast, without turning or basting, 2 to 2½ hours or until thermometer reads 140 degrees (rare). (If medium-rare meat is preferred, internal temperature should be 160 degrees; well-done, 170.) Allow lamb to rest at room temperature for 20 minutes before carving. Juices should run red when meat is pricked with a fork.

While lamb is standing, drain fat from roasting pan. Add to the meat juices the cooked carrots, onions, garlic, stock, and reserved mustard coating. Simmer over low heat for 15 minutes—until liquid is reduced. Pour this sauce over the carved meat and pass extra sauce separately.

SERVES 6 TO 8

Crown Roast of Pork with Macademia Nut Stuffing

Roast

1 tablespoon salt
dash of pepper
1½ tablespoon lemon juice
2 tablespoons chopped parsley
1 clove garlic, minced
1 tablespoon olive oil
½ teaspoon basil
2 tablespoons finely chopped onion
1 6- to 7-pound crown roast of pork
½ cup butter, melted

Stuffing

1 cup butter
1½ cups chopped onion

1½ cloves garlic, chopped
1½ cups chopped celery
3 cups fresh diced pineapple
1½ cups peeled and diced tart apple
1½ cups peeled and diced papaya
¾ teaspoon pepper
1½ teaspoons salt
1½ cups chopped macadamia nuts
7 to 8 cups diced bread, crusts
   removed

Garnishes

watercress or parsley sprigs
papaya and pineapple wedges

Preheat oven to 350 degrees.

To prepare roast: Mix salt, pepper, lemon juice, parsley, garlic, olive oil, basil, and onion into a paste. Cut slits on inside of roast and place some paste in each slit. Rub outside of roast with more of the paste. Place roast on rack in a large roasting pan and set aside.

To prepare stuffing: Melt butter and sauté onion, garlic, and celery. Add fruits and seasonings, and simmer until heated through. Toss lightly with nuts and bread. Place stuffing inside the crown, saving any extra stuffing to heat and serve separately.

Roast meat covered, allowing 30 minutes per pound, or until meat thermometer reads 175 degrees. Baste with melted butter every 20 minutes. Uncover during last hour to brown. Place roast on heated serving platter and garnish.

SERVES 12

Pork Chops and Apples in Mustard Sauce

2 onions, chopped
2 pounds apples, cored, peeled, and
   sliced thin
4 pork loin chops, about ¾ inches
   thick

salt and freshly ground pepper to taste
2 tablespoons butter
¼ cup dry white wine
1 cup sour cream
⅓ cup Dijon-style mustard

Preheat oven to 400 degrees. Lightly butter a 9-x-9-inch baking dish.

Spread the onions and apples in prepared baking dish and bake for 15 minutes.

Trim fat from pork chops and sprinkle with salt and pepper. Sauté chops in butter over medium heat until lightly browned on each side—about 7 minutes per side. Remove from sauté pan and arrange in baking dish over the apples and onions. Deglaze the sauté pan with the white wine, reducing by half, and drizzle over the chops. Bake about 45 minutes, or until chops are tender and no longer pink when slashed near the bone.

Combine sour cream and mustard with salt and pepper to taste, and pour over the chops and apples. Bake 15 minutes longer.

SERVES 4

Rio Pork Roast

1 3- to 5-pound loin of pork
1 teaspoon salt
1 garlic clove, halved
½ cup flour
1 cup apricot jam, currant jelly, or
   apple jelly

1 cup catsup
1 cup crushed tortilla chips
¼ cup flour

Preheat oven to 325 degrees.

Rub roast with the salt and garlic, then dredge roast in flour. Bake until meat thermometer reads 160 degrees—approximately 30 to 35 minutes per pound. Remove from oven.

Combine jam and catsup and spread mixture over the roast. Return roast to oven and baste frequently with jam–catsup mixture. When the thermometer reads about 165 degrees, sprinkle the top of the roast with crushed tortilla chips. Continue to roast until the thermometer reaches 170, and remove the roast to a heated platter. Skim fat from pan, spoon the pan drippings into a sauceboat, and serve separately.

SERVES 6 TO 10

Calf's Liver in Mustard and Vinegar Sauce

¾ cup heavy cream
1 tablespoon Dijon-style mustard
2 tablespoons chopped fresh tarragon
    or 1 tablespoon dried tarragon
½ teaspoon salt
¼ teaspoon freshly ground pepper
2 pounds calf's liver, cut into 1-inch
    slices
2 tablespoons unsalted butter
1 tablespoon olive oil

salt and pepper to taste
chopped parsley for garnish

Sauce

1 tablespoon unsalted butter
4 cups thin-sliced onions
½ teaspoon thyme
¼ cup white wine vinegar
1 tablespoon unsalted butter, softened
1 tablespoon flour

Combine cream, mustard, tarragon, salt, and pepper in a small bowl. Cover and set aside. Sauté liver in mixture of butter and oil in a large skillet until light brown—about 2 minutes (liver should be rare). Season with salt and pepper and remove from pan.

To prepare sauce: Add butter to drippings in skillet. Stir in onions and thyme and sauté, stirring frequently, until brown. Reduce heat to low and simmer, covered, until onions are very soft—about 10 minutes. Stir in vinegar. Increase heat to high. Boil, uncovered, until vinegar evaporates. Stir in reserved cream mixture and cool until slightly thickened, which will take 3 to 5 minutes. In a small bowl, combine butter and flour with a fork. Add to onion mixture gradually, whisking constantly until smooth. Taste and adjust seasonings. Return liver to skillet. Reduce heat to low and heat liver thoroughly, stirring gently. Arrange on serving platter and garnish with parsley.

SERVES 6

Almost as familiar as family, Pasqualina Verdi offers her farm produce for sale at Pike Place Market in downtown Seattle.

Vegetables

━━

Asparagus and Crookneck Squash with Herb Mayonnaise

A simple picnic dish that can be made elegant enough for a gourmet dinner simply by changing the presentation.

1 pound asparagus spears of uniform
   size
½ pound crookneck squash
1 cup mayonnaise
1 tablespoon minced parsley
1 tablespoon minced watercress

1 tablespoon minced chives or green
   onions
1 tablespoon chervil
2 teaspoons tarragon wine vinegar or
   a pinch of tarragon and 2 teaspoons white wine vinegar

Use medium-thick asparagus if the vegetables are going to be dipped in the mayonnaise; if mayonnaise is to be spread over the vegetables, choose more slender stalks. Trim off asparagus bottoms with a diagonal cut and cut squash in strips or bite-size slices. Steam asparagus and squash separately until each is tender but slightly crisp. Drain and rinse in ice-cold water. Arrange attractively in a serving dish or a container for a picnic. Combine remaining ingredients, blend, and ladle on asparagus or serve separately.

SERVES 4

Asparagus Fans

5 asparagus spears per person
red- or green-leaf lettuce

walnut oil
hard-cooked eggs, minced

Choose asparagus spears that are uniform in size, wash, and remove tough ends. Steam spears a few at a time and arrange, fan shape, on beds of lettuce on salad plates. Drizzle with a little walnut oil and sprinkle hard-cooked eggs across asparagus.

Madison Park Asparagus

1¼ pounds asparagus
½ pound mushrooms
3 tablespoons butter

dash of salt and pepper
⅓ cup slivered almonds, toasted

Wash asparagus and drain on paper towels. Cut each spear diagonally into approximately 1½-inch lengths, discarding end of each stalk. Rinse and gently dry mushrooms, cutting smaller ones in halves and larger ones in quarters.

Melt butter in a large skillet over medium heat and add asparagus. Increase temperature to medium-high, cover pan, and cook 2 minutes, stirring once or twice. Uncover pan, raise temperature to high and add mushrooms, salt, and pepper. Stir constantly but gently until liquids evaporate, sprinkle with toasted almonds, and serve.

SERVES 6

Green Beans in Red-Pepper Butter

Red-Pepper Butter
2 tablespoons butter
2 red bell peppers
¾ cup unsalted butter
¼ cup chopped onion
juice of 1 lemon

salt and pepper to taste
Beans
3 pounds Italian green beans, fresh or
    5 10-ounce packages frozen
3 red bell peppers
2 tablespoons unsalted butter

To prepare butter: Melt butter in a medium saucepan over medium-high heat. Seed and shred peppers, add to butter, and sauté until tender but slightly crisp. Remove peppers with slotted spoon and set aside. Purée unsalted butter with onion in a blender or food processor. Add the sautéed peppers, lemon juice, salt, and pepper, and process until smooth—about 30 seconds. Remove to a bowl and set aside.

To prepare beans: Steam beans until tender but slightly crisp. Drain well, soak in ice water 2 to 3 minutes, and drain again. Core, seed, and julienne the 3 remaining peppers and set aside. (The dish may be prepared ahead of time to this point.)

Ten minutes before serving, melt unsalted butter in a large saucepan over medium heat. Add julienned peppers and sauté 2 minutes. Reduce heat to low and add green beans and half the red-pepper butter, stirring to blend well. Cover and simmer until heated thoroughly—3 to 4 minutes. Transfer to a serving bowl and serve immediately, with remaining pepper butter served separately.

SERVES 12

Dilly Beans

2 pounds green beans

Wash and trim green beans, and pack upright in 4 sterilized 1-pint glass canning jars. To each pint add:

¹/₈ teaspoon ground red pepper	Brine
1 clove garlic	*2 cups cider vinegar*
½ teaspoon dill	*2 cups water*
	¼ cup salt
	pinch of alum

Bring brine to a boil in a medium saucepan. Ladle brine over beans in each of the jars and seal with lids. Store in a cool dark place for at least 3 weeks.

YIELD: 4 PINTS

English Walnut Broccoli

1 pound broccoli	*1 cup milk*
7 tablespoons butter	*⅓ cup water*
2 tablespoons flour	*¼ cup seasoned bread stuffing*
2 teaspoons chicken stock base	*⅓ cup chopped English walnuts or*
(powdered seasoning for dissolving in water)	*other nuts*

Preheat oven to 350 degrees. Butter a 1½-quart casserole.

Cut broccoli into bite-size flowerets, discarding stems. Steam flowerets about 4 minutes, until tender but slightly crisp. Transfer to prepared casserole and set aside. Melt ¼ cup butter in a saucepan. Blend in flour and stock base and cook over low heat for 5 minutes. Gradually add milk in a steady stream, stirring constantly. Cook until slightly thickened and pour over broccoli.

Heat the water and remaining butter in the previously used saucepan and stir in bread stuffing. When all liquid has been absorbed, spoon stuffing over broccoli and top with walnuts. (This dish may be prepared ahead to this point and refrigerated overnight.) Bake for 15 minutes, or until broccoli has reached desired tenderness.

SERVES 4

Brussels and Bells

2 pounds Brussels sprouts of uniform size, trimmed and washed
2 large red bell peppers
6 tablespoons butter

1 teaspoon basil
1 teaspoon Dijon-style mustard
salt and pepper to taste

Steam Brussels sprouts until tender when pierced with a fork. (Do not overcook! Overcooking causes a strong flavor that many people dislike.) Immediately rinse in very cold water, drain, and refrigerate in covered container. Remove seeds from peppers and slice into strips. Sauté pepper strips in 1 tablespoon of butter for 3 minutes, or until tender, and remove from heat.

Combine remaining butter with basil, mustard, salt, and pepper in a large skillet over medium-low heat. Add Brussels sprouts and stir until coated with butter mixture and heated thoroughly. Add the pepper strips, toss, and cook for 2 to 3 minutes, stirring frequently. Transfer to a heated dish and serve.

SERVES 12

A Bucket of Brussels

1 pound Brussels sprouts of uniform size
3 tablespoons butter
¼ teaspoon salt
1 teaspoon crushed basil

¼ cup chopped parsley
¼ cup chopped chives or green onions, green part only
2 to 3 tablespoons toasted wheat germ

Wash Brussels sprouts thoroughly. Trim stems and discard any loose outer leaves. (Small, bite-size Brussels sprouts are the most desirable—if larger, halve them.) Steam until tender but slightly crisp and set aside.

Melt butter in a small saucepan over medium heat. Add salt, basil, parsley, and chives and stir until bubbly. Add Brussels sprouts and toss until coated and warm. Spoon into a glass or enameled bucket and sprinkle with toasted wheat germ.

SERVES 4 TO 6

Flemish Red Cabbage

3 tablespoons butter
3 tablespoons chopped onion
8 cups shredded red cabbage (about 2
    pounds)
2 cups coarsely grated apples

1 teaspoon salt
¼ cup firmly packed brown sugar
½ cup red wine vinegar
pepper to taste

Melt butter in a large skillet over medium heat, add onion, and sauté until tender. One or 2 cups at a time, stir in cabbage until all 8 cups are thoroughly blended with onion. Cover and cook at medium temperature for 5 minutes. Mix in grated apples and salt. Cover and cook another 10 to 15 minutes or until cabbage is tender.

Combine brown sugar, vinegar, and pepper, and add to cabbage when cabbage has reached desired tenderness. Cover, increase the temperature to heat thoroughly, and reduce temperature to keep cabbage warm until ready to serve.

SERVES 4 TO 6

Marsha's Stuffed Cabbage

1 medium head green cabbage
2½ tablespoons butter
1 onion, chopped
½ cup cooked rice
½ teaspoon salt

¹/₈ teaspoon pepper
2¼ cups grated Cheddar cheese
8 ounces (1 cup) tomato sauce
grated Parmesan cheese and parsley
    for garnish

Wash cabbage and steam entire head until tender throughout—approximately 25 minutes. Test for doneness with a skewer. Remove and drain.

Preheat oven to 425 degrees. Grease an 8-x-8-inch baking dish.

When cabbage is cool enough to handle, cut an opening approximately 3 inches deep and 4 inches in diameter in the top, leaving base intact. Chop part of the removed center and reserve it for filling.

Melt butter in large skillet. Add chopped onion, chopped cabbage, rice, salt, and pepper, and sauté until lightly browned. Remove from the heat, stir in the Cheddar cheese, and put into the opening in the cabbage. (The dish may be prepared ahead to this point.) Place cabbage in prepared baking dish and pour tomato sauce over it. Sprinkle with Parmesan and bake for 15 minutes. To serve, place on serving dish, slice into wedges, and garnish with parsley.

SERVES 4 TO 6

Toasted Carrots

8 large carrots, peeled and quartered lengthwise	1 teaspoon firmly packed brown sugar
1/8 teaspoon salt	1 cup wheat germ

Preheat oven to 350 degrees. Grease a baking sheet. Steam carrots until tender but slightly crisp. Rinse with cold water. Combine salt and sugar in a plastic bag and add carrots, a few at a time, and shake until all carrots are coated. Roll each carrot stick in wheat germ, then place on prepared baking sheet. Bake 15 minutes, or until golden.

SERVES 8

Cointreau Carrots

16 medium carrots or 1½ pounds French carrots	3 tablespoons Cointreau
3 to 6 tablespoons butter	3 tablespoons minced parsley
1 tablespoon lemon juice	8 ounces mandarin oranges (optional)

If using medium-sized carrots, wash, peel, and slice very thin by hand or in a food processor. If using French carrots, cut in half lengthwise and trim to uniform size. Sauté carrots in butter over low heat until tender but slightly crisp. Add lemon juice and Cointreau and simmer until the alcohol evaporates—about 1 minute. Sprinkle with parsley, toss gently with mandarin oranges, and serve.

SERVES 6

Carrots Delicious

10 medium carrots
4 to 6 large Golden Delicious apples
1/3 cup firmly packed brown sugar

3 tablespoons butter
salt and pepper to taste

Preheat oven to 350 degrees. Butter a 9-x-13-inch baking dish.

Wash and peel carrots and cut into julienne strips by hand or with a food processor. Peel, core, and slice apples into eighths. Steam apples and carrots together until tender but slightly crisp. Make a sauce by combining brown sugar and butter in a saucepan and stirring until sugar has dissolved. Transfer apples and carrots to prepared baking dish, cover with sauce, and toss gently. Sprinkle with salt and pepper, cover, and bake 35 minutes.

SERVES 10

Carrot-Cucumber Relish

Serve this instead of pickle relish as a condiment with meats. Or find occasions for giving to friends as a colorful gift.

12 medium carrots
10 cucumbers
4 yellow or Walla Walla sweet onions
1/4 cup salt

5 cups sugar
3 cups cider vinegar
1 tablespoon celery seeds
1 tablespoon mustard seeds

Peel vegetables, seed cucumbers, and grate or mince (separately) in a food processor. Measure out 3 cups of each. Add salt, allow to stand 3 hours, and drain.

Sterilize 5 1-pint or 10 1/2-pint canning jars with lids.

In a large pot, combine sugar, vinegar, and spices and bring to boil. Add vegetables and simmer 20 minutes. Spoon into sterilized jars, wipe rims, and tighten lids.

Place a wine rack in bottom of a boiler. Fill boiler with water to about jar height. When water boils, lower jars into boiler. The jars must not touch each other or the sides of the boiler and should be 2 inches apart. Add more boiling water so there will be about 1 inch above jar lids, and continue to add boiling water as water evaporates. Boil, uncovered, for 10 minutes, timing from when water begins to boil after jars have been added. Remove jars from boiler by using tongs on sides of jars, not on the lids. Cool on wood or on a rack. Check seals after 24 hours.

YIELD: 5 PINTS

Carrots with Glazed Grapes

1½ pounds carrots
½ cup butter
½ teaspoon ground coriander
½ teaspoon salt

1 to 2 tablespoons firmly packed
    brown sugar
1 pound seedless grapes or Red
    Emperor grapes, halved and
    seeded

Peel and cut carrots into bite-size pieces. Melt ¼ cup butter in large skillet, and add coriander, salt, and carrots. Cover and cook over medium heat approximately 8 minutes. Remove carrots with slotted spoon. Add remaining butter and stir in brown sugar. Return carrots to skillet and add grapes, tossing gently to combine with carrots and coat with glaze.

SERVES 8

Carrot Flan with Honey–Butter Glaze

An eye-catching addition to any menu.

Butter Pastry
*Prepare and refrigerate according to
    instructions in Individual Mush-
    room Tarts (page 248)*

Carrot Filling
3 pounds carrots

1 tablespoon sugar
¼ cup butter
salt, pepper, and nutmeg to taste

Honey–Butter Glaze
2 tablespoons honey
1 tablespoon butter

Preheat oven to 350 degrees.

Remove pastry from refrigerator and roll out on a lightly floured surface or pastry cloth. Using a 9-inch flan or quiche pan with removable bottom, gently press pastry into pan sides and bottom. Cover pastry with foil and weight with pastry weights or dried beans to prevent bubbles during baking. Bake for 30 to 45 minutes or until sides are golden, then increase temperature to 400 degrees. Remove foil and weights and continue baking an additional 3 to 4 minutes—until bottom is golden. Remove and set on rack to cool.

To prepare filling: Peel carrots and cut into ¼- to ⅛-inch slices. Steam or microwave until tender but slightly crisp. Remove 2½ cups of the largest, most uniform slices and return remaining carrots to continue cooking until very tender. In a mixing bowl or food processor, combine this second batch of carrots with sugar, butter, and seasonings, and thoroughly mash or purée. (Filling may be prepared ahead and refrigerated up to 24 hours.) Fill cooled pastry shell with puréed filling and overlap reserved carrot slices on top to form a decorative spiral pattern.

To prepare glaze: Melt honey and butter and stir to the consistency of syrup. Brush over carrot filling and bake flan for 10 minutes or until heated thoroughly. Remove the sides of the pan and carefully transfer flan to a serving platter. Cool 10 minutes before slicing.

SERVES 8

Marinated Cauliflower and Shallots

1 medium, well-formed cauliflower	salt and pepper to taste
¾ cup vegetable oil or olive oil	1 tablespoon parsley
½ cup white vinegar	2 to 3 lettuce leaves for garnish
3 tablespoons minced shallots	red bell pepper strips for garnish
2 tablespoons lemon juice	(optional)
1 clove garlic, minced	

Separate cauliflower into bite-size flowerets. Steam only until slightly tender—do not overcook. Plunge into ice water to stop further cooking. Make a marinade by combining oil, vinegar, shallots, lemon juice, garlic, and seasoning. Place cauliflower in a wide, shallow container and add marinade.

Just before serving, arrange lettuce leaves on a serving dish to form a bed for the cauliflower. With a slotted spoon remove cauliflower from marinade. Drain each spoonful thoroughly and arrange on lettuce. Garnish with red pepper strips and some of the minced shallots from marinade.

SERVES 8

Note: Reserve the marinade for another salad or for drizzling over a hot green vegetable.

Cauliflower Deluxe

1 large cauliflower
1 cup sour cream
3 tablespoons mayonnaise
1 tablespoon chopped parsley
¼ teaspoon salt

pepper to taste
¼ cup dry white wine
¾ cup grated Monterey jack cheese
⅓ cup grated Parmesan cheese
paprika to taste

Preheat oven to 350 degrees. Butter a 1½-quart casserole.

Rinse cauliflower and break into flowerets. Steam until tender but slightly crisp. Combine sour cream, mayonnaise, parsley, salt, pepper, and wine in a food processor or blender, processing for 15 seconds. Transfer mixture to a bowl and add Monterey jack. Fold in cauliflower. Pour into prepared dish, top with Parmesan, and bake for 20 minutes, or until bubbly and golden brown on top. Garnish with paprika.

SERVES 6

Leeks Vinaigrette

12 small leeks
3 whole cloves
2 cups dry vermouth or dry white
    wine

Vinaigrette
2 teaspoons Dijon-style mustard with
    tarragon

2 teaspoons salt
½ teaspoon freshly ground pepper
¼ teaspoon sugar
¼ cup tarragon wine vinegar
1 cup olive oil
2 tablespoons minced fresh tarragon

Wash and trim leeks to 6 inches above white part. Split in half to 1 inch above root ends, not allowing leeks to separate completely. Combine cloves and vermouth in a medium saucepan and bring to a boil over high heat. Reduce heat, add leeks, and poach gently 5 to 8 minutes. Drain, transfer to a shallow bowl, cover, and refrigerate.

To prepare the vinaigrette: Combine mustard, salt, pepper, and sugar in a blender. Add vinegar and continue blending. With blender running, add oil in a steady stream. When liquid has thickened, add tarragon and mix 3 to 4 seconds more. Refrigerate, covered. (Vinaigrette may be prepared up to a week in advance.)

To serve, arrange leeks on a platter and pour some of the vinaigrette over them. Serve remaining vinaigrette separately.

SERVES 6

Mushrooms Metropolitan

1 pound mushrooms	¼ teaspoon salt
2 tablespoons butter	freshly ground pepper to taste
½ cup sour cream	½ cup freshly grated Parmesan cheese
1 tablespoon flour	¼ cup minced parsley

Preheat oven to 425 degrees.

Slice or halve the mushrooms and sauté in butter in a large skillet for 2 to 3 minutes. Using a wire whisk, combine the sour cream, flour, salt, and pepper in a small mixing bowl. Stir into skillet with mushrooms and heat until sauce bubbles but does not curdle. Spoon into an oven-proof dish, sprinkle with cheese and parsley, and bake 10 minutes.

SERVES 4 TO 6

Individual Mushroom Tarts

Butter Pastry

1 cup flour
¼ teaspoon salt
2 teaspoons powdered sugar
½ cup butter
½ of a slightly beaten egg yolk
   (approximately 1 teaspoon)

Filling

12 ounces button mushrooms, sliced
   thin
5 green onions, minced
1½ cups heavy cream
1 teaspoon tarragon (2 teaspoons if
   fresh)
salt and pepper to taste
4 cherry tomatoes and parsley for
   garnish

Preheat oven to 350 degrees.

To prepare pastry: Sift flour, salt, and sugar into a large bowl. Cut butter into flour. Add egg yolk and mix *by hand* until just blended. Form dough into a ball and refrigerate at least an hour or overnight before rolling out. After dough has been refrigerated, divide into 4 sections. Gently roll out each section on a floured surface and press into individual tart pans. Bake 10 minutes, or until golden. Remove and cool. When cooled, carefully remove pastry from pans. Set on paper towels until ready to fill (or freeze until needed).

To prepare filling: Combine mushrooms, green onions, and cream in a skillet. Simmer over medium heat, stirring occasionally, until cream is absorbed and mixture has thickened—10 to 15 minutes. Be sure cream does not burn. Add tarragon, salt, and pepper. Remove from heat and spoon into tart shells. Garnish with cherry tomatoes and/or parsley. Serve warm.

SERVES 4

Hot Potatoes

2 large baking potatoes
2 tablespoons olive oil
2 ounces Monterey jack cheese, grated
1½ tablespoons green chili salsa

3½ tablespoons sour cream
1 teaspoon butter
paprika for garnish

Preheat oven to 425 degrees.

Scrub potato skins, pat dry, and oil generously. Pierce each potato and bake on a cookie sheet for 1 hour. Cool 10 minutes and cut each potato in half lengthwise. Scoop out most of the pulp, leaving enough so skins can hold their shape. Set skins aside.

Reduce oven temperature to 350 degrees. Mix the potato pulp with the cheese, salsa, and sour cream, whipping by hand to blend. Do not overmix—you want some texture. Spoon potato filling into the skins and bake for 10 to 15 minutes. Remove, dot with butter, and sprinkle with paprika. Place under broiler until butter is bubbly.

SERVES 4

Pippin Canoes

Canoes
4 large baking potatoes
4 to 6 tablespoons butter

Applesauce
12 to 14 Pippin or other apples

¼ cup lemon juice
½ cup sugar (optional)
dash cinnamon
additional sugar to taste

Preheat oven to 375 degrees.

Scrub potatoes and bake until tender. Melt butter.

To prepare applesauce: Peel, core, and quarter apples. Add lemon juice and sugar. Place in a large kettle and add just enough water to prevent scorching. Cover and cook over medium heat, stirring occasionally, adding more water if necessary. When apples have reached the desired consistency, taste to adjust sweetness and add cinnamon. Set aside to cool, but do not refrigerate.

When potatoes are baked, remove them from oven, butter the skins, and cut in half lengthwise. Increase oven temperature to 450 degrees. Scoop out and discard most of the potato, leaving just enough to support the skins. Brush butter on inside of each "canoe" and return to oven, baking until crisp. Remove, fill with applesauce, and serve 8 edible canoes.

SERVES 4 OR 8

Variations: Cut scooped-out skins into strips before re-baking and serve with peanut butter and chutney or guacamole as an hors d'oeuvre. As alternative fillings try puréed vegetables, cheese, guacamole, or taco salad.

Spinach Rockefeller

2 10-ounce packages frozen chopped
    spinach
2 eggs
¼ cup minced green onion
¼ cup freshly grated Parmesan cheese
½ teaspoon minced garlic

½ teaspoon minced thyme
⅛ teaspoon freshly ground pepper
½ teaspoon salt
6 to 10 ¼-inch slices of large firm
    tomatoes
¼ cup garlic-flavored bread crumbs

Preheat oven to 375 degrees. Grease a baking sheet.

Cook spinach according to package directions. Drain and squeeze out excess liquid, and set aside on paper towels. Beat eggs in a small bowl. Add green onions, Parmesan, garlic, thyme, pepper, and salt, and blend thoroughly.

Arrange tomato slices with at least 1 inch between them on baking sheet. Add spinach to egg mixture and stir to combine all ingredients. With a slotted spoon, scoop out enough spinach mixture to cover a slice of tomato, allowing excess liquid to drain out before placing spinach on the tomato. Leave a small border of tomato showing. Top spinach with bread crumbs and bake 15 minutes, or until spinach is set. Remove from oven and use a spatula to transfer carefully to plates.

SERVES 6 TO 8

Variation: Place a fresh oyster or minced clams on each tomato slice before adding topping.

Herb-Spinach Soufflé

1 10-ounce package frozen chopped
   spinach
2 tablespoons butter, softened
1 cup cooked rice
1 cup grated sharp Cheddar cheese
2 eggs, lightly beaten

⅓ cup milk
2 tablespoons minced onion
½ teaspoon salt
½ teaspoon Worcestershire sauce
¼ teaspoon crushed rosemary

Preheat oven to 350 degrees and grease a 1½-quart soufflé dish with 1 tablespoon of butter.

Cook spinach according to package directions. Drain well, squeeze out excess water, combine with remaining butter and other ingredients, and transfer to prepared soufflé dish. (Soufflé may be refrigerated at this point to be baked later in the day.) Place soufflé dish in a larger pan with at least 2 inches of water in the bottom and bake for 30 to 45 minutes. Be sure center is set before removing from oven.

SERVES 6 TO 8

Spaghetti Squash Sauté

1 eggplant, peeled and cubed
1 teaspoon salt
1 spaghetti squash (approximately 3 to
   4 pounds)
½ to 1 tablespoon olive oil
½ to 1 tablespoon butter

salt and pepper to taste
2 cloves garlic, minced
2 tablespoons (approximately) olive oil
½ cup minced parsley
½ cup freshly grated Parmesan cheese

Salt eggplant cubes and set aside. Cut spaghetti squash in half, remove seeds, and steam 20 to 25 minutes. Remove skin and separate squash with fork (squash will resemble spaghetti). Sauté in a mixture of olive oil and butter for about 5 minutes, adding salt and pepper.

Sauté garlic and cubed eggplant in olive oil until eggplant is soft. Toss with parsley. Place warm squash on platter. Spoon eggplant over top and sprinkle generously with cheese.

SERVES 6 TO 8

Sneaky Squash Fries

1 pound spaghetti or butternut squash	Garnishes (choose 1)
⅔ cup safflower oil	salt and pepper
¾ cup milk	parsley and garlic salt
½ cup flour	cinnamon and sugar
	tomato salsa

Peel, seed, and slice squash into strips or wedges as if for French fries. Dry wedges with paper towels. Heat oil very hot in a skillet; if using an electric skillet, heat to 325 degrees. Dip wedges into milk, then into flour. Shake off excess and sauté until crisp and golden. Drain on paper towels and keep warm in oven until all wedges have been sautéed. Serve with 1 of the garnishes or create your own.

SERVES 6

Spaghetti Squash with Orange–Nut Butter

2 medium-size spaghetti squash (about 3 pounds each)	2 tablespoons orange juice
1 cup chopped filberts, pecans, almonds or a combination	2 tablespoons firmly packed brown sugar or honey
½ cup butter	½ teaspoon ground nutmeg
1 tablespoon freshly grated orange zest	

Preheat oven to 325 degrees. Lightly oil a large baking sheet.

Pierce squash shells in 5 or 6 places with a fork. Place squash on baking sheet and bake until shells are soft when pressed—about 2 hours. Turn squash over after 1 hour in oven. While squash is baking, toast nuts in oven for about 15 minutes. Blend butter with grated zest, juice, and brown sugar. Add nutmeg and set aside.

When squash is done, cut in half lengthwise, remove seeds carefully, and scoop out squash. If any half-shell is firm enough, save it to use as a serving container. Toss squash with butter mixture and toasted nuts and place in shell or dish. Serve immediately or keep warm in 200-degree oven.

SERVES 12 TO 14

Yellow and Green Strudel

1 pound zucchini
6 tablespoons butter, melted
3 to 4 green onions, chopped
10 to 12 ounces peas, fresh or frozen
1 cup ricotta or cottage cheese
½ cup freshly grated Parmesan cheese

1 egg, lightly beaten
1 tablespoon fresh dill
3 to 4 sheets phyllo
½ cup toasted bread crumbs
sesame seeds for garnish (optional)

Preheat oven to 350 degrees. Lightly oil a baking sheet.

Scrub zucchini and shred in a food processor or julienne by hand. Put 2 tablespoons butter in a medium skillet and sauté green onions and peas until tender. Remove from heat and blend in zucchini, cheeses, egg, and dill.

Brush phyllo sheets with most of remaining melted butter. Stack the sheets and sprinkle the top with bread crumbs. Place vegetable-cheese mixture in center of phyllo sheets in a loaf shape. Fold short ends of phyllo over mixture, then fold phyllo sides over it, and place strudel seam side down on prepared baking sheet. Brush top with melted butter and sprinkle with sesame seeds.

Put on prepared baking sheet and bake until pastry is golden—approximately 15 minutes. Slice into individual servings and place on a warm platter. If desired, arrange slices in a circle and fill center with rice, rice salad, or colorful garnishes.

SERVES 4

Variation: To reduce calories, use ricotta cheese, reduce Parmesan to ⅓ cup, and use only 1 sheet phyllo.

Zucchini with Pesto

In Italy, pesto is often thinned with 1 or 2 tablespoons of hot water from the pasta before being mixed with the pasta—a useful tip for when you prepare pesto for your own pasta recipe. In the meantime, zucchini takes on a new look when combined with pesto.

6 medium zucchini
2 tablespoons butter
½ tablespoon olive oil

Pesto
1½ cups fresh basil leaves
½ cup parsley

½ cup pine nuts or walnuts
¼ teaspoon salt
½ teaspoon pepper
1½ teaspoons minced garlic
½ cup olive oil
½ cup freshly grated Parmesan cheese

To prepare pesto: In a blender or food processor, combine all ingredients except cheese. Blend at high speed until smooth, stopping the blender every few seconds to push the herbs down with a rubber spatula. Pesto should be thin enough to run off the spatula easily. Transfer to a bowl and stir in the Parmesan. (Pesto may be prepared ahead of time and refrigerated.)

Peel zucchini and cut into 2-inch julienne strips. Sauté in butter and olive oil in a large saucepan, stirring gently. When zucchini is tender but slightly crisp, drain and transfer to a heated platter and place in a warm oven.

Add half the pesto to the saucepan and return to medium heat until warmed thoroughly. Remove zucchini from oven and put into the saucepan, tossing gently until coated. Add more pesto if desired, or heat remaining sauce separately and offer as an accompaniment. Serve zucchini on a heated platter immediately after adding sauce.

SERVES 8

Zucchini and Rice Monterey

1 large zucchini, grated
1½ teaspoons salt
2 cups cooked rice
1 7-ounce can diced green chilis
4 cups grated Monterey jack cheese
    (about ¾ pound)

1½ cups sour cream
1 teaspoon oregano
2 tablespoons chopped green bell
    pepper
3 tablespoons chopped green onions
2 tablespoons chopped parsley

Salt zucchini and set aside for 30 minutes in a glass bowl. Preheat oven to 350 degrees. Butter a baking dish.

In a large mixing bowl, combine remaining ingredients. Squeeze excess liquid from zucchini, add zucchini to rice, and spoon the mixture into prepared dish. (Mixture may be refrigerated at this point and baked the next day.) Bake for 30 minutes, uncovered, or until heated through.

SERVES 8 TO 10

Zucchini-Stuffed Tomatoes

4 medium tomatoes
2 cups grated zucchini
⅓ cup chopped onion
1 cup grated Swiss or Gruyère cheese

¾ teaspoon salt
¼ teaspoon pepper
¼ teaspoon basil

Preheat oven to 350 degrees.

Slice tops off tomatoes and scoop out insides, discarding seeds but reserving some pulp. Drain liquid from pulp. Sprinkle insides of tomatoes with ½ teaspoon salt and invert tomatoes to drain on paper towels, allowing to stand for 30 minutes. Pat dry. In medium bowl, combine drained tomato pulp with zucchini, onion, cheese, remaining salt, pepper, and basil. Place tomatoes on a baking sheet and fill each with zucchini mixture. Bake for 10 minutes and serve.

SERVES 4

Mint-and-Rice-Stuffed Tomatoes

12 medium or 6 large tomatoes
2 cups uncooked brown or white rice
   (or a combination)
¾ cup olive oil

1 large Walla Walla sweet or yellow
   onion
6 tablespoons chopped fresh mint
2 teaspoons oregano
salt and pepper to taste

Preheat oven to 350 degrees.

Slice tops off tomatoes, and remove seeds and pulp, leaving sides intact. Chop pulp and set aside to be added to rice. Salt inside of each tomato and invert onto paper towels to drain.

Cook rice and drain when barely tender. Rinse briefly in cold water, return to pan, and stir in ½ cup olive oil. Chop onion thoroughly. Add onion, mint, oregano, tomato pulp, salt, and pepper to rice and mix well. (Dish may be prepared ahead to this point.) Fill tomatoes with rice mixture and place close together in a shallow baking dish. Pour remaining olive oil carefully around tomatoes and add water to surround the bottom third of the tomatoes. Bake 35 minutes, or until tender. Cool slightly and serve.

SERVES 6 OR 12

Green Tomatoes in Sour Cream

¼ cup butter
8 large green tomatoes, cut into ½-inch
   slices
curry powder to taste
paprika to taste
sugar (optional)

salt to taste
3 large onions (a combination of
   yellow, red, and white), cut into
   ¼-inch slices
¼ cup minced parsley

2 cups sour cream thinned with ½ cup   ¼ cup wheat germ or bread crumbs
   milk   ½ cup freshly grated Parmesan cheese

Preheat oven to 350 degrees.

Melt butter in a large skillet over medium-high heat. Add tomatoes and simmer for 10 minutes, turning once, until tomatoes are limp, adding more butter if necessary. Transfer tomatoes to 1½-quart oven-proof serving dish, sprinkle with curry powder, paprika, sugar, and salt, and set aside. Layer onions over tomatoes, repeat seasonings, and sprinkle with parsley. Spread sour cream evenly over top. Blend wheat germ with the cheese and sprinkle over sour cream. Bake for 20 minutes or until sour cream begins to bubble.

SERVES 6

Green Tomato Sauce

Freeze several batches in the summer and use as a hostess gift all year long.

7 hot yellow peppers (more for a
   hotter sauce)
1½ pounds green tomatoes
¼ small onion   salt and pepper to taste
1 medium bunch parsley or fresh   ½ small red tomato
   coriander   ½ cup water

Wash green tomatoes, drop into boiling water to cover, and boil 5 minutes. Remove from water and cool several minutes. Peel and quarter onion. Remove stems from parsley or coriander. Clean peppers and remove seeds and stems.

In a blender or food processor, combine green tomatoes, red tomato, onion, parsley, peppers, and seasonings. Blend to a chunky (not puréed) consistency, adding water as soon as desired consistency is reached. For a thinner sauce, add a little extra water.

YIELD: ABOUT 3 PINTS

Marinated Tomatoes

4 to 6 firm tomatoes or 2 baskets   1 clove garlic
   cherry tomatoes   1 teaspoon seasoning salt
4 tablespoons vegetable oil   ½ teaspoon thyme
4 tablespoons wine vinegar

Slice tomatoes and layer in a glass bowl. Combine remaining ingredients, pour over tomatoes, chill, and serve.

SERVES 6 TO 8

Vegetable Pâté

This unique pâté is worth the effort!

Pâté

3 10-ounce packages frozen chopped
  spinach, defrosted
12 eggs
3 teaspoons salt
½ teaspoon ground nutmeg
½ teaspoon freshly ground pepper
2 28-ounce cans plum tomatoes
1 small yellow onion, minced

¼ teaspoon basil
2 large red or Walla Walla sweet
  onions (about 1 pound)
1 tablespoon butter
1 cup heavy cream

Sauce
1 cup sour cream
2 to 3 teaspoons prepared horseradish

Preheat oven to 425 degrees. Prepare a 5-x-9-inch loaf pan by cutting a piece of foil to fit the bottom. Butter foil and sides of pan.

Spinach Layer: Squeeze moisture out of spinach. In a medium bowl, beat 4 eggs; add 1 teaspoon salt, nutmeg, and ¼ teaspoon pepper. Blend in spinach, mix well, and set aside.

Tomato Layer: Seed, *thoroughly* drain, and finely chop the tomatoes. In a large skillet over medium heat, combine tomatoes and yellow onion and simmer until the tomato and onion liquids have evaporated completely. Set aside to cool. In a small bowl, beat 4 eggs, 1 teaspoon salt, and basil. Add to tomato mixture, mix well, and set aside.

Onion Layer: Uniformly chop the large onions. Melt butter in the skillet over medium heat, add onions, and sauté until limp. Add cream and simmer gently, stirring often until cream is absorbed and mixture thickens—about 20 minutes. Cool. In a small bowl, beat remaining eggs, salt, and pepper. Add to onion mixture and set aside.

Spread half the spinach mixture on bottom of prepared loaf pan. Top with all of the tomato mixture, then the onion mixture and remaining spinach. Spread gently to cover. Butter another piece of foil and cover top of pâté, buttered side down. Place loaf pan in a larger (9-x-13-inch) pan and fill the larger pan with 1½ inches of boiling water. Bake pâté 1 hour and 20 minutes, or until knife inserted in center comes out clean. (Be sure to pull back foil when testing for doneness.) When pâté is done, lift loaf pan from water and set on a rack to cool for 10 minutes. Remove foil from top.

When pâté has cooled, run a spatula around sides to loosen. Invert a serving plate over top and turn loaf pan over to unmold. Lift off bottom foil and cool pâté to room temperature. (At this point pâté and sauce may be refrigerated for up to 2 days. Cover both carefully with plastic wrap. Before serving bring to room temperature or warm in oven.) To serve, cut pâté into ½- to ¾-inch slices.

To prepare sauce: Combine sour cream and horseradish. Pass sauce separately.

SERVES 8 TO 10

Rumanian Vegetables

1 cup sliced carrots, ¼-inch thick
1 cup cut green beans, 1½-inch lengths
1 cup peeled and diced potato
½ cup diagonally sliced celery
2 tomatoes, cut in wedges
1 small zucchini, cubed or sliced
½ red onion, sliced thin
½ head cauliflower, cut into flowerets
½ cup frozen peas, partially thawed
1 cup beef broth
⅓ cup olive oil
1 teaspoon salt
½ teaspoon savory
¼ teaspoon tarragon
¼ teaspoon basil
¼ teaspoon oregano
3 cloves garlic

Preheat oven to 350 degrees.

Toss vegetables together and place in a 9-x-13-inch baking dish. Combine remaining ingredients and bring to a boil in a medium saucepan. Pour over vegetables, cover, and bake for about 1 hour.

SERVES 10 TO 12

Vegetable Sauté

A last-minute dish to make with whatever vegetables might be on hand. Try it in place of an ordinary salad. A great partner for a steak dinner.

¼ pound spinach leaves or green
    beans
6 slices lean bacon
4½ tablespoons butter
1 Walla Walla sweet or red onion,
    chopped
2 medium zucchini in ¼-inch slices
½ pound mushrooms, sliced
½ teaspoon salt
⅛ teaspoon pepper
¼ cup freshly grated Parmesan cheese
½ cup cashew nuts (optional)
¼ cup toasted sesame seeds (optional)

Remove spinach stems and slice leaves in strips. (If using green beans, cut into 1-inch lengths.) Fry bacon in a large skillet. When crisp, drain, crumble, and set aside. Pour off drippings and wipe skillet with paper towels.

Melt butter in the same skillet, add onion, and sauté until tender (3 minutes). Increase heat to medium-high and add zucchini. Cook, stirring briskly, until tender but slightly crisp. Add mushrooms and sauté 1 minute longer. Add spinach strips or green beans, salt, pepper, and bacon. Heat thoroughly for about 1 minute. Sprinkle grated cheese on top, garnish with cashews or sesame seeds, and serve immediately.

SERVES 4 TO 6

Moveable Feast Vegetable Sauce

To serve warm over any blanched vegetable or cold as a dip for crudités.

½ cup butter
3 egg yolks
½ teaspoon salt

1 teaspoon tarragon
1 tablespoon minced shallots or onion
2 tablespoons white wine vinegar

Melt butter in a small saucepan and set aside. Combine remaining ingredients in a blender or food processor and process for 5 seconds. With motor still running, pour melted butter in a steady stream into egg mixture.

YIELD: 1 CUP

Cheese-Herb Butter

½ cup butter
¼ cup minced parsley
½ teaspoon Italian herbs
¼ teaspoon salt

½ small clove garlic
¼ teaspoon freshly ground pepper
⅓ cup grated Parmesan cheese

In a food processor, combine ingredients and process until smooth. Refrigerate until ready to serve. To serve, heat and pour over hot cooked vegetables.

YIELD: ABOUT 1½ CUPS

Wild apple blossoms near Conway, in the Skagit River Valley north of Seattle, with an abandoned dairy barn presiding over the tranquility.

Desserts, Sorbets, & Sweets

>==<

Scottish Shortbread

1 cup butter, softened
¾ cup powdered sugar
⅓ cup plus 1 tablespoon cornstarch

1⅓ cups flour
pinch of salt
⅓ cup sugar

Preheat oven to 325 degrees.

Cream together butter and powdered sugar. Sift together cornstarch, flour, and salt; gradually beat into butter–sugar mixture. Pat dough into 2 ungreased 9-inch springform pans and prick all over with a fork. Bake for 20 minutes, lower heat to 300 degrees, and continue baking 25 to 30 minutes more—until light golden brown. Remove from oven, cut immediately into 16 pieces per pan, and sprinkle with sugar. Cool; then remove sides of pan.

YIELD: 32 PIECES

Note: If dough sticks to fingers when being pressed into pan, chill it about 5 minutes, then continue pressing. Dough will be thin—about ¼ inch thick—barely enough to cover the bottoms of the pans.

Lemon-Glazed Shortbread

First Layer
1½ cups flour
½ cup firmly packed brown sugar
½ cup butter

Second Layer
2 eggs
1 cup firmly packed brown sugar
1½ cups coconut

1 cup chopped nuts
2 tablespoons flour
½ teaspoon baking powder
½ teaspoon vanilla extract
¼ teaspoon salt

Frosting
1 cup powdered sugar
1 tablespoon butter, melted
juice and grated zest of 1 lemon

Preheat oven to 350 degrees.

To prepare first layer: Combine ingredients and mix until crumbly. Press into a 9-x-13-inch baking pan. Bake for 10 minutes, remove from oven, and reduce oven heat to 325 degrees.

To prepare second layer: Beat eggs lightly; and add brown sugar and beat well. Stir in remaining ingredients, and spread over baked mixture. Bake for 15 minutes.

To prepare frosting: Combine ingredients and spread over cookies while still warm. Cut cookies into bars and refrigerate.

YIELD: 4 DOZEN

Grandma's Whoppers

1 cup butter
1 cup sugar
1 cup firmly packed brown sugar
2 eggs
1 teaspoon vanilla extract
2 cups flour

1 teaspoon baking soda
1 teaspoon baking powder
¼ teaspoon salt
1 cup corn flakes, wheat flakes, or
    other unsweetened cereal flakes
1 cup rolled oats (oatmeal)

Preheat oven to 325 degrees.

Beat together butter, sugar, brown sugar, eggs, and vanilla. Sift together flour, baking soda, baking powder, and salt. Stir into butter mixture. Mix in flaked cereal and oats. Drop by heaping tablespoons onto baking sheets, about 3 inches apart. Bake for 20 minutes.

YIELD: ABOUT 20 4-INCH COOKIES

Variation: For variety, add raisins, chocolate or flavored chips, or nuts. For a more crunchy cookie, increase the flakes to 3 cups.

Garden-Fresh Cookies

⅔ cup butter, softened
1¼ cup firmly packed brown sugar
2 eggs
1 teaspoon vanilla extract
1 tablespoon grated lemon zest
½ cup buttermilk or sour milk
2 cups flour
1 teaspoon baking powder

1 teaspoon baking soda
1 teaspoon salt
1 teaspoon cinnamon
¼ teaspoon nutmeg
2 cups rolled oats (oatmeal)
1 cup currants
½ cup chopped walnuts
2 cups grated carrots or zucchini

Preheat oven to 400 degrees. Butter 2 cookie sheets.

Cream together butter and brown sugar; add eggs, vanilla, lemon zest, and buttermilk. Stir until well mixed. In another bowl, sift together flour, baking powder, baking soda, salt, cinnamon, and nutmeg. Add flour mixture, and then stir in oats, currants, nuts, and grated carrots. Drop by tablespoons onto prepared cookie sheets. Bake about 12 minutes, or until lightly browned.

YIELD: ABOUT 5 DOZEN

Waterford Crystal Cookies

1 cup butter
1 cup vegetable oil
1 cup sugar
1 cup powdered sugar
2 eggs

4 cups flour
1 teaspoon baking soda
1 teaspoon cream of tartar
½ teaspoon salt
1 tablespoon vanilla extract

Cream together the first 4 ingredients, then add remaining ingredients, mixing well. Refrigerate for 2 hours.

Preheat oven to 350 degrees; butter 2 cookie sheets.

Form dough into small balls on prepared pans. Flatten with the greased bottom of a Waterford crystal glass or any glass with a pattern in the base (or a cookie stamp) dipped in sugar. Bake for 10 to 12 minutes.

YIELD: ABOUT 5 DOZEN

Variation: Add 1 teaspoon lemon juice and grated zest of 1 lemon to batter. Sprinkle with nutmeg after stamping.

Disappearing Marshmallow Brownies

½ cup butterscotch chips
¼ cup butter
¾ cup flour
⅓ cup firmly packed brown sugar
1 teaspoon baking powder
¼ teaspoon salt

½ teaspoon vanilla extract
1 egg
1 cup miniature marshmallows
1 cup semisweet chocolate chips
¼ cup chopped nuts

Preheat oven to 350 degrees. Butter a 9-inch-square pan.

Melt butterscotch chips and butter in a heavy 3-quart saucepan over medium heat, stirring constantly. Remove from heat; cool to lukewarm. Add flour, brown sugar, baking powder, salt, vanilla, and egg to butterscotch mixture; mix well. Fold marshmallows, chocolate chips, and nuts into batter just until combined, using about 5 strokes. Spread in prepared pan and bake for 20 to 25 minutes; *do not overbake.* Center will become firm after cooling. Cut when cool.

YIELD: 12 TO 18

Chocolate-Caramel Cookies

First Layer

1 cup butter
½ cup sugar
2 cups flour
1 teaspoon baking powder

Second Layer

1 cup butter

1 cup firmly packed brown sugar
¼ cup light corn syrup
1 14-ounce can sweetened condensed
  milk

Third Layer

6 ounces semisweet chocolate

Preheat oven to 350 degrees.

To prepare first layer: Cream together butter and sugar. Gradually add flour and baking powder, beating well after each addition. Pat into a 9-x-13-inch pan. Bake for 15 to 20 minutes, or until light brown. Cool.

To prepare second layer: Melt butter, brown sugar, corn syrup, and milk in saucepan. Bring to a boil and stir constantly for 8 minutes—to 238 degrees on a candy thermometer. Pour onto first layer and cool.

To prepare third layer: Melt chocolate and immediately pour over second layer. Cool cookies until very firm before cutting into squares.

Note: Do not freeze these cookies!

YIELD: 4 DOZEN

Duwamish Mud Bars

2 cups flour
2 cups sugar
½ teaspoon salt
1 cup butter
¼ cup unsweetened cocoa
1 cup water
2 eggs
½ cup buttermilk
1 teaspoon baking soda
1 teaspoon vanilla extract

Topping:
1 cup butter
pinch of salt
¼ cup unsweetened cocoa
6 tablespoons buttermilk
3¾ cups powdered sugar (1 pound)
¼ cup chopped nuts
1 teaspoon vanilla extract

Preheat oven to 350 degrees. Butter a 10-x-15-x-1-inch jelly-roll pan.

Sift together flour, sugar, and salt. Over low heat, melt together butter, cocoa, and water. Beat together eggs, buttermilk, baking soda, and vanilla. Add butter mixture to egg mixture, then stir in dry ingredients. Pour into prepared pan, bake for 15 minutes and keep warm.

To prepare topping: Combine and cook over medium heat butter, salt, cocoa, and buttermilk. Remove from heat and add powdered sugar, nuts, and vanilla. Slowly pour hot topping over cake while cake is hot, spreading with a spatula if necessary. Carefully cut into bars while still warm. Cool before serving.

YIELD: 6 DOZEN

Raspberry Bars

1¼ cups flour
½ teaspoon salt
1 teaspoon sugar
1 teaspoon baking powder
½ cup butter
1 egg
¾ cup thick raspberry jam

Topping
2 eggs
1½ cups sugar
2 teaspoons vanilla extract
6 tablespoons butter, melted
2½ cups flaked coconut

Preheat oven to 350 degrees. Butter a 9-x-13-inch pan.

Combine flour, salt, sugar, and baking powder. Using plastic blade of food processor, or with electric beater, blend in butter and egg. Pat this dough into prepared pan. Spoon jam on dough.

To prepare topping: Beat eggs until thick and lemon-colored. Beat in sugar, vanilla, and melted butter. Add coconut and spoon over jam-covered dough. Bake for 30 to 35 minutes; cut into squares when cool.

YIELD: 4 DOZEN

Apple Bars

2 cups flour
½ cup firmly packed brown sugar
¾ cup butter
¼ teaspoon salt
½ cup chopped walnuts (optional)

Filling

1 teaspoon cinnamon
¼ cup sugar

1 tablespoon flour
5 cups peeled, cored, and grated
    apples

Icing

1 cup powdered sugar
1 teaspoon vanilla or maple extract
1 tablespoon milk

Preheat oven to 350 degrees.

Combine flour, brown sugar, butter, salt and walnuts in a food processor. Or combine dry ingredients in a small bowl and cut in butter with a pastry cutter or 2 knives and blend until crumbly. Reserve 1 cup of pastry and press the remainder into a 9-x-13-inch pan.

To prepare filling: Combine the cinnamon and sugar, mix with flour and grated apples, and spread on top of pastry. Crumble the reserved pastry over the top and bake for 25 minutes.

To prepare icing: Combine ingredients and drizzle over top of warm pastry. Cut into bars and serve.

YIELD: 4 DOZEN

Apple Cake

4 cups peeled, cored, and chopped
    apples
1 cup chopped walnuts or other nuts
2 cups flour
2 cups sugar
2 teaspoons baking soda
2 teaspoons cinnamon
1 teaspoon salt
2 eggs
½ cup vegetable oil

2 teaspoons vanilla extract

Cinnamon Sauce

¼ cup butter
1 cup powdered sugar
1 teaspoon vanilla extract
½ teaspoon cinnamon
¼ teaspoon nutmeg
½ cup water

Preheat oven to 375 degrees. Butter and flour a 9-x-13-inch pan.

Combine apples and nuts in a large bowl and sift dry ingredients over top. Mix eggs, oil, and vanilla together; add to the apple–flour mixture and mix until well blended. Bake in prepared pan for 45 minutes; cool.

To prepare sauce: In a saucepan, cream together butter and powdered sugar; add vanilla, cinnamon, and nutmeg. Gradually add water and stir over medium heat until thickened. Serve over warm apple cake.

SERVES 8 TO 10

Note: For richer flavor, allow the cake to stand for 24 hours. Whipped cream, ice cream, or Caramel Sauce (page 302) can be substituted for the Cinnamon Sauce.

Bavarian Apple Torte

½ cup butter
⅓ cup sugar
½ teaspoon vanilla extract
1 cup flour
½ teaspoon salt

Filling
8 ounces cream cheese
¼ cup sugar

1 egg
½ teaspoon vanilla extract

Topping
¼ cup sugar
1 teaspoon cinnamon
2 cups peeled tart cooking apples in
⅛-inch-thick slices, or other fresh
fruit
½ cup strained apricot preserves

Preheat oven to 375 degrees. Butter a 9-inch spring-form pan.

Cream together butter and sugar until fluffy, then beat in vanilla. Add flour and salt, blend, and spread in prepared pan.

To prepare filling: Beat cream cheese until fluffy; add sugar, egg, and vanilla, and beat until smooth. Spread evenly over dough.

To prepare topping: Combine sugar and cinnamon. Dip each apple slice into this mixture and arrange slices over filling in 2 overlapping circles. Warm strained apricot preserves and brush over apples.

Bake torte for 45 to 55 minutes, or until golden. Cool to lukewarm before removing from pan; serve warm or cold.

SERVES 10 TO 12

Mount St. Helens Spectacular

½ cup butter
1 cup sugar
2 eggs

2 1-ounce squares unsweetened
chocolate, melted
½ cup flour

1 teaspoon vanilla extract
1 quart favorite ice cream, softened
5 egg whites

10 tablespoons sugar
¼ cup brandy (optional)

Preheat oven to 325 degrees. Butter an 8-inch spring-form pan.

Cream together butter and sugar; beat in eggs. Add chocolate, mixing well. Add flour and combine thoroughly, then add vanilla. Pour batter into prepared pan and bake for 30 minutes. Allow to cool completely in the pan, then mold ice cream into a cone or mountain shape on top of the cooled brownie. Place in freezer to harden. When completely frozen, use a knife dipped in hot water to loosen ice cream and brownie from the sides of the pan and release the spring-form side. Place the mountain and base on a foil-covered cookie sheet and return to freezer.

Beat egg whites at high speed until frothy. Gradually add sugar and continue beating until meringue holds stiff peaks. Cover brownie and ice cream with meringue and return to freezer. When frozen, cover with plastic wrap.

At serving time, remove plastic and place mountain in 500-degree oven for 2 minutes, or until lightly browned. Remove from oven and let stand 10 minutes before serving. To have your own Mount St. Helens eruption, place a small stainless-steel cup or half an eggshell on top of the ice cream before spreading with meringue. Cover the ice cream and sides of the cup or egg shell with meringue, *but* leave the opening clear. While the mountain stands prior to serving, heat brandy, pour into cup or shell, and flame at the table.

SERVES 12

Variation: Instead of ice cream, use 1 pint heavy cream, whipped, and 10 ounces frozen raspberries, thawed. Fold the berries into the whipped cream and freeze in a bowl with a diameter smaller than 8 inches. Unmold onto cooled brownie and proceed as above.

Rum–Espresso Mousse Cake

5 tablespoons rum
1¼ cups strong espresso
3 tablespoons sugar
1 16-ounce day-old pound cake, or Queen Anne Pound Cake (following recipe)
2 teaspoons rum (optional)

4 eggs, separated
1 teaspoon sugar
10 ounces semisweet chocolate, chips or chopped
1 teaspoon butter
1 cup heavy cream
chocolate-covered coffee beans or walnuts for garnish

Line bottom and sides of a 9-inch spring-form pan with buttered waxed paper, extending it above the rim.

Combine rum, coffee, and 3 tablespoons sugar. Cut pound cake into ¼-inch slices and dip in rum–coffee mixture. Place slices on bottom and along sides of the baking pan, reserving some slices for the top.

Beat egg yolks together with 1 teaspoon sugar until the yolks turn pale yellow. Melt 6 ounces of chocolate; mix into beaten egg yolks and cool. Whip egg whites until they form stiff peaks. Combine 1 tablespoon egg whites with yolks and chocolate; fold in remaining whites and spoon mixture over pound cake. Cover with remaining slices of pound cake dipped in rum–coffee mixture and refrigerate overnight.

The following day, turn the pan over onto a flat serving platter, remove spring-form, carefully peeling off waxed paper. To frost, melt remaining 4 ounces of chocolate with 1 teaspoon butter and cover entire surface of cake with a thin coat. Refrigerate until chocolate hardens—about 45 minutes. Whip cream with rum and decorate cake, using a pastry bag fitted with a decorating tip; garnish with chocolate coffee beans or walnuts. Cut with a serrated knife.

SERVES 10

Queen Anne Pound Cake

1 cup butter, softened
3 cups sugar
6 eggs
1 cup sour cream
3 cups sifted flour

dash salt
¼ teaspoon baking powder
2 teaspoons vanilla extract
powdered sugar for dusting

Preheat oven to 350 degrees. Generously butter a Bundt pan or loaf pan.

Cream butter and blend in sugar. Add eggs one at a time, beating thoroughly each time. Blend in sour cream. Sift flour with salt and baking powder, and add to sour cream mixture a little at a time, blending well after each addition. Add vanilla, pour into prepared pan, and bake for 1 hour and 25 minutes, or until skewer inserted in center comes out clean. Let cool 5 minutes, then invert on rack and cool completely. Remove from pan and wrap tightly in foil for 24 hours. Dust with powdered sugar before serving.

SERVES 8

Sunshine Sponge Cake

6 eggs, separated
¾ teaspoon cream of tartar
1½ cups sugar
½ cup water

1 teaspoon vanilla extract or ½ tea-
    spoon lemon extract and ½ tea-
    spoon almond extract
1 cup cake flour
¼ teaspoon salt

Preheat oven to 325 degrees.

Beat egg whites with cream of tartar until stiff peaks form. Set aside. Bring sugar and water to a boil in a medium saucepan, and cook until mixture reaches 234 degrees on a candy thermometer. Slowly, but in a steady stream, pour sugar syrup into egg whites, continuing to beat until cool, about 5 minutes. Beat egg yolks, add flavoring, and fold into egg-white mixture. Sift flour and salt together and fold into egg mixture, ⅓ cup at a time. Gently pour or spoon batter into an un-greased 10-inch tube pan and bake for 1 hour.

SERVES 8 TO 10

French Almond Torte

1 cup butter
¾ cup sugar
4 ounces almond paste
1 egg yolk
1 teaspoon almond extract

2 cups sifted flour
1 egg white
½ cup sliced almonds, lightly toasted
sorbet or fresh berries (optional)

Preheat oven to 350 degrees. Butter an 8-inch spring-form or cake pan.

Cream together butter and sugar. Crumble and add almond paste and mix with egg yolk and almond extract. Stir in flour and press into prepared pan. Beat egg white until foamy, spread over dough, and cover with almonds. Bake for 30 minutes.

SERVES 8 TO 10

Note: The torte is best if made a day in advance. Cut into small slices, as this is very rich. Serve as is or accompanied by a sorbet or fresh berries.

Orange-Cranberry Cake

2¼ cups flour	grated zest of 2 oranges
1 cup sugar	2 eggs, beaten
¼ teaspoon salt	¼ cup vegetable oil
1 teaspoon baking powder	1 cup buttermilk
1 teaspoon baking soda	
1 cup pecans, chopped or coarsely ground	Topping
	¾ cup orange juice
1 cup dates, chopped	1 cup sugar
1½ cups fresh whole cranberries	

Preheat oven to 350 degrees. Butter a 10-inch tube pan, 2 9-x-5-inch loaf pans, a 9-x-13-inch baking pan, or 4 8-x-4-inch loaf pans.

Sift together flour, sugar, salt, baking powder, and baking soda into a large bowl. Add pecans, dates, cranberries, and orange zest, and toss. Combine eggs, oil, and buttermilk in a small bowl, and add to first mixture, mixing thoroughly. Pour into prepared pan or pans and bake 50 to 60 minutes for a tube pan or large loaf pans, or 30 minutes for a 9-x-13-inch pan or small loaf pans. Remove from oven and let stand 15 minutes.

To prepare topping: Combine juice and sugar in a saucepan over low heat, stirring until sugar is dissolved. Pour over cake. Let cake stand *in pan* over night. Unmold carefully. This cake freezes beautifully and will keep for up to a year.

SERVES 10 TO 12

Variation: Instead of the orange-juice topping, drizzle ¾ cup orange liqueur over the cake.

Rhubarb Meringue Squares

1 cup butter, softened	¼ teaspoon salt
2¼ cups flour	5 cups rhubarb in ¼-inch pieces
2½ cups plus 2 tablespoons sugar	¾ teaspoon cream of tartar
6 eggs, separated	2 teaspoons vanilla extract

Preheat oven to 350 degrees.

Cream the butter. Combine 2 cups flour with 2 tablespoons sugar. Slowly blend flour–sugar mixture into butter, creaming until smooth. Pat dough onto bottom and sides of a 9-x-13-inch pan and bake for 10 minutes.

Meanwhile, beat egg yolks with a wire whisk. Combine 2 cups sugar and remaining flour with salt and add slowly to egg yolks, mixing thoroughly. Stir in rhubarb, pour into crust and bake for 45 minutes.

Beat egg whites with cream of tartar until soft peaks form. *Slowly* add remaining sugar, beat until stiff, and add vanilla. Spread mixture over rhubarb, covering it completely. Return to oven and bake an additional 10 minutes, or until meringue is golden brown. Cool, cut into squares, and serve.

SERVES 6 TO 8

Holiday Nut Cake

½ cup sifted flour
½ cup sugar
½ teaspoon baking powder
½ teaspoon baking soda
2 cups whole, shelled Brazil nuts
    (½ pound)
3 cups whole, shelled walnuts
    (¾ pound)

3 cups pitted dates (¾ pound)
1 cup maraschino cherries (contents of
    1 8-ounce jar), drained
2 eggs
½ teaspoon vanilla extract
1 cup heavy cream, whipped, or 1 pint
    vanilla ice cream (optional)

Preheat oven to 325 degrees. Butter a 9-x-5-inch loaf pan.

In a large bowl, sift together flour, sugar, baking powder, and baking soda. Add nuts, dates, and cherries to flour mixture and stir until coated. Beat eggs well and add vanilla, then carefully stir into flour mixture. Spoon into prepared pan and bake for 60 minutes. Serve with whipped cream or ice cream.

SERVES 12

Chocolate-Chip Orange Cake

¾ cup butter, softened
1½ cups sugar
2 eggs
1½ teaspoons vanilla extract
2½ cups sifted flour
2½ teaspoons baking powder
1 teaspoon salt
1½ cups milk
½ cup semisweet chocolate chips
1 tablespoon finely grated zest
    of orange

Orange Filling
1 cup sugar
6 tablespoons cornstarch
dash salt
1 teaspoon finely grated zest of orange
1⅓ cups orange juice
4 egg yolks, lightly beaten
3 to 4 tablespoons butter

Chocolate Glaze
½ cup semisweet chocolate chips
2 tablespoons butter
1 tablespoon light corn syrup

Preheat oven to 350 degrees. Butter and flour 2 round cake pans 9 inches in diameter and 1½ inches deep.

Thoroughly cream butter and sugar. Add eggs, beating well, then vanilla. Sift together flour, baking powder, and salt, and add alternately with milk to butter mixture, beating well after each addition. Fold in chocolate chips and orange zest. Pour batter into prepared pans and bake for 30 to 35 minutes. Cool cakes in the pans 10 minutes, then remove and cool completely before filling.

To prepare filling: Combine sugar, cornstarch, and salt in a saucepan; stir in orange zest and juice. Cook over medium heat and stir until thick and bubbly, then stir about half the hot mixture into beaten egg yolks. Add this mixture to saucepan; cook and stir until very thick, about 1 to 2 minutes. Remove from heat and stir in butter. Cover surface with waxed paper, cool, and chill. Split cake layers in half horizontally and spread orange filling between layers and between cakes, but not on top.

To prepare glaze: Combine ingredients in a small saucepan; heat and stir over low heat until chocolate melts. Spread over top of cake, allowing chocolate to drizzle down sides.

SERVES 12

Chocolate Mousse Cake

Meringue Layers
⅓ cup unsweetened cocoa
1¾ cups powdered sugar
5 egg whites
pinch cream of tartar
¾ cup sugar

Mousse
13 ounces semisweet chocolate
7 egg whites
¼ teaspoon cream of tartar
3 cups heavy cream, chilled
1½ teaspoons vanilla extract

Preheat oven to 300 degrees. Using an inverted 8-inch-square cake pan as a guide, outline 3 squares on sheets of parchment paper; cut out and place on baking sheets.

To prepare meringue: Sift together cocoa and powdered sugar and set aside. In a large bowl, beat egg whites with a pinch of cream of tartar until soft peaks form. Slowly add sugar, 2 tablespoons at a time. Beat until meringue holds very stiff peaks. Fold in cocoa mixture and divide meringue onto the 3 squares, spreading evenly. Bake 1 hour and 15 minutes; for even baking, rotate baking sheets in oven. Place meringue on racks to cool.

To prepare mousse: Melt chocolate in a double boiler over hot water and cool until lukewarm. In a large bowl, beat egg whites with cream of tartar until stiff peaks form. In another bowl, whip the cream with vanilla, again beating until stiff peaks form. Carefully fold chocolate into egg whites, and fold in cream. Mixture will measure about 9 cups.

Put a meringue square on a 10-inch-diameter cake stand and spread with mousse. Top mousse with second meringue layer, spread thickly with more mousse, and top with third meringue. Transfer the remaining mousse to a pastry bag fitted with a decorative tip and decorate third meringue with rows of overlapping figure-8s. Cover cake and chill for 6 hours or overnight. Cake may be kept up to 48 hours.

SERVES 12

Chocolate–Almond–Carrot Torte

1 cup almonds
¼ cup semisweet chocolate chips
6 eggs, separated
1 cup sugar
1 tablespoon grated zest of orange
¾ teaspoon ground cinnamon
¼ teaspoon salt
½ cup fine dry bread crumbs

1 cup grated carrot

Chocolate Frosting
2 tablespoons butter
⅛ cup semisweet chocolate chips
1 cup powdered sugar
3 tablespoons hot water

Preheat oven to 350 degrees. Generously butter 9- or 10-inch spring-form pan.

Whirl almonds in a blender or food processor until finely ground, and sprinkle bottom of pan with 2 tablespoons of them. Whirl chocolate chips in blender or food processor until ground and set aside. In a large bowl, beat egg whites until foamy. Add ¼ cup sugar, 1 tablespoon at a time, beating until stiff, glossy peaks form; set aside. In a small bowl, beat egg yolks together with remaining sugar, orange zest, cinnamon, and salt until thick. Stir in crumbs and remaining almonds. Press excess liquid out of carrot and gently stir into egg-yolk mixture.

Fold half of carrot mixture into egg whites, then fold in chocolate and remaining carrot mixture until blended. Spread batter into prepared pan and bake for about 45 minutes, or until skewer inserted into center comes out clean. Cool thoroughly in pan, then remove and spread with frosting.

To prepare frosting: Melt butter and chocolate chips in a small pan over low heat. Stir in powdered sugar and hot water, beating with a spoon until smooth. Drizzle over cake.

SERVES 12

Chocolate Truffle Cake

1 cup sugar
¼ cup butter
2 eggs, separated
1 teaspoon vanilla extract
2 ounces unsweetened chocolate,
    melted and cooled
1¼ cups sifted flour
½ teaspoon baking powder
½ teaspoon baking soda
½ teaspoon salt
¾ cup milk

Filling
½ cup semisweet chocolate chips
1 cup heavy cream
½ cup slivered almonds, toasted

Chocolate Glaze
1 ounce unsweetened chocolate
2 tablespoons butter
1½ cups sifted powdered sugar
1 teaspoon vanilla extract
2 to 3 tablespoons boiling water
slivered almonds, toasted, for garnish

Preheat oven to 350 degrees. Butter 2 cake pans 9 inches in diameter and 1½ inches deep.

Cream together sugar and butter. Add egg yolks and vanilla, beat until fluffy, and stir in chocolate. Sift together flour, baking powder, baking soda, and salt. Add to chocolate mixture alternately with milk, beating well after each addition. Beat egg whites until stiff and fold into mixture. Turn into prepared pans and bake for 15 to 18 minutes. Cool 10 minutes, then remove from pans.

To prepare filling: Melt chocolate chips and cool. Whip the cream until fluffy, add the melted chocolate, and continue beating until stiff. Fold in slivered almonds. Place a cake on a serving dish; spread top with filling and put second layer on top of the filling.

To prepare glaze: Melt chocolate with butter and stir in powdered sugar and vanilla. Gradually add boiling water, beating until smooth. Spread over the cake top and garnish with toasted slivered almonds.

SERVES 12

Very Chocolate Cheesecake

Crust

4 ounces chocolate wafers, crushed
3 tablespoons butter, sliced and frozen
2 tablespoons instant coffee
3 tablespoons sugar
½ cup flaked coconut

Filling

3 eggs
1 cup sugar
24 ounces cream cheese, softened
⅛ teaspoon salt

1 cup sour cream
1 teaspoon vanilla extract or Grand
   Marnier
2 cups semisweet chocolate chips,
   melted

Topping

1 cup heavy cream
2 tablespoons powdered sugar
chocolate shavings or chocolate-
   coffee beans for decoration
   (optional)

Preheat oven to 375 degrees.

To prepare crust: Combine wafers and butter, add coffee, sugar, and coconut, and mix well. Press evenly into 9-inch spring-form pan and freeze for 10 minutes while preparing filling.

To prepare filling: Beat eggs with sugar until light. Beat in cream cheese until smooth, then add remaining ingredients and again beat until smooth. Pour into crust and bake for 60 minutes; *do not overbake.* Cool in pan on rack; cake will become firm as it cools. Refrigerate.

To prepare topping: Beat cream with powdered sugar until stiff peaks form. Spread on cooled cake or apply with pastry bag. Remove sides of spring-form pan and decorate cake with chocolate shavings or chocolate-covered coffee beans, if desired.

SERVES 12 TO 14

Note: For the best flavor and texture, this cheesecake should be made the day before it is to be served.

Fudge–Almond Cheesecake

Crust

1 cup graham cracker crumbs
½ cup ground toasted almonds
½ cup butter, melted
1 tablespoon Amaretto

Filling

24 ounces cream cheese, softened
1 cup sugar
3 eggs
1½ teaspoons almond extract
1 teaspoon vanilla extract

Topping

1 cup semisweet chocolate chips

3 tablespoons butter

½ cup whole almonds, toasted

Preheat oven to 350 degrees.

To prepare crust: Combine cracker crumbs, almonds, and butter; add Amaretto, and press into bottom and halfway up sides of 8- or 9-inch spring-form pan.

To prepare filling: Beat cream cheese until smooth and creamy, add sugar and blend well. Beat in eggs, 1 at a time, then add extracts. Pour into crust and bake for 40 minutes. Turn off oven, open door, and allow cake to cool in oven. When cool, remove cake from pan.

To prepare topping: Melt together chocolate chips and butter, and swirl over filling. Garnish with almonds.

SERVES 12 TO 14

Note: For the best flavor and texture, the cheesecake should be made the day before it is to be served.

Cheddar Cheese Cheesecake

Crust

1 cup flour

¼ cup sugar

½ teaspoon grated zest of lemon

1½ cups butter

2 egg yolks, lightly beaten

½ teaspoon vanilla

Cheese Filling

16 ounces cream cheese, softened

1 cup grated Cheddar cheese
   (4 ounces)

¾ cup sugar

2 tablespoons flour

2 eggs

¼ cup milk

Glaze

3 cups peeled and sliced apples

½ cup apple juice

¼ cup sugar

¼ teaspoon cinnamon

3 teaspoons cornstarch

½ teaspoon vanilla extract

Preheat oven to 400 degrees.

To prepare crust: Combine flour, sugar, and lemon zest; cut in butter until crumbly. Add egg yolks and vanilla, and mix well. Pat a third of the dough on the bottom of a 9- or 10-inch spring-form pan with sides removed. Bake for 5 minutes and cool. Butter the sides of pan and attach to bottom. Pat remaining dough halfway up sides of pan and set aside.

Reduce oven temperature to 375 degrees.

To prepare filling: Beat together cream cheese and Cheddar until fluffy and well blended. Combine sugar and flour; add to cheese mixture. Add eggs and beat until blended, then gently stir in milk. Pour into crust-lined pan, bake for 40 minutes, and cool for 15 minutes. Loosen sides of cake from pan with narrow spatula, cool 30 minutes more, remove sides from pan, and cool completely.

To prepare glaze: Poach sliced apples in ¼ cup of the apple juice until tender but slightly crisp; *do not overcook.* Add sugar and cinnamon. Stir cornstarch into remaining apple juice, and pour mixture over apple slices. Add vanilla and cook until clear and thick. Cool, then arrange apple slices on top of cheesecake. Spoon remaining glaze over apples and chill.

SERVES 12

Note: For the best flavor and texture, the cheesecake should be made the day before it is to be served.

Lemon Fluff Pie

1 tablespoon unflavored gelatin
1 cup sugar
½ teaspoon salt
4 eggs, separated
⅓ cup lemon juice
⅔ cup water

1 teaspoon grated zest of lemon
½ cup heavy cream, whipped
1 baked 9-inch pie crust
heavy cream, whipped, and grated
   zest of lemon for garnish

In a saucepan, thoroughly mix gelatin, ½ cup sugar, and salt. Beat together egg yolks, lemon juice, and water and stir into gelatin mixture. Cook and stir over medium heat until just boiling. Remove from heat and stir in lemon zest. Chill mixture, stirring occasionally, until *partially* set.

Beat egg whites until soft peaks form. Add remaining sugar and beat again until stiff peaks form and sugar dissolves. Fold into gelatin mixture. Fold in whipped cream, pour into crust and chill. Just before serving, frost with a thin layer of whipped cream and sprinkle with lemon zest.

SERVES 8

Pumpkin-Bourbon Pie

3 cups canned pumpkin
1¼ cups sugar
¾ teaspoon ground cloves
¾ teaspoon ginger
¾ teaspoon nutmeg
½ teaspoon salt
dash mace (optional)
4 eggs
¾ cup milk
⅓ cup plus 2 tablespoons bourbon
1¾ cups heavy cream
1 unbaked 10-inch, deep-dish pie crust

Apricot Glaze
6 ounces apricot preserves
1 tablespoon brandy

Pecan Topping
⅔ cup firmly packed brown sugar
¼ cup melted butter
1 tablespoon heavy cream
⅛ teaspoon salt
¾ cup chopped pecans
½ cup pecan halves

Preheat oven to 425 degrees.

To prepare glaze: Place apricot preserves in a double boiler over hot water until preserves liquefy. In a blender or food processor, combine preserves and brandy. Set aside.

Combine pumpkin, sugar, cloves, ginger, nutmeg, salt, mace, eggs, milk, ⅓ cup bourbon, and ¾ cup cream in a large bowl and mix thoroughly. Paint pie shell with 2 teaspoons of apricot glaze, pour in pumpkin mixture, and bake for 15 minutes. Reduce heat to 350 degrees and bake 40 to 50 minutes longer, or until filling has set. Cool pie to lukewarm.

To prepare topping: Combine all ingredients except last. Pour mixture evenly over filling and decorate with pecan halves. Broil 3 to 4 inches from heat until surface begins to bubble; *avoid burning.*

Whip remaining cup cream, fold in remaining 2 tablespoons bourbon, and serve on wedges of warm pie.

SERVES 8 TO 10

Kentucky Pecan Pie

1 cup light corn syrup
1 cup firmly packed brown sugar
⅛ teaspoon salt
⅓ cup butter, melted
1 teaspoon vanilla extract
½ teaspoon instant espresso or instant
   coffee

3 whole eggs, lightly beaten
1 heaping cup pecan halves
1 unbaked 9-inch pie crust
1 cup heavy cream, whipped, for
   garnish

Preheat oven to 350 degrees.

Combine first 6 ingredients and mix well. Add eggs and beat. Mix in the pecans with a fork, pour into crust, and bake for 45 minutes. Cool, garnish with whipped cream, and serve.

SERVES 8

Chocolate Walnut Pie

Narrow fifty-five-mile-long Lake Chelan, squeezed between steep mountains, is a favorite area for backpackers in the summer and, in the winter, for boaters who hope to catch sight of mountain goats. An anytime favorite is this pie created by Merry Collette of Campbell's Resort at the end of the lake.

dough for crust for top and bottom of pie	*3 teaspoons vanilla extract*
5 eggs	*1¼ cups flour*
2¼ cups sugar	*2¼ cups semisweet chocolate chips*
½ cup butter, melted	*2¼ cups chopped walnuts*
	ice cream and crème de cacao

Preheat oven to 350 degrees. Prepare pie crust and line the bottom of a 9-inch pie plate with half the dough. Combine eggs, sugar, and butter; stir in vanilla, flour, chocolate chips, and walnuts. Pour into crust and cover with remaining crust. Seal edges, pierce top with a fork, and bake for 1 hour and 10 minutes. Serve warm or cool with ice cream drizzled with crème de cacao.

SERVES 6 TO 8

Chocolate Mousse Pie

Crust

3 cups (12 ounces or 1½ packages) chocolate wafer crumbs
½ cup unsalted butter, melted

Filling

1 pound semisweet chocolate
2 eggs
4 egg yolks
3 cups heavy cream

6 tablespoons powdered sugar
4 egg whites, at room temperature

Chocolate Leaves

8 ounces semisweet chocolate
1 scant tablespoon vegetable shortening
stiff waxy leaves (camellias work well)
1 cup heavy cream
sugar to taste

To prepare crust: Combine crumbs and butter. Press on bottom and completely up sides of 10-inch spring-form pan. Refrigerate 30 minutes or chill 10 minutes in freezer.

To prepare filling: Soften chocolate in top of double boiler over simmering water. Let cool to lukewarm, (about 95 degrees). Add whole eggs and mix well. Add yolks and mix until thoroughly blended. Whip cream with powdered sugar until soft peaks form. Beat egg whites until stiff but not dry. Stir a little of the cream and egg whites into the chocolate mixture to lighten, then fold in remaining cream and egg whites until completely incorporated. Pour into crust and chill at least 6 hours or overnight.

To prepare leaves: Melt chocolate and shortening in top of double boiler. Using spoon, generously coat undersides of leaves. Chill or freeze until firm. Whip the cream with sugar until very stiff.

Using a sharp knife, loosen pie crust on all sides and remove spring-form. Spread all but about ½ cup whipped cream over top of mousse; pipe remaining cream into rosettes in center of pie. Separate chocolate from leaves, starting at stem end of leaf. Arrange in an overlapping pattern around rosettes. Cut pie into wedges with a thin, sharp knife.

SERVES 10 TO 12

Note: This dessert can be prepared ahead and frozen; thaw overnight in the refrigerator.

Apple Cream Pie

2 cups peeled and diced apples
¾ cup sugar
2 tablespoons flour
1 egg, beaten
1 cup buttermilk
1 teaspoon vanilla extract
1 unbaked 9-inch pie crust

Topping
½ cup sugar
1 teaspoon cinnamon
¼ cup butter
3 tablespoons flour

Preheat oven to 400 degrees.

Combine apples, sugar, and flour; add the egg, buttermilk, and vanilla. Pour into pie crust and bake for 30 minutes.

To prepare topping: Cut together all ingredients with a fork until crumbly. Sprinkle on hot pie; bake for 10 more minutes. Remove from oven and cool.

SERVES 6

Raspberry Bavarian Pie

Crust
⅓ cup butter
2½ tablespoons sugar
⅓ teaspoon salt
1 egg yolk
1 cup flour
⅓ cup finely chopped almonds

Filling
2 egg whites

1 10-ounce package frozen raspberries, thawed and drained
1 cup sugar
1 tablespoon lemon juice
¼ teaspoon vanilla extract
¼ teaspoon almond extract
⅛ teaspoon salt
1 cup heavy cream
½ cup raspberry purée for garnish

Preheat oven to 400 degrees.

To prepare crust: Butter a 10-inch pie pan. Cream together butter, sugar, and salt until fluffy. Add egg yolk, beat thoroughly, and mix in flour and almonds. Press into prepared pie pan and bake 12 minutes; cool.

To prepare filling: Place all ingredients except last 2 in a large bowl. Beat with an electric mixer until mixture thickens and expands in volume—up to 15 minutes. Whip cream and fold into raspberry mixture, and spoon resulting mixture into pastry. Freeze at least 8 hours. Thaw partially before serving and top with raspberry purée.

SERVES 10

Cheese-topped Apple Pie

⅔ to 1 cup sugar, depending upon desired tartness
1 teaspoon cinnamon
1 teaspoon nutmeg
6 to 7 medium apples, peeled and sliced
1 unbaked 9-inch pie crust

Topping
⅓ cup sugar
½ cup flour
¼ cup butter
1 cup grated Cheddar cheese

Preheat oven to 425 degrees.

Stir sugar, cinnamon, and nutmeg together and combine with apples. Pour into crust. Mix topping ingredients together, sprinkle over apples, and pat down. Bake for 10 minutes; decrease oven temperature to 350 degrees, and bake for 50 minutes more.

SERVES 6

Variation: Without crust, this recipe becomes apple crisp.

Rhubarb Custard Pie

1¾ pounds rhubarb, cut up (about 5
   cups)
dash of cinnamon
1½ cups sugar
3 tablespoons flour

3 large eggs
dash of salt
1 unbaked 9-inch pie crust
whipped cream or ice cream

Preheat oven to 400 degrees.

Combine rhubarb, cinnamon, ½ cup sugar, and 1 tablespoon flour and set aside. Beat eggs with remaining sugar, remaining flour, and salt. Add this mixture to the rhubarb, mixing well. Pour into unbaked crust and bake for 10 minutes, being careful not to brown too much. Reduce heat to 350 degrees and bake for an additional 45 to 60 minutes. Serve with whipped cream or ice cream.

SERVES 6 TO 8

Ice Cream Pie

Crust
1½ cups finely chopped pecans
¼ teaspoon salt
¼ cup sugar
1 egg white, beaten until stiff peaks
   form

Filling
1 pint vanilla ice cream, softened
1 pint coffee ice cream or flavor of
   your choice, softened

Sauce
⅔ cup firmly packed brown sugar
1 egg yolk
¼ cup condensed milk
⅓ cup corn syrup
¼ cup butter
1 teaspoon vanilla extract
salt

Preheat oven to 350 degrees.

To prepare crust and filling: Fold pecans, salt, and sugar into beaten egg white; spread into pie pan and bake 10 minutes until brown. Cool completely. When crust has cooled, add ice cream in layers, or using a scoop, make circles, alternating the flavors. Swirl circles together with a knife and freeze.

To prepare sauce: Combine ingredients and heat until thickened in top of a double boiler; serve over wedges of pie.

SERVES 6 TO 8

Note: If coffee ice cream is not available, make a substitute by adding 1 tablespoon instant coffee to 1 tablespoon of water and mixing into 1 quart of vanilla ice cream.

Sorbets

The sorbet is a versatile dish that may be served as a palate refresher during the course of a meal, as a dessert, or as a complement to other dishes at a brunch or luncheon.

Razz-Ma-Tazz Apple Sorbet

⅔ cup sugar
⅔ cup water
10 ounces frozen raspberries and
   liquid, sweetened and thawed

3 large tart apples (such as Granny
   Smith), peeled, cored, and pared
2 tablespoons lemon juice
3 tablespoons Calvados, apple brandy,
   or apple jack

Combine sugar and water in a small saucepan and stir over medium-high heat until sugar is completely dissolved. Remove from heat just before the syrup comes to a boil, transfer to a bowl, and chill.

Purée raspberries in a food processor or blender. If necessary, press raspberries through a sieve to remove seeds. Add raspberries to sugar syrup and combine with remaining ingredients. Freeze mixture in either an ice-cream maker or a freezer. If using a freezer, finish the sorbet by partially thawing it and beating until smooth and fluffy in a blender, food processor, or with a mixer. Refreeze. Place in refrigerator approximately a half-hour before serving.

SERVES 6 TO 8

Very Peary Cranberry Sorbet

⅔ cup sugar
⅔ cup water
1 to 1½ cups whole cranberries, puréed
1 29-ounce can pears, drained and puréed

3 tablespoons Pear William, pear brandy, or eau de vie de poire
zest of 1 medium orange, finely minced
2 tablespoons lemon juice

Combine sugar and water in a small saucepan and stir over medium-high heat until the sugar is completely dissolved. Remove from heat just before the syrup boils, transfer to a bowl, and chill.

Combine the chilled sugar syrup with remaining ingredients and freeze mixture in either an ice-cream maker or a freezer. If using a freezer, finish the sorbet by partially thawing it and beating in a blender, food processor, or with a mixer until smooth and fluffy. Re-freeze. Place in refrigerator approximately a half-hour before serving.

SERVES 6 TO 8

Note: For this recipe, home-canned or commercially canned pears are preferred to fresh ones because they provide a more pronounced flavor.

Screwdriver Brunch Sorbet

¾ cup sugar
¾ cup water
3 medium oranges, peeled, seeded, and puréed

½ teaspoon finely minced zest of orange
¼ cup lemon juice
1 teaspoon orange extract
2 ounces vodka

Combine sugar and water in a small saucepan and stir over medium-high heat until the sugar is completely dissolved. Remove from heat just before the syrup comes to a boil, transfer to a bowl, and chill. In another bowl, blend remaining ingredients and chill.

Add the sugar syrup to the orange mixture and freeze in either an ice-cream maker or a freezer. If using a freezer, finish the sorbet by partially thawing it and then beating it in a blender, food processor, or with a mixer until smooth and fluffy. Refreeze. Place in refrigerator approximately a half-hour before serving.

SERVES 6 TO 8

South-of-the-Border Sorbet

½ cup sugar
½ cup water
2 large ripe avocados, peeled, seeded,
    and puréed
⅓ cup lime juice
2 tablespoons tequila
Tabasco sauce to taste (minimum of
    10 drops)

salt to taste
hollow lime halves for serving
    (optional)
lettuce leaves, cherry tomatoes,
    kumquats, and celery sticks for
    garnish

Combine sugar and water in a small saucepan and stir over medium-high heat until the sugar is completely dissolved. Remove from heat just before syrup comes to a boil, transfer to a bowl, and chill. Blend avocados, juice, tequila, Tabasco, and salt in another bowl, and chill.

Add the sugar syrup to the avocado mixture and freeze in either an ice-cream maker or a freezer. If using a freezer, finish the sorbet by partially thawing it and then beating it in a blender, food processor, or with a mixer until smooth and fluffy. Refreeze. Place in refrigerator approximately a half-hour before serving.

Serve the sorbet in hollowed-out lime halves and surround with garnishes or colorful blossoms. To hollow out lime halves, squeeze out the juice, turn limes inside out, and peel away any extra pulp, which should come out in a few large pieces.

SERVES 6 TO 8

Pink Grapefruit Sorbet

1⅓ cups sugar
1⅓ cups water
2½ cups pink grapefruit juice
2 tablespoons lemon juice

½ teaspoon finely minced grapefruit
    zest
1 tablespoon grenadine

Combine sugar and water in a small saucepan and stir over medium-high heat until the sugar is completely dissolved. Remove from heat just before syrup comes to a boil, transfer to a bowl, and chill. Combine remaining ingredients in another bowl, and chill.

Add the sugar syrup to the grapefruit mixture and freeze in either an ice-cream maker or a freezer. If using a freezer, finish the sorbet by partially thawing it and then beating it in a blender, food processor, or with a mixer until smooth and fluffy. Refreeze. Place in refrigerator approximately a half-hour before serving.

SERVES 10 TO 12

Rum-Lime Sorbet

8 to 10 ripe limes
3½ cups water

1¾ to 2 cups superfine sugar
⅓ to ½ cup dark rum

Remove the zest from 3 of the limes, using a zester or potato peeler (take care not to get any pith, or your sorbet will have a bitter taste). Coarsely chop the zest. Juice the limes to yield 1 cup of juice. Cover and refrigerate.

In a saucepan, boil water and add sugar and chopped zest, stirring constantly until sugar is dissolved. Cover and simmer for 30 minutes, then cool and pour into a 2-quart jar. Place in the freezer for about 15 minutes. Stir in the lime juice and strain the mixture to remove bits of zest. Pour this mixture into the cannister of an ice-cream maker and churn according to manufacturer's instructions.

When the ice-cream maker stops, check the sorbet for ice crystals. If there are some, process the sorbet in a food processor or blender for a few seconds, then return to the freezer in a covered container.

About 1½ hours before serving, remove sorbet from freezer and place in refrigerator. Shortly before serving, stir in 3 tablespoons of rum; refreeze for 10 to 15 minutes if the mixture becomes too soft. Serve the sorbet in chilled glasses. Make a little indentation in the top of each serving, pour ¾ teaspoon rum into each hollow, and serve immediately.

SERVES 12

Note: If prepared the day before serving, the sorbet will develop a more intense flavor.

Creamy Pear Ice

3 large pears (Bartletts are best)
½ cup pineapple juice
1 cup sugar
½ teaspoon salt

3 ounces cream cheese, softened
½ cup heavy cream
2 tablespoons lemon juice
butter cookies for garnish

Peel, core, and quarter each pear. Place pears and pineapple juice in a food processor, and process until they make a smooth purée. Gradually add all other ingredients except cookies and continue processing until well blended. Pour into a loaf pan or other container, cover, and freeze overnight.

Several hours before serving, cut the ice into chunks and place in food processor. Blend quickly until smooth, spoon into container, cover, and freeze again before serving. Serve in clear glass stemware with crisp butter cookies.

SERVES 6 TO 8

Five-Fruit Sherbet

5 ripe bananas, sliced
grated zest of 2 oranges
1 cup orange juice
½ cup lemon juice

2 cups sugar
3 cups cranberry–apple juice
3 egg whites

Mash bananas with a fork or in a food processor. Stir in orange zest, orange and lemon juice, sugar, and cranberry–apple juice. Pour into a 10-x-15-inch baking pan and freeze 1 to 2 hours, or until mushy.

Beat egg whites until stiff. Spoon fruit mixture into a large bowl and beat well with electric mixer at low speed. Gently fold in beaten egg whites, return to pan, and refreeze 1 to 2 hours more or until mushy. Beat the mixture again, cover with foil, and refreeze. To serve, let frozen sherbet stand at room temperature about 15 minutes before spooning into glasses.

SERVES 14 TO 15

Frozen Daiquiri Soufflé

10 eggs, separated
2 cups sugar
½ cup lime juice
½ cup lemon juice
grated zest of 2 lemons
grated zest of 2 limes
pinch of salt

2 tablespoons unflavored gelatin
½ cup light rum
2 cups heavy cream
½ cup heavy cream, whipped, for
*   garnish*
10 to 12 candied violets for garnish
*   (optional)*

Beat egg yolks until light. Gradually add sugar and beat until smooth. Add juices, zests, and salt and mix until blended. Place mixture in a heavy saucepan and cook, stirring constantly, over low heat until mixture is thick and coats a spoon. Remove from heat. Soften gelatin in rum and add to hot custard, stirring until dissolved. Cool. Attach a collar to a 6-cup soufflé dish and butter both collar and dish (or use individual dessert dishes).

Beat whites until stiff and whip cream until stiff. Fold custard into egg whites, then fold in cream. Pour into dish and freeze. Decorate with rosettes of piped cream and candied violets. Serve directly from freezer after removing collar.

SERVES 10 TO 12

Rolling-Can Ice Cream

1 egg
½ cup sugar
1½ pints heavy cream
1 teaspoon vanilla extract
½ cup crushed fruit or crushed
    peppermint candy

peppermint extract or other flavoring
    to taste
1 1-pound coffee can with lid
1 3-pound coffee can with lid
ice and rock salt

Lightly beat egg and slowly add sugar. Stir in cream, vanilla, fruit or candy, and flavoring until well blended. Pour this mixture into the 1-pound can and put on lid. Place the 1-pound can inside the 3-pound can. Fill space between the cans with alternating layers of ice and rock salt. Put lid on the large can and roll on a hard surface (i.e., a driveway or path) for 1 hour, opening the cans every 15 minutes to stir the ice cream. Pour out the water and add more ice and rock salt as necessary.

YIELD: 4 CUPS

Note: If not all the mixture can be put in at first, add remaining mixture when inside can is opened for stirring.

Northwest Blackberry Ice Cream

4 eggs
2 cups sugar
5 cups puréed and strained fresh
    blackberries

1 quart heavy cream
2 teaspoons vanilla extract
½ teaspoon salt
rock salt and crushed ice

In a large mixing bowl, beat eggs until frothy. Gradually add sugar and beat at medium speed for 2 to 3 minutes. Add blackberries, cream, vanilla, and salt and mix well. Pour into ice-cream maker and pack with rock salt and ice; churn according to directions and store in freezer. Allow the ice cream to soften a little before serving.

YIELD: 3 QUARTS

Lime Cream

1 cup sugar
2 tablespoons cornstarch
½ teaspoon mace
⅛ teaspoon salt
1 cup water
¼ cup lime juice
1 egg, lightly beaten

1 teaspoon grated zest of lime
1 teaspoon vanilla extract
a drop of green food coloring
1 cup heavy cream, whipped
4 twists of lime peel for garnish
baked pie crust (optional)

Stir together sugar, cornstarch, mace, and salt; add water and cook until thickened. Add lime juice and cook a minute longer. Combine egg with 2 tablespoons of the hot mixture; stir and add to remaining hot mixture. Cook 1 to 2 minutes, stirring constantly. Remove from heat; add lime zest, vanilla, and food coloring and cool. Fold in whipped cream and serve in long-stemmed glasses or in a pie crust, garnished with lime twists.

SERVES 4

Ice Cream Bonbons

1 tablespoon unflavored gelatin
2 tablespoons water
3 tablespoons Grand Marnier,
    Cointreau, Kahlua, or other
    liqueur

1 quart vanilla ice cream, softened
4 ounces semisweet chocolate
1 ounce vegetable shortening

Sprinkle gelatin over water and dissolve over low heat. Cool and add liqueur. Using an electric mixer, combine ice cream and liqueur mixture and place in freezer for several hours or overnight.

Chill a cookie sheet in freezer. Using a melon baller, quickly make ice cream balls; place on chilled tray, insert attractive picks, and return to freezer until firm.

Melt chocolate with shortening in top of double boiler, stirring well. Pour chocolate into a small drinking glass and cool slightly. Dip ice cream balls into chocolate, coating thoroughly, and return to freezer.

YIELD: ABOUT 30 BALLS

Amaretto-Ricotta Mousse

Frangipane
½ cup butter
1½ cups sugar
3½ cups slivered almonds

Crust
24 1-inch Amaretto cookies, crushed
½ cup frangipane
1 cup graham-cracker crumbs
⅓ cup butter, melted

Filling
1½ tablespoons unflavored gelatin
4 tablespoons Amaretto
1 cup sugar
1 cup double-strength espresso coffee, hot
30 ounces ricotta cheese
2 cups heavy cream
sugar to taste
2 tablespoons slivered toasted almonds for garnish
¼ cup frangipane for garnish

To prepare frangipane: Melt together butter and sugar in a saucepan. When mixture is melted and bubbly, add almonds. Sauté until brown, remove from pan to cool, and process just enough to mix.

YIELD: ABOUT 3 CUPS

Preheat oven to 400 degrees. Butter a 10-inch spring-form pan.

To prepare crust: Combine cookies, frangipane, and cracker crumbs and set aside half of the mixture. Stir butter into remainder and press into bottom and halfway up sides of the spring-form pan. Bake for 5 minutes, remove from oven, and cool.

To prepare filling: Sprinkle gelatin over the Amaretto and allow to soften. Stir gelatin mixture and sugar into the hot espresso, stir to dissolve, and cool slightly. Beat the ricotta until smooth and stir into espresso mixture. Whip 1 cup of the cream until stiff, fold into the cheese mixture, and pour half of the resulting mixture into the cooled crust; sprinkle with reserved crumb mixture and top with remaining filling. Chill several hours or overnight, then remove spring-form pan.

Whip the remaining cream until stiff, adding sugar. Spread the whipped cream on the mousse or force it through a pastry bag. Sprinkle with toasted almonds and frangipane.

SERVES 12

Note: Keep frangipane in freezer and use on other desserts.

Royal Crown Mousse

1 to 1½ packages ladyfingers
¼ cup cream sherry or orange juice
12 ounces semisweet chocolate chips
1 pound cream cheese, softened
1½ cups firmly packed brown sugar
¼ teaspoon salt

4 eggs, separated
1 teaspoon vanilla extract
1 cup heavy cream
whipped cream and shaved chocolate
  curls for garnish

Preheat oven to 375 degrees.

Split ladyfingers lengthwise and arrange, cut sides down, on an oven rack. Bake for 5 minutes or until lightly brown, then cool and brush with sherry or orange juice. Line sides of an 8- or 9-inch spring-form pan with the ladyfingers.

Melt chocolate chips and cool. Blend cream cheese with ¾ cup brown sugar and salt. Beat in egg yolks 1 at a time, then stir in chocolate. Add vanilla and remaining brown sugar. Beat egg whites until stiff. Whip cream. Fold both into chocolate mixture. Turn mixture into pan lined with ladyfingers and chill overnight. To serve, remove sides of pan and surround base of mousse with whipped cream piped through a pastry bag fitted with a decorating tip. Garnish with chocolate curls.

SERVES 10 TO 12

Frozen Lemon Mousse
with Raspberry Topping

Crust
30 lemon or vanilla wafers (approximately)

Filling
4 eggs, separated
½ cup lemon juice
1 cup sugar
1½ tablespoons zest of lemon
⅛ teaspoon cream of tartar
⅛ teaspoon salt

1½ cups heavy cream
lemon-peel twists for garnish

Raspberry Topping
1 cup fresh raspberries or 1 10-ounce
  package frozen raspberries,
  thawed and drained
3 to 4 tablespoons sugar (preferably
  superfine)
2 tablespoons kirsch or Grand Marnier

To prepare crust: Butter sides of an 8- or 9-inch spring-form pan. Line bottom and sides of pan with wafers.

To prepare filling: In a large bowl, thoroughly blend egg yolks, lemon juice, sugar, and lemon zest. Let stand at room temperature. Beat egg whites until foamy. Add cream of tartar and salt and continue beating until stiff. Whip cream until stiff. Gently fold whites and cream into yolk mixture and carefully spoon into pan. Cover with foil and freeze 8 hours. Unmold and thaw 30 to 40 minutes before serving. Garnish with lemon-peel twists.

SERVES 15

To prepare topping: Pureé ingredients in a food processor or blender and chill. Serve topping in a bowl or spoon over the mousse as it is served.

YIELD: ABOUT 1 CUP

Variations: Substitute Blueberry Sauce (page 302) for Raspberry Topping. For a different crust, crush wafers or graham crackers to make 1½ cups. Mix with ¼ cup each melted butter and chopped pecans; pat into a metal pie pan, pressing firmly, and bake for 10 minutes at 325 degrees; let cool before filling with the lemon mixture.

Swedish Raspberry Cream

1²⁄₃ pounds raspberries or black-
    berries
6 cups water
1 vanilla bean, split
¾ to 1 cup sugar

6 tablespoons potato starch
½ cup cold water
1 cup heavy cream
½ cup sliced almonds

Boil berries, water, and vanilla bean together for 30 minutes. Strain and return 6 cups of liquid to pot. Add sugar and return barely to a boil. Meanwhile, dissolve potato starch in cold water. Remove liquid from heat and add potato-starch mixture in a slow stream while whisking rapidly; the raspberry liquid will thicken immediately. Serve warm with chilled cream and almonds, or serve cold with warm cream and almonds.

SERVES 6

Oranges Orientale

zest of 1 orange, cut into very thin
    julienne strips
1½ cups sugar
½ cup water

2 tablespoons honey
7 large naval oranges
½ cup Cointreau or Grand Marnier

In a small saucepan, barely cover orange zest with water and simmer 10 minutes. Drain thoroughly with cold water.

Place the sugar, ½ cup water, and honey in another saucepan. Heat, stirring, until sugar dissolves, and boil to 230 degrees on a candy thermometer. Remove from heat, add the zest, and stir gently. Let stand about 30 minutes, then add liqueur. Peel the oranges and take out the sections, removing all membrane. Arrange sections in a serving dish, top with glazed peel and syrup, and refrigerate 3 to 4 hours before serving.

SERVES 6

Christmas Custard

4 cups milk
½ cup flour
1½ cups sugar
3 eggs, separated

1 pint heavy cream
2 teaspoons vanilla extract
½ cup brandy or bourbon
nutmeg for garnish

Combine 1½ cups milk and flour until smooth. Pour 2½ cups milk into a heavy saucepan; add sugar and stir until dissolved. Slowly add flour–milk mixture, stirring constantly over low heat; cook and continue to stir until thickened.

Beat egg yolks until foamy. Combine yolks with ¼ cup milk–custard mixture, add to custard mixture, and stir well. Cook 1 minute more, then remove from heat. Cool, cover, and refrigerate. (Custard may be prepared ahead to this point.)

In a large bowl, whip egg whites until stiff and fold into cooled custard mixture. Whip cream until thick but not stiff, and fold into custard mixture. Divide in half and pour into 2 large serving pitchers. Add vanilla to 1 pitcher for the nonalcoholic dessert; add liquor to the other. Serve in parfait glasses, brandy snifters, demitasse cups, or any other unusual containers. Sprinkle nutmeg on top to garnish.

YIELD: 24 4-OUNCE SERVINGS

Baked Apples in Custard with Cinnamon Sauce

4 cups water
3 tablespoons lemon juice
6 medium red or Golden Delicious
   apples
½ cup chopped unsalted macadamia
   nuts
½ cup currants
½ cup firmly packed brown sugar
1 cup apple juice

Custard
3 eggs, lightly beaten

¼ cup sugar
¼ teaspoon salt
2 cups whole milk, scalded
½ teaspoon vanilla extract

Cinnamon Sauce
½ cup butter
¼ teaspoon cinnamon
2 tablespoons water
1 cup firmly packed brown sugar
1 cup apple juice

Preheat oven to 350 degrees.

Combine water and lemon juice. Remove peel from top ¼ inch of apples. Remove cores and seeds, being careful to leave bottoms intact. Dip each apple in lemon–water mixture to prevent browning.

Combine nuts, currants, and brown sugar; pack mixture into centers of apples. Place stuffed apples in a 7-x-11-inch baking dish, add apple juice, cover, and bake for 50 minutes, or until apples are tender but not mushy. While apples bake, prepare custard and sauce.

To prepare custard: Combine eggs, sugar, and salt in a heavy sauce-pan; slowly stir in milk. Stirring constantly, cook over low heat *only* until mixture coats a metal spoon, being careful not to let mixture boil. Stir in vanilla.

To prepare sauce: Melt butter; add cinnamon, water, brown sugar and apple juice. Bring mixture to a boil; boil briefly and keep warm.

To serve, divide custard evenly among 6 large brandy snifters or bowls. Place an apple in each dish and drizzle cinnamon sauce over each.

SERVES 6

Note: Custard and sauce may be prepared ahead; chill custard with plastic wrap touching the surface to prevent skin from forming.

Variation: Slice apples and poach with currants in apple juice. Place in sherbet glasses, top with custard sauce, serve with Caramel Sauce (page 302), and sprinkle with macadamia nuts.

Lemon Crème Caramel

1½ cups sugar
¼ cup water
pinch of cream of tartar
3½ cups milk
1 cup heavy cream
5 eggs

5 egg yolks
2 tablespoons lemon juice
1 tablespoon finely minced zest of
   lemon
1½ teaspoons vanilla extract

In a heavy pan, combine ¾ cup sugar, water, and cream of tartar; cook mixture 20 to 30 minutes, or until it becomes a deep, golden caramel color. Pour the sauce into the bottom of a 9-x-5-x-3-inch loaf pan.

Preheat oven to 325 degrees.

Scald milk and cream in a saucepan. In a large bowl, beat together eggs, egg yolks, and remaining sugar until mixture is light and frothy. Pour hot milk and cream into eggs slowly, stirring constantly. Add lemon juice, zest, and vanilla; strain mixture onto caramel sauce and set loaf pan into a deep, larger baking pan. Pour hot water into the baking pan until it reaches two-thirds up the sides of the loaf pan. Place a heavy sheet of foil over the loaf pan, and bake custard for 1 hour. Remove loaf pan from baking pan and take off foil. Cool custard and chill at least 4½ hours. Release the edges of the custard from pan and invert onto a serving dish.

SERVES 4 TO 6

Ivory Chocolate Parfait

4 egg yolks
½ cup sugar
3 tablespoons light rum
dash of salt

16 ounces cream cheese, softened
2 to 3 ounces semisweet chocolate,
   grated

Beat egg yolks with sugar, rum, and salt until thick and creamy. Beat cream cheese until creamy and gradually add egg-yolk mixture, beating until smooth and fluffy. Put a spoonful of the mixture into the bottom of a parfait glass. Top with a generous sprinkling of grated chocolate and repeat to make 2 to 3 layers each of cheese and chocolate, ending with chocolate. (The number of layers will depend on size of serving and glass.) Cover and chill 1 hour or more.

SERVES 6 TO 8

Vanilla Cream with Butterscotch Sauce

Pudding
1 cup sugar
1 tablespoon unflavored gelatin
2¼ cups heavy cream
2 cups sour cream
1 teaspoon vanilla extract

Butterscotch Sauce
⅔ cup firmly packed light brown
   sugar
1 cup heavy cream
¼ teaspoon salt
1 tablespoon butter
1 teaspoon vanilla extract

To prepare pudding: In a saucepan, mix sugar with gelatin, stir in cream, and let stand for 5 minutes to soften gelatin. Heat for a few minutes, stirring until sugar and gelatin are completely dissolved. Chill until slightly thickened, about 1 hour, stirring occasionally. Fold in sour cream and vanilla, pour into 8 individual molds or a single large mold and chill for several hours. Unmold and serve with butterscotch sauce.

To prepare sauce: Combine brown sugar, cream, salt, and butter, and bring to a boil; reduce heat and simmer until thick. Stir in vanilla and serve hot.

SERVES 8

Variation: Serve with fresh strawberries instead of Butterscotch Sauce.

Old-fashioned Caramel Apples

2 cups sugar
1 cup firmly packed brown sugar
⅔ cup light corn syrup
⅔ cup butter
1 cup heavy cream

1 teaspoon salt
2 teaspoons vanilla extract
8 apples, chilled
sugar for dipping

Combine sugars, corn syrup, butter, cream and salt in a saucepan and stir over high heat until mixture reaches 242 to 248 degrees on a candy thermometer. Remove from heat and add vanilla. Dip the cold apples into caramel mixture, then dip in sugar to prevent sticking, and set on waxed paper—or roll them in snow.

SERVES 8

Variation: Quartered apples may be dipped in caramel and served for dessert. The caramel coating is also delicious over ice cream.

Bananas Flambé

¼ cup butter
½ cup firmly packed brown sugar
2 to 3 tablespoons lemon or lime juice
4 firm, ripe bananas, peeled and
　　quartered lengthwise

½ teaspoon cinnamon
¼ cup banana liqueur
½ cup white rum
1 pint French vanilla ice cream, slightly
　　softened

In a shallow, flat chafing dish or large, attractive skillet, melt butter and combine with brown sugar; cook over medium heat until bubbly. Sprinkle juice over bananas, and arrange bananas in the chafing dish in a single layer. Sauté bananas, turning once, until tender—about 5 minutes. Sprinkle with cinnamon and pour in banana liqueur.

　　Warm rum until steaming, then ignite it with a long match and pour over bananas. Remove from heat, baste bananas until flame burns out, and serve immediately. Top each serving with a spoonful of French vanilla ice cream.

SERVES 4

Caramel Pears

¼ cup butter
½ cup sugar
4 to 6 pears, peeled, cored, and halved
　　lengthwise

½ teaspoon vanilla extract
dash of salt
½ cup heavy cream
2 tablespoons kirsch

Preheat oven to 475 degrees.

　　Melt butter in an 8-inch pie pan. Sprinkle sugar over butter and add pears, face down. Bake for 20 minutes, basting pears frequently. Remove from oven and reduce oven temperature to 350 degrees. Combine remaining ingredients, pour over pears, and bake about 20 minutes more—until sauce is slightly thickened and caramelized. Remove pears from oven, cool, and serve slightly warm.

SERVES 6

Chocolate Truffles

6½ ounces dark chocolate (the better
　　the quality, the better the truffles)
¼ cup butter
3 tablespoons heavy cream

3 tablespoons powdered sugar
1 tablespoon brandy
sifted unsweetened cocoa

Break chocolate into very small pieces. Melt butter in a saucepan, add chocolate, remove from heat, and stir until chocolate is melted. Add cream and powdered sugar and stir well. Add brandy and beat with a wooden spoon until smooth and glossy. Refrigerate until firm enough to handle. Roll, a teaspoonful at a time, into tiny balls, roll in sifted cocoa, and refrigerate. Serve in tiny paper cups.

YIELD: ABOUT 30

Ms. C's Fudge

4½ cups sugar
1 15½-ounce can evaporated milk
3 cups semisweet chocolate chips

1 cup butter
2 cups chopped walnuts
1 tablespoon vanilla extract

Butter a 9-x-13-inch baking pan.

Combine sugar and evaporated milk in a large, heavy saucepan. Bring to a rolling boil, stirring constantly, and boil for 6 minutes. Remove from heat and quickly add remaining ingredients. Stir until butter and chips are melted and pour into prepared pan.

YIELD: 4 POUNDS

Chocolate-covered Almond Brittle

2 cups butter
2 cups sugar
½ pound blanched almonds

1 pound semisweet chocolate
2 cups ground or finely chopped
    walnuts

Melt butter in a skillet over high heat or (easier) in an electric skillet on highest heat. When butter is just melted, but not brown, add sugar and stir until dissolved. Bring mixture to a boil and cook 5 minutes over highest heat, stirring constantly. Add chopped almonds, and cook and stir until mixture forms a brittle ball when ½ teaspoon is dropped into cold water. Pour into a 9-x-13-inch pan; score while warm into ½-x-1-inch rectangles. When cool, break into pieces.

Melt chocolate in a double boiler. Dip pieces of almond brittle in warm chocolate; allow excess chocolate to drop off, then roll pieces in ground walnuts and set aside on waxed paper until the chocolate hardens.

YIELD: ABOUT 2 POUNDS

Rich Rum Sauce for Fresh Fruit

6 egg yolks
¾ cup sugar
1 teaspoon lemon juice

⅓ cup dry sherry
1 cup heavy cream
¼ cup light rum

Combine egg yolks, sugar, and juice in a heavy saucepan over low heat. Beat well, add sherry, and continue to beat until sauce thickens. Remove from heat and cool. Whip the cream until stiff. Fold cream and rum into sauce, and refrigerate until ready to serve.

YIELD: 2½ CUPS

Whiskey Sauce for Fresh Fruit

1½ cups sour cream
¼ cup firmly packed brown sugar
1 tablespoon bourbon

1 tablespoon Irish whiskey
⅓ cup raisins

Combine first 4 ingredients in a bowl, whisk until thoroughly blended and smooth, and stir in raisins. Cover and refrigerate a minimum of 8 hours. Serve over fresh fruit.

YIELD: 2 CUPS

Grand Marnier Sauce for Summer Fruit

5 egg yolks
½ cup plus 1 tablespoon sugar

¼ cup Grand Marnier
1 cup heavy cream

Combine egg yolks and ½ cup sugar in a 2-quart mixing bowl that will rest fairly snugly on the rim of a saucepan. Put about 2 inches of water in the saucepan and bring to a boil. Beat the yolks vigorously and rest the mixing bowl on the saucepan, making sure that the bowl does not touch the bottom of the saucepan, and stir in 2 tablespoons Grand Marnier. Let the sauce cool, then refrigerate.

Before serving, beat cream with remaining tablespoons of sugar until it forms gentle peaks. Fold cream into the cold sauce and stir in the remaining Grand Marnier. Serve on any summer fruit.

SERVES 8 TO 10

Caramel Sauce

1 cup butter
1 cup evaporated milk

1 cup firmly packed brown sugar
1 cup sugar

Melt butter over medium heat; add milk and both kinds of sugar. Cook until slightly thick, stirring constantly.

YIELD: 2 CUPS

Blueberry Sauce

Especially recommended as a topping for Frozen Lemon Mousse (page 293).

1 cup sugar
1½ tablespoons cornstarch
dash salt

1 cup water
3 cups blueberries (if frozen, partially
    thawed and drained)

In a medium saucepan, mix sugar, cornstarch, and salt. (If frozen blueberries are used, add an additional teaspoon of cornstarch.) Stir in water until smooth and cook over moderate heat until thick and clear. Add blueberries, bring to a boil, remove from heat immediately and chill. (This sauce can be made a day ahead.)

YIELD: 4 CUPS

Index

TO ORDER ADDITIONAL COPIES SEND:

$22.55 per copy for Washington residents (includes sales tax, postage and handling)

$20.95 per copy for out-of-state residents (includes postage and handling)

Make your check payable to and send to either:

JLS Publication
Seattle Classic Cookbook/CB
1803 42nd Ave. East
Seattle, WA 98112

Madrona Publishers
P.O. Box 22667
Seattle, WA 98122